First World War
and Army of Occupation
War Diary
France, Belgium and Germany

35 DIVISION
Headquarters, Branches and Services
Adjutant and Quarter-Master General
21 June 1915 - 18 March 1919

WO95/2470/3

The Naval & Military Press Ltd
www.nmarchive.com
Published in association with The National Archives

Published by

The Naval & Military Press Ltd

Unit 10 Ridgewood Industrial Park,

Uckfield, East Sussex,

TN22 5QE England

Tel: +44 (0) 1825 749494

www.naval-military-press.com

www.nmarchive.com

This diary has been reprinted in facsimile from the original. Any imperfections are inevitably reproduced and the quality may fall short of modern type and cartographic standards.

© Crown Copyright
Images reproduced by permission of The National Archives, London, England, 2015.

Contents

Document type	Place/Title	Date From	Date To
Heading	WO95/2470/2 35 Div HQ Gen. Staff A & QM Gen.		
Heading	35th Division 'A' & 'Q' Branch 1915 Jun-Mar 1919		
Heading	A & Q 35 Div. Vol. 1915 Jun-1916 Jun		
War Diary		21/06/1915	21/06/1915
War Diary		24/07/1915	24/07/1915
War Diary		28/08/1915	28/08/1915
War Diary		10/09/1915	10/09/1915
War Diary		10/10/1915	10/10/1915
War Diary		28/01/1916	31/01/1916
War Diary		09/02/1916	01/06/1916
War Diary	In The Field	01/06/1916	05/06/1916
War Diary		31/05/1916	31/05/1916
War Diary	In The Field	06/06/1916	10/06/1916
War Diary		08/06/1916	09/06/1916
War Diary	In The Field	11/06/1916	30/06/1916
Heading	A. & Q. 35th Division. July 1916		
War Diary		01/07/1916	01/07/1916
War Diary	In The Field	02/07/1916	27/07/1916
War Diary		24/07/1916	28/07/1916
War Diary	In The Field	28/07/1916	31/07/1916
Heading	A. & Q. 35th Division August 1916		
War Diary		01/08/1916	03/09/1916
Miscellaneous	Position of Divisional H.Q. and Unit 35th Division in Now Area (No. 3)	04/08/1916	04/08/1916
Miscellaneous	Distribution of Billets 35th Division.	11/08/1916	11/08/1916
Miscellaneous	Distribution of Billets 35th Division.	17/08/1916	17/08/1916
War Diary		03/09/1916	31/01/1917
War Diary		01/03/1917	31/03/1917
Miscellaneous			
War Diary		01/04/1917	31/05/1917
Operation(al) Order(s)	35th Division. Administrative Order No. 7. App. A.	16/05/1917	16/05/1917
Operation(al) Order(s)	35th Division. Administrative Order No. 8. App. B.	17/05/1917	17/05/1917
War Diary		01/06/1917	31/07/1917
Miscellaneous	35th Division Administrative Staff.	03/08/1917	03/08/1917
War Diary		01/08/1917	28/02/1918
Heading	35th Division Administrative. A. & Q. 35th Division. March 1918		
Miscellaneous	35th Div. No. A.A. 21	23/04/1918	23/04/1918
War Diary		01/03/1918	31/07/1918
Miscellaneous	D.A.G., 3rd Echelon.	08/09/1918	08/09/1918
War Diary		01/08/1918	31/10/1918
Heading	War Diary of Headquarters 35 Division Administrative Staff From Nov 1918 To March 1919. Vol 33 to 37		
War Diary		01/11/1918	30/11/1918
War Diary		00/12/1918	00/12/1918
War Diary		00/01/1919	00/01/1919
War Diary		06/02/1919	25/02/1919
War Diary		18/03/1919	18/03/1919
War Diary		01/11/1918	30/11/1918
War Diary		00/12/1918	00/12/1918

War Diary	00/01/1919	00/01/1919
War Diary	06/02/1919	25/02/1919
War Diary	18/03/1919	18/03/1919

WO 95
2470/2
35 Div
HQ
Gen Staff
A & QM Gen.

35TH DIVISION

'A' & 'Q' BRANCH

1915 JUN ~~APR 1916~~-MAR 1919

A & B
3 & 2
3

Vol 1

1915 JUNE — 1916 JUNE

Army Form C. 2118

WAR DIARY

35th DIVISION.
ADMINISTRATIVE STAFF.

Instructions regarding War Diaries and Intelligence Summaries are contained in F.S. Regs., Part II. and the Staff Manual respectively. Title Pages will be prepared in manuscript.

(Erase heading not required.)

Place	Date	Hour	Summary of Events and Information	Remarks and references to Appendices
	21.6.15.		Major BELLAIRS, R.A. appointed D.A.A. & Q.M.G. - 1st member of Divisional Staff on forming of Division.	
	24.7.15.		Major-General R.J. PINNEY, joined Division as G.O.C.	
	28.8.15.		Division left MASHAM for SALISBURY, Hd.Qrs Division at MARLBOROUGH.	
	10.9.15.		Hd.Qrs. moved from MARLBOROUGH to CHISLEDON.	
	10.10.15.		Hd.Qrs moved from CHISLEDON to CHOLDERTON.	
	28.1.16.		Embarkation of the 35th Division commenced.	
	31.1.16.		Divisional Hd.Qrs established at LE NIEPPE.	
	9.2.16.		Divisional Hd.Qrs moved to LAMBRES.	
	11.2.16.		LORD KITCHENER inspected Division.	
	18.2.15.		Divisional Hd.Qrs moved to LESTREM.	
	21.2.16.		Casualties for 21st. Attached 38th Division. 23rd Manchesters wounded O.R. 1. 18th Lancs. Wounded CAPTAIN HARRY AUSTIN HUTSON. O.R. 1.	
			Attached 19th Division. 17th West Yorks. O.R. killed 1. 17th Royal Scots. O.R. wounded 2.	
	22.2.16.		Casualties for 22nd.	
			17th Lancs. Fusrs. died of wounds, 2/Lieut.D.A.C. LAYMAN.Wounded O.R. 4. 23rd Manchesters. Wounded O.R. 2 (including 1 accidentally).	
	24.2.16.		Casualties for 24th.	
			Attached 19th Division. 17th Royal Scots. O.R. wounded one.	

1875 Wt. W593/826 1,000,000 4/15 J.B.C. & A. A.D.S.S./Forms/C. 2118.

Army Form C. 2118

WAR DIARY
~~INTELLIGENCE SUMMARY~~

(Erase heading not required.)

Instructions regarding War Diaries and Intelligence Summaries are contained in F. S. Regs., Part II. and the Staff Manual respectively. Title Pages will be prepared in manuscript.

Place	Date	Hour	Summary of Events and Information	Remarks and references to Appendices
	24.2.16.		Casualties for 24th (Contd)	
			17th West Yorks O.R. killed one.	
			Attached 38th Division.17th Lancs. Fus. killed O.R. one.	
	25.2.16.		Casualties for 25th.	
			Attached 19th Division.17th West Yorks O.R. wounded 1	
			Attached 38th Division.17th Lancs. Fus. O.R. wounded 1.	
			23rd Manchesters O.R. wounded 2.	
	26.2.16.		Casualties for 26th.	
			Attached 19th Division.17th Royal Scots. O.R. wounded 1.	
			Attached 38th Division.14th Glosters wounded LIEUT.H.C.KINRED, O.R. 3, all accidental by rifle-	
			18th Lancs. wounded O.R. 3. -grenade.	
			23rd Manchesters LIEUT. W.M. REID.wounded.	
	27.2.16.		Casualties for 27th.	
			Attached 19th Division.17th West Yorks O.R. wounded 1.	
			Attached 38th Division.23rd Manchesters wounded O.R. 2. including 1 at duty.	
	28.2.16.		Casualties 28th.	
			Attached 38th Division.17th Lancs. Fus. wounded O.R. 1 - self inflicted.	
			15th Cheshires wounded O.R. 1.	
	29.2.16.		Casualties for 29th.	
			Attached 19th Division.18th H.L.I. O.R. wounded 1.	
			Attached 38th Division.15th Bn. Cheshires, killed O.R. 1.	
			An enemy prisoner was admitted to 107th Field Amb. He was taken from a captured flying-machine.	

1875 Wt. W593/826 1,000,000 4/15 J.B.C. & A. A.D.S.S./Forms/C. 2118.

WAR DIARY

~~INTELLIGENCE SUMMARY~~

(Erase heading not required.)

Army Form C. 2118

Place	Date	Hour	Summary of Events and Information	Remarks and references to Appendices
	1.3.16.		**Casualties 1st.** Attached 19th Division. 18th H.L.I. O.R. wounded 1. 19th D.L.I. O.R. wounded 2. Attached 38th Division. 14th Glosters killed O.R. 1.	
	2.3.16.		**Casualties for 2nd.** Attached 19th Division. 18th H.L.I. O.R. wounded 1. 19th D.L.I. O.R. wounded 1. 15th Cheshires killed O.R. 2. 19th N.F. killed OR. Bomb accident occurred on bombing ground 23rd Manchstrs Attached 38th Division. 23rd Manchesters / As result of accident Capt. R.C. BODGE, 17th Lancs. Fus Brigade Bomb officer was killed: Lieut. DURANDEAU 23rd Manchester Regt and 2 other ranks 23rd Manchester Regt were wounded, Accident believed to be due to defective bomb. Attached 19th Division. 18th H.L.I. O.R. killed 1. 19th D.L.I. O.R. wounded accidentally 1.	
	3.3.16.		**Casualties for 3rd.** Attached 38th Division. 20th Lancs. Fus. O.R wounded 1. 15th Cheshires killed O.R. 1. 14th Glosters O.R. killed 1.	
	4.3.1.6.		**Casualties for 4th.** Attached 19th Division. 204th Field Co. R.E. O.R. wounded 1. 205th Field Co. R.E. O.R. wounded 1. 20th Lancs. Fus. killed 2/Lieut. F.P. ROBERTSON. 19th D.L.I. O.R. wounded 1. Attached 38th Division. 14th Glosters killed O.R. 1. wounded O.R. 3. 35th Div. Signal Co. O.R. wounded accidentally 1.	
	5.3.16.		**Casualties for 5th.** Attached 19th Division. 205th Field Co. R.E. O.R. wounded 1. 19th D.L.I. O.R. wounded 3. Attached 38th Division. 15th Cheshires O.R. wounded 1 accidentally self inflicted. 14th Glosters wounded O.R. 2.	

Army Form C. 2118

WAR DIARY
INTELLIGENCE SUMMARY
(Erase heading not required.)

Instructions regarding War Diaries and Intelligence Summaries are contained in F. S. Regs., Part II. and the Staff Manual respectively. Title Pages will be prepared in manuscript.

Place	Date	Hour	Summary of Events and Information	Remarks and references to Appendices
	6.3.16.		Casualties. 159th Bde R.F.A. O.R. wounded one. 17th Lancs. Fus. O.R. wounded one accidentally. 20th Lancs. Fus. O.R. wounded one. 19th D.L.I. wounded one. Attached 19th Division.	
	7.3.16.		Casualties. 14th Glosters killed O.R. one. 15th Cheshires wounded O.R. three. Attached 38th Division.	
	8.3.16.		Casualties.8th. 17th Royal Scots 2 killed, 1 died of wounds, 2 wounded (1 reported self-inflicted.) 17th West Yorks 1 wounded, self inflicted. 18th H.L.I. Major C.B.LUMSDEN died of syncope owing to exposure and exhaustion. 14th Glosters, accidentally wounded O.R. 5 (4 slightly at duty) grenade explosion. 104th Brigade O.R. 2 wounded (18th L.F).	
	9.3.16.		159th Bde R.F.A. O.R. wounded 1. 17th Royal Scots O.R. wounded 1. 17th West Yorks O.R killed one wounded 2, 17th Lancs. Fus. wounded one (accidentally) 23rd Manchesters wounded one.	
	10.3.16.		Casualties. 16th Cheshires killed O.R. one, wounded O.R. 2. 15th Sherwoods, wounded O.R.2. 18th Lancs. Fus wounded one. 23rd Manchester R. wounded one. 17th Royal Scots O.R. killed three, wounded 3. 17th West Yorks O.R. wounded 2.	

1875 Wt. W593/826 1,000,000 4/15 J.B.C. & A. A.D.S.S./Forms/C.2118.

WAR DIARY
INTELLIGENCE SUMMARY

(Erase heading not required.)

Army Form C. 2118

Instructions regarding War Diaries and Intelligence Summaries are contained in F.S. Regs., Part II. and the Staff Manual respectively. Title Pages will be prepared in manuscript.

Place	Date	Hour	Summary of Events and Information	Remarks and references to Appendices
	11.3.16.		Casualties. 106th Bde H.Q. O.R. wounded 2 accidentally. 17th Royal Scots C.R. wounded one, 17th Lancs. Fus. O.R. wounded 2. 18th Lancs. Fus. O.R. wounded 2. 159th Bde R.F.A. O.R. died of wounds 1 (reported wounded 5.3.16) 35th Divl. R.E. wounded Lieut. L.J. MACLEAN, 204th Field Co R.E.	
	12.3.16.		Casualties. 19th Northld. Fus. O.R. wounded 1. at duty. 17th Lancs. Fus. O.R. wounded 1. 20th Lancs. Fus. O.R. wounded 1. 23rd Manchesters O.R wounded 1. 17th West Yorks Lieut. C.W. BANKS wounded at duty. 19th D.L.I. wounded 1. 18th H.L.I. 2 killed 3 wounded. 159th Bde R.F.A.No.27011 Gr.J. Macalister wounded.	
	13.3.16.		Casualties. 17th Lancs. Fus. Lieut WILLIAM NUTTALL wounded, O.R 3 killed 2 wounded. 18th Lancs. Fus. O.R. wounded 1. 23rd Manchesters O.R. 2 wounded. 16th Cheshires killed O.R. 2 wounded O.R. 6. 17th Royal Scots 1 wounded (accidentally) 18th H.L.I. wounded 5. (Major A.G.HILLS 15th Ches. evac to England s/s "David")	
	14.3.16.		Casualties. 17th Lancs. Fus. O.R. killed 1 wounded 1. 20th Lancs Fus. O.R. wounded 1 23rd Manchesters O.R. killed 1. wounded 1. 16th Cheshires killed O.R. 1 wounded 2. 19th Northld. Fusilrs O.R. wounded 1. 19th D.L.I. 17 wounded. 18th H.L.I. killed 4, wounded 30, 21 missing believed killed. 15th Sherwoods O.R. wounded 1. The casualties in the 18th H.L.I. and the 19th D.L.I. were due to the blowing up of an enemy mine.	

Army Form C. 2118

WAR DIARY

~~INTELLIGENCE SUMMARY~~

(Erase heading not required.)

Instructions regarding War Diaries and Intelligence Summaries are contained in F.S. Regs., Part II. and the Staff Manual respectively. Title Pages. will be prepared in manuscript.

Place	Date	Hour	Summary of Events and Information	Remarks and references to Appendices
	14.3.16.		Additional casualties up to 4 p.m.	
			18th H.L.I. killed 4, wounded 7, missing believed killed 5.	
	15.3.16.		Casualties.	
			17th Lancs. Fus wounded Capt F.J.M.CHRISTIE & 2nd Lieut V.A.FARRAR, O.R. wounded 3.	
			23rd Manchesters C.R. wounded 1.	
			16th Cheshires killed O.R. 1.	
			19th D.L.I. wounded O.R. 3.	
			18th H.L.I. wounded O.R. 2.	
	16t3.16.		Casualties.	
			17th Lancs. Fus. O.R. wounded 2.	
			23rd Manchesters Lieut. F. WATSON wounded.	
			17th W.Yorks Shell shock 1 man,	
			18th H.L.I. 2.Lt. J.H.G.BORLAND wounded.	
			17th W.Yorks O.R. wounded 1.	
	17.3.16.		Casualties.	
			17th Lancs. Fus. O.R. wounded 1.	
	18.3.16.		Casualties.	
			18th Lancs. Fus. O.R. wounded 1.	
			20th Lancs. Fus. O.R. killed 1 wounded 3 (incl. 1 self inflicted 1 accidental)	
	19.3.16.		Casualties.	
			18th Lancs. Fus. O.R. wounded 3	
			20th Lancs. Fus. O.R. killed 1, wounded 4.	
			23rd Manchesters wounded at duty 2nd Lieut. E.L.DUNAND. O.R.wounded 6.	
	20.3.16.		Casualties.	
			18th Lancs. Fus. Lieut JOHN YOUNG R.A.M.C. attd. wounded at duty. O.R. wounded 3.	
			20th Lancs. Fus. O.R. wounded 2.	

Army Form C. 2118

WAR DIARY
INTELLIGENCE SUMMARY
(Erase heading not required.)

Instructions regarding War Diaries and Intelligence Summaries are contained in F.S. Regs., Part II. and the Staff Manual respectively. Title Pages will be prepared in manuscript.

Place	Date	Hour	Summary of Events and Information	Remarks and references to Appendices
	21-3-16.		Casualties. 18th Lancs. Fus. O.R. killed 1 wounded 1. 20th Lancs. Fus. O.R. wounded 1. 163rd R.F.A. attd c/157 O.R. wounded 1. 16th Cheshires O.R. 1 previously reported wounded now died of wounds.	
	22-3-16.		Casualties. 20th Lancs. Fus. O.R. 1 killed. 23rd Manch. R. O.R. 1 killed, 1 wounded (at duty). 204th Coy R.E. O.R. wounded 1.	
	23-3-16.		Casualties. 18th Lancs. Fus. O.R. 1 killed.(accidental) 20th Lancs. Fus. 2nd Lt W.H.DUCKWORTH wounded, O.R. 2 wounded.	
	24-3-16.		Casualties. Nil.	
	25-3-16.		Casualties. 17th Lancs. Fus. 2nd Lt E.H.WILLIAMS wounded, O.R. killed 1 wounded 11. (4 at duty.) 20th Lancs. Fus. O.R. killed 1. wounded 3. X 35 Trench Morter Batty O.R. 1. wounded.	
	26-3-16.		Casualties. 17th Lancs. Fus. The 4 men reported yesterday wounded at duty have now been admitted to hospital. 18th M. Fus. O.R. wounded 1. 20th Lancs. Fus. O.R. wounded 2.	
	27-3-16.		Casualties. Nil.	

Army Form C. 2118

WAR DIARY
or
INTELLIGENCE SUMMARY
(Erase heading not required.)

Instructions regarding War Diaries and Intelligence Summaries are contained in F. S. Regs., Part II. and the Staff Manual respectively. Title Pages will be prepared in manuscript.

Place	Date	Hour	Summary of Events and Information	Remarks and references to Appendices
	28-3-16.		Casualties. "C" Batty 158th Brigade R.F.A. killed 2nd Lt E.F.R.BALDERSON. 15th Cheshires. O.R. wounded 1. 17th West Yorks. O.R. killed 1. The Division took over line from CHAPIGNY M 24. to FERME LA CORDONN-ERIE N10., taken over from 8th Division/Div. Qrs. moved from LESTREM to SAILLY.	
	29-3-16.		Casualties. 163rd F.A. Bde. O.R. wounded 1. 17th Royal Scots. O.R. wounded 3. 17th West Yorks. O.R. killed 1. wounded 3. 20th Lancs. Fus. killed 1. (self inflicted).	
	30-3-16.		Casualties. 159th F.A. Bde. O.R. wounded 1. 15th Sherwoods. 2nd Lt S. E. BRIDGWATER killed. O.R. wounded 2. 14th Glosters O.R. wounded 1. (at duty). 17th West Yorks. O.R. wounded 1. 181st Tunnelling Co R.E. 2nd Lt S. WRIGHT (at duty) O.R. wounded 1. 19th Northld. Fus. O.R. wounded 1.	
	31-3-16.		Casualties. 17th Royal Scots. O.R. wounded 4. 18th High. L.I. O.R. wounded 2. (1 accidental) 16th Cheshires. O.R. killed 1. wounded 3. (1. at duty). 14th Glosters. O.R. killed 1. wounded 2.	

Army Form C. 2118

WAR DIARY

Headquarters, 35th Division.

INTELLIGENCE SUMMARY Administrative Staff.

(Erase heading not required.)

Place	Date	Hour	Summary of Events and Information	Remarks and references to Appendices
	1.4.16.		Casualties.– 16th Cheshires wounded O.R. 1, 14th Glosters killed O.R. 1, 159th F.A. Bde wounded O.R. 1, 17th W.Yorks wounded Major J.H. GILL, O.R. 3, 19th Durh. L.I. killed O.R. 1, wounded 4.	
	2.4.16.		Casualties.– 16th Cheshires O.R. wounded 1 (at duty), 14th Glosters O.R. died of wounds 1, 181st Tun. Co R.E. O.R. wounded 1, 204th Co. R.E. O.R wounded 1. 19th Durh. L.I. O.R. killed 1, wounded 3, 18th High. L.I. O.R. killed 1, wounded 1.	
	3.4.16.		Casualties. 20th North. Fus. attd 181st Tun. Co.R.E. O.R. killed 1, 16th Cheshires O.R. killed 1, wounded 1 (at duty), 14th Glosters O.R. wounded 1 (at duty), 15th Sherwoods O.R. wounded 1, 19th Durh. L.I. O.R. killed 1, 19th Durh. L.I. attd 106/1 Trench Mortar Battery O.R. wounded 1.	
	4.4.16.		Casualties. 16th Cheshires O.R. wounded 1, 14th Glosters O.R. wounded 1 (self inflicted), 15th Sherwoods O.R. wounded 1. 172nd Tun. Co. attd 181st Tun Co.R.E. O.R. wded 1.	
	5.4.16.		Casualties. 23rd Manch. R. killed O.R. 1, wounded 3 (1 at duty), 15th Cheshires killed O.R. 1, 15th Sherwoods wounded O.R. 1.	
	6.4.16.		Casualties. 17th Lancs. Fus.O.R. wounded 2, 23rd Manc. Reg. O.R. wounded 1, 203rd Co. R.E. wounded 2/Lt. W.S. LAIDLAW, wounded (at duty) Capt. K.W. PYE. 19th Northd. Fus. O.R. wounded 1 (accidental)	
	7.4.16.		Casualties. 15th Cheshires O.R. wounded 1 (at duty), 15th Sherwoods O.R.wounded 1, 17th Lancs. Fus O.R. wounded 1, 18th Lancs. Fus. O.R.wounded 1, 20th Lancs.Fus. O.R. killed 1, 23rd Manch. R. O.R. wounded 1.	
	8.4.16.		Casualties. 23rd Manch.R. wounded Lieut. M.H. ROSE, wounded at duty 2/Lt. L.D. FITZGERALD, O.R. wounded 4 (2 at duty), 14th Glosters wounded O.R. 1.	
	9.4.16.		Casualties. 18th Lancs. Fus.O.R.wounded O.R. 1, 16th Cheshires wounded O.R. 1 (at duty) 14th Glosters wounded O.R. 2 (1 accidental), 19th Durham L.I. wounded O.R. 1 accidental) 15th Cheshires wounded O.R. 1 (accidental)	

WAR DIARY

INTELLIGENCE SUMMARY

(Erase heading not required.)

Army Form C. 2118

Instructions regarding War Diaries and Intelligence Summaries are contained in F. S. Regs., Part II. and the Staff Manual respectively. Title Pages will be prepared in manuscript.

Place	Date	Hour	Summary of Events and Information	Remarks and references to Appendices
	10.4.16.	Casualties.	18th Lan. Fus. killed O.R. 3 wounded O.R. 3, 20th Lan.Fus. wounded 2/Lt. H. QUINNEY, killed O.R. one, 14th Glosters wounded O.R. 2 (1 at duty), 15th Sherwoods wounded O.R. 1, 19th Northld. Fus. wounded O.R. 2.	
	11.4.16.	Casualties.	159th F.A. Bde killed believed accidental Capt A.C. WHYTE, court of enquiry being held, 17th Lan. Fus. killed O.R. 1, wounded O.R. 1, 18th Len. Fus. wounded Major M.H. LOWTHER-CLARK, 16th Cheshires killed O.R. 3 wounded O.R. 2 (1 at duty), 15th Sherwoods wounded O.R. 1.	
	12.4.16.	Casualties.	c/159th F.A. Bde O.R. killed 1, wounded 6, 18th Lan. Fus. O.R. wounded 1, 16th Cheshires O.R. wounded 2, 14th Glosters O.R. killed 1.	
	13.4.16.	Casualties.	17th Lan. Fus. O.R. wounded 2, 23rd Manch.R. accidentally injured 2 (collapse of dugout), 17th Royal Scots killed O.R. 3, wounded O.R. 3, 17th W.Yorks killed O.R. 1 wounded O.R. 1.	
	14.4.16.	Casualties.	17th R.Scots O.R. died of wounds 1, 18th High L.I. O.R. wounded 1, 15th Sherwoods previously reported wounded now died of wounds O.R. 2, 17th Lan. Fus. O.R. wounded 2 (at duty) X 35 T.M.Battery, O.R. wounded 1 (accidentally report follows), 19th N. Fus. O.R. wounded 1.	
	15.4.16.	Casualties.	18th Lan. Fus. O.R. 1 injured by horse, accidentally kicked, 23rd Manch.R. O.R. wounded 3 (1 at duty), 17th R.Scots O.R. killed 1 wounded 3, 17th W.Yorks O.R. wounded 1, 19th Northld. Fus wounded (at duty) 2/Lt. E.O. PRETHEROE.	
	16.4.16.	Casualties.	23rd Manch.R. O.R. killed 1 wounded 1 (self inflicted) 17th W.Yorks O.R.wounded 1 (accidentally), 19th Durh. L.I. O.R. wounded 1.	
	17.4.16.	Casualties.	23rd Manch. R. wounded Capt. T.H.DIXON, O.R. wounded 5 (2 accidentally), (1 at duty) Suppl. 14th. 17th R.Scots attd. 181st Tunnelling Co. R.E. O.R. wounded 1(accdtly) Attd 38th Div.17th. 19th Durh. L.I. O.R. killed 1.	
	18.4.16.	Casualties.	Attd. 38th Div. 19th Durh. L.I. wounded O.R. 1, 18th High. L.I. killed O.R. 1.	

Army Form C. 2118

WAR DIARY

INTELLIGENCE SUMMARY

(Erase heading not required.)

Instructions regarding War Diaries and Intelligence Summaries are contained in F.S. Regs., Part II. and the Staff Manual respectively. Title Pages will be prepared in manuscript.

Place	Date	Hour	Summary of Events and Information	Remarks and references to Appendices
	19.4.16.		Casualties. 158th F.A. Bde wounded (believed accidental) 2/Lieut. G. DARBY. Attd. 38th Div. 17th W.Yorks O.R. killed 1, 19th Durh.L.I. O.R. wounded 1. Attd 35th Div. 2nd Aust. Batt. O.R. wounded 1.	
	20.4.16.		Divisional H.Q. moved from SAILLY to LESTREM on the Division taking over the line from S.21.d. to M.35.d. FERME DU BOIS and NEUVE CHAPELLE Sector.	
	21.4.16.		Casualties. 15th Cheshires O.R. wounded 5, 18th High. L.I. O.R. wounded 1, 204th Fd.Coy. R.E. wounded accidentally Lieut. E.W. SEEMAN.	
	22.4.16.		Casualties. 15th Cheshires O.R. killed 2, 14th Glosters O.R. wounded 1 (at duty) 17th R.Scots O.R. killed 1, 18th High.L.I. O.R. wounded 1, 17th W.Yorks attd 106/2 T.M.Battery O.R. wounded 1, Z.35 T.M.B. O.R. wounded 1, 9th M.G. Squadn. O.R. killed 1, 19th Northd.Fus. O.R. wounded 2 (1 at duty)	
	23.4.16.		Casualties. 15th Sherwoods O.R. wounded 1. 19th Northd.Fus. wounded O.R. 1.	
	24.4.16.		Casualties. 15th Cheshires O.R. wounded O.R. 1 accidental (report follows) 15th Sherwoods killed Major H.W. THELWALL, A/159 F.A. Bde wounded 2nd Lieut. R. COCHRANE, 19th Northld. Fus. wounded O.R. 1, 17th R. Scots wounded O.R. 1, 19th Durham L.I. wounded O.R. 1 (accidentally)	
	25.4.16.		Casualties. 14th Glosters O.R. killed 1, 16th Cheshires O.R. wounded 2 (1 at duty), 17th W.Works O.R. wounded 4, 19th Durham L.I. O.R. wounded 2.	
	26.4.16.		Casualties. 16th Cheshires O.R.killed 1, 14th Glosters O.R. wounded 1, 17th R.Scots O.R. wounded 1 (accidentally) 19th Durh. L.I. O.R. wounded 1, 18th High.L.I.O.R. killed 1 wounded 3.	
			Casualties. 19th Northld. Fus. O.R. killed 1 wounded (accidentally) O.R.1, 19th Durh.L.I. O.R. wounded 1, 18th High. L.I. O.R.killed 2, 16th Cheshires O.R. wounded 2 (1 at duty) 14th Glosters O.R. wounded 1, 15th Sherwoods O.R.wounded 1.	

Army Form C. 2118

WAR DIARY
INTELLIGENCE SUMMARY
(Erase heading not required.)

Place	Date	Hour	Summary of Events and Information	Remarks and references to Appendices
	27.4.16.	Casualties.	19th Northld. Fus. O.R. wounded 1, 15th Cheshires O.R. wounded 2, 16th Cheshires O.R. killed 3 wounded 14, 18th High. L.I. wounded O.R. 1.	
	28.4.16.	Casualties.	15th Cheshires O.R. wounded 1, 15th Sherwoods O.R. wounded 1, 17th West Yorks wounded Lieut. A.B. COHEN, 17th R.Scots O.R. wounded 2 19th Dur. L.I. O.R. wounded 5, 18th High. L.I. O.R. killed 1 wounded 2.	
	29.4.16.	Casualties.	23rd Manch.R. O.R. wounded 1, 9th M.G. Squadron O.R. wounded 1, 14th Glosters O.R. wounded 2 (accidentally), 19th Durh. L.I. O.R. wounded 1, 18th High. L.I. O.R. wounded 1.	
	30.4.16.	Casualties.	17th Lancs.Fus. O.R. wounded 2 (one at duty) 15th Cheshires O.R. killed 1 wounded 1 15th Sherwoods O.R. killed 1 wounded 2.	

13. 5. 16.

Beaumont,
Capt.
D.A.A. & Q.M.G.
35th Division.

Army Form C. 2118

35/244/a

Vol 3

WAR DIARY
~~INTELLIGENCE SUMMARY~~

(Erase heading not required.)

ADMINISTRATIVE STAFF,
35th DIVISION.

Instructions regarding War Diaries and Intelligence Summaries are contained in F. S. Regs., Part II. and the Staff Manual respectively. Title Pages will be prepared in manuscript.

Place	Date	Hour	Summary of Events and Information	Remarks and references to Appendices
	1.5.16.		Casualties. 203rd Field Co. R.E. wounded O.R. 1, 20th Lancs.Fus. O.R. wounded 1, 18th High. L.I. O.R. wounded 1 (accidentally), 15th Cheshires O.R killed 1 wounded 3 (1 at duty), 15th Sherwoods O.R. wounded 2, 35th Div. Signals R.E. wounded 2 killed 1.	
	2.5.16.		Casualties. 17th Lancs.Fus. O.R. wounded 1, 23rd Manch.R. O.R. wounded 3, 15th Cheshires O.R. killed 1 wounded 5 (1 at duty), 15th Sherwoods O.R. killed 1 wounded 1, 17th W.Yorks O.R. wounded 1 (accidentally; at duty).	
	3.5.16.		Casualties. 15th Cheshires wounded O.R. 1, 16th Cheshires killed O.R. 1 wounded O.R. 3, 14th Glosters wounded O.R. 1, 19th N.F. wounded O.R. 1, 18th Lancs. Fus. wounded 2/Lieut. H.M. BARNS O.R. 1 (at duty).	
	4.5.16.		Casualties. 16th Cheshires O.R. wounded 5 (1 at duty), 14th Glosters O.R. wounded 2 (1 at duty) 19th Northd. Fus. O.R. wounded 1.	
	5.5.16.		Casualties. 20th Lancs.Fus. O.R. killed 1, 19th Northld.Fus.O.R.killed 1, 15th Cheshires O.R wounded 1. 16th Cheshires wounded Capt. G.G.EARL, O.R. wounded 5 (2 at duty), 14th Glosters O.R. killed 1, 106th M.G.Coy O.R. wounded 1. The Commander-in-Chief, General Sir.D.HAIG, visited Divisional Headquarters at LESTREM.	
	6.5.16.		Casualties. 15th Cheshires O.R wounded 2, 20th Lancs.Fus. O.R. killed 1, 19th Northd.Fus.O.R. wounded 1.	

1875 Wt. W593/826 1,000,000 4/15 J.B.C. & A. A.D.S.S./Forms/C. 2118.

Army Form C. 2118

WAR DIARY
~~INTELLIGENCE~~ SUMMARY
(Erase heading not required.)

Instructions regarding War Diaries and Intelligence Summaries are contained in F.S. Regs., Part II. and the Staff Manual respectively. Title Pages will be prepared in manuscript.

Place	Date	Hour	Summary of Events and Information	Remarks and references to Appendices
	7.5.16.		Casualties. 16th Cheshires O.R. wounded 1, 17th Lancs.Fus Capt. E.T.COWAN wounded, O.R. killed 1 wounded 1, 18th Lancs Fus. attd Vickers M.G.Sect. O.R. wounded 1, 17th W.Yorks O.R. wounded 2. 159th F.A. Bde wounded 1.	
	8.5.16		Casualties. 11th Hussars attd 23rd Manch.R. wounded Major J.Fitz.G. BANNATYNE, 23rd Manch.R. O.R.killed 1 wounded 6 (3 at duty) 18th Lancs.Fus at td Vickers M.G.Sect. O.R. wounded 1 (accidentally), 19th Northd.Fus. O.R. wounded 1, 17th R. Scots O.R. wounded 3, 17th W.Yorks O.R. wounded 4 19th D.L.I. O.R. wounded 1, 18th High.L.I. O.R. wounded 1.	
	9.5.16.		Casualties. 17th Lancs.Fus. wounded O.R. 1, 20th Lancs.Fus. killed O.R. 3 wounded 2, 23rd Manch.R. killed O.R. 6 wounded 16, 17th W.Yorks wounded O.R. 2, 106th M.G.Coy wounded O.R. 2.	
	10.5.16.		Casualties. 17th Lancs.Fus. wounded O.R. 2, 20th Lancs.Fus. wounded O.R. 1, 17th R.Scots killed O.R. 1, 17th W.Yorks killed Capt. A.B. CRAWFORD O.R. 1 15 8th F.A.Bde wounded O.R.1 (self. inflicted).	
	11.5.16.		Casualties. 23rd Manch.R. wounded O.R. 3, 19th D.L.I. wounded O.R. 1, 18th High. L.I. wounded O.R. 2. 19th D.L.I. attd. 173rd Co. R.E. killed O.R. 2.	
	12.5.16.		Casualties 17th R.Scots killed O.R. 1 (acedtly on point duty), 19th Northd.Fus. wounded O.F. 1, 19th D.L.I. killed O.R. 1 wounded 5, 106th M.G.Coy wounded O.R. 3	
	13.5.16.		Casualties. 17th R.Scots wounded O.R. 1, 18th H.L.I.wounded O.R. 3, 18th Lancs Fus. killed -	

1875 Wt: W593,826 1,000,000 4/15 J.B.C. & A. A.D.S.S./Forms/C. 2118.

Army Form C. 2118

WAR DIARY
of
INTELLIGENCE SUMMARY
(Erase heading not required.)

Instructions regarding War Diaries and Intelligence Summaries are contained in F. S. Regs., Part II. and the Staff Manual respectively. Title Pages will be prepared in manuscript.

Place	Date	Hour	Summary of Events and Information	Remarks and references to Appendices
	13.5.16.		Casualties (Contd).	
	14.5.16.		Capt. G.H.S. de M. WILLIAMS wounded O.R. 1, 23rd Manch.R. killed O.R. 1.	
			Casualties.	
			19th Durh.L.I. killed O.R. 2 wounded 1.	
	15.5.16.		Casualties.	
			19th Northd.Fus. killed O.R. 1 wounded 1, 15th Cheshires wounded O.R.1, 16th Cheshires wounded O.R. 1, 14th Glosters wounded O.R. 1, 17th R.Scots killed O.R. 1 wounded 1, 17th W.Yorks wounded O.R. 2. 106th M.G.Coy. injured accidentally O.R. 1. 19th D.L.I. wounded O.R. 1.	
	16.5.16.		Casualties.	
			19th Northd.Fus. wounded O.R. 1, 17th R.Scots wounded O.R. 1, 17th W.Yorks wounded O.R. 2 (includes 1 accidental by M.G. Bullet jam), 18th H.L.I. wounded O.R.1, 14th Glosters wounded O.R.1 15th Sherwoods killed O.R. 1, 158th F.A.Bde wounded O.R. 1.	
	17.5.16.		Casualties.	
			17th R.Scots killed O.R. 4 wounded 4, 17th W.Yorks killed O.R. 2 wounded 2, 16th Cheshires wounded O.R. 1, 14th Glosters wounded O.R. 2.	
	18.5.16.		Casualties.	
			17th W.Yorks killed O.R. 2 wounded 2m 18th H.L.I. wounded O.R. 3, 106th M.G.Coy wounded 2/Lt. W.N.MORRIS O.R. 1.	
	19.5.16.		Casualties.	
			17th R.Scots killed O.R. 1, 17th W.Yorks wounded Capt. G.H.MASON O.R. 1, 19th D.L.I. wounded O.R.3 18th H.L.I. killed O.R. 1, 15th Cheshires killed O.R. 1, 16th Cheshires wounded O.R.1 (accdtl)	

1875 Wt. W593/826 1,000,000 4/15 J.B.C. & A. A.D.S.S./Forms/C. 2118.

WAR DIARY or INTELLIGENCE SUMMARY

Army Form C. 2118

(Erase heading not required.)

Place	Date	Hour	Summary of Events and Information	Remarks and references to Appendices
	19.5.16.		Casualties (Contd) 14th Glosters wounded Lt.L.A.MATTOCK O.R. 3 all accidental, 15th Sherwoods wounded Lt.G.H.BOOT O.R. 2 (all accidental) (Grenade explosion).	
	20.5.16.		Casualties. 17th R.Scots wounded O.R. 1, 17th W.Yorks wounded O.R. 2, 19th D.L.I. killed O.R. 2 wounded 1, 18th HLI wounded O.R. 1, 15th Cheshires wounded O.R. 1, 14th Glosters wounded O.R. 1 (at duty) 19th Northd.Fus. killed 2/Lt. B.J. WILLIAMS.	
	21.5.16.		Casualties. 19th D.L.I. wounded O.R. 6 (includes 4 accidental), 18th H.L.I. wounded O.R. 1, 15th Cheshires wounded O.R. 2 (1 accidental 1 self-inflicted), 16th Cheshires wounded O.R. 3, 14th Glosters wounded O.R. 1, 15th Sherwoods wounded O.R. 2.	
	22.5.16.		Casualties. 204th Field Coy. R.E. killed O.R. 1, 18th H.L.I. wounded Lieut & Adjt. W.J.LYLE, 15th Cheshires wounded O.R. 2, 15th Sherwoods wounded O.R. 1 (at duty) 19th Nortd.Fus. wounded O.R. 3, 16th Cheshires wounded O.R. 2.	
	23.5.16.		Casualties. 16th Cheshires wounded O.R. 1, 14th Glosters wounded O.R. 1, 106th M.G.Coy wounded O.R. 1 (accidentally), 23rd Manch.R. wounded O.R. 2, 19th Northd Fus. wounded O.R. 2.	
	24.5.16.		Casualties. 17th Lancs.Fus. killed O.R. 1 wounded 1, 20th Lancs.Fus. wounded O.R. 1 (at duty), 204th Field Coy. R.E. killed O.R. 1, 16th Cheshires wounded O.R. 2, 14th Glosters wounded O.R. 7 (includes 3 at duty), 15th Sherwoods killed O.R. 1.	

WAR DIARY

INTELLIGENCE SUMMARY

(Erase heading not required.)

Army Form C. 2118

Instructions regarding War Diaries and Intelligence Summaries are contained in F. S. Regs., Part II. and the Staff Manual respectively. Title Pages will be prepared in manuscript.

Place	Date	Hour	Summary of Events and Information	Remarks and references to Appendices
	25.5.16.		Casualties. 16th Cheshires wounded O.R. 3 (at duty), 14th Glosters killed O.R. 1 wounded 1, 18th Lancs. Fus wounded O.R. 1.	
	26.5.16.		Casualties. 19th D.L.I. wounded O.R. 2, 16th Cheshires wounded Capt. S.C.BACON, killed O.R. 1 wounded 4, 15th Sherwoods wounded O.R. 1 (accidental rifle shot), 105th M.G.Coy wounded O.R. 1, 17th Lancs. Fus. killed O.R. 2 wounded 3, 18th Lancs.Fus. wounded O.R. 1, 23rd Manch.R. wounded 2/Lt. L.D. FITZGERALD (accidentally by Very Light Pistol)	13
	27.5.16.		Casualties. 17th Lancs.Fus. killed O.R. 1, 18th Lancs.Fus. killed Lieut.K.D.EAST O.R. 2 wounded 1, 16th Cheshires wounded O.R. 1, 14th Glosters killed O.R. 1 wounded 1, 15th Sherwoods wounded O.R. 5, B/159 Bde R.F.A. killed O.R. 1 wounded 6.	
	28.5.16.		Casualties. 17th W.Yorks wounded O.R. 1, 17th Lancs.Fus. wounded 2/Lt. G.WATSON, 18th Lancs.Fus. killed O.R. 1 wounded 1 (accidental), 23rd Manch.R. wounded O.P. 1, 19th Northd.Fus. wounded O.R. 1, 15th Cheshires wounded O.R. 4 (1 accidental), 16th Cheshires wounded O.R. 1, 15th Sherwoods wounded O.R. 1, 204th Field Coy R.E wounded O.R. 1,	35
	29.5.16.		Casualties. 159 Bde R.F.A. wounded 2/Lt. C.M.DAVENPORT, 17th W.Yorks wounded O.R. 2, 19th D.L.I. wounded O.R. 1, 15th Cheshires wounded O.R. 5, 15th Sherwoods wounded O.R. 1, 18th Lancs. Fus. wounded O.R. 1, 20th Lancs. Fus. killed O.R. 1, 23rd Manch.R. wounded O.R. 2 (1 accidental).	
	30.5.16.		Casualties. 15th Cheshires killed O.R. 1 wounded 5 (3 at duty), 14th Glosters wounded O.R. 1, 15th Sherwoods	

Army Form C. 2118

WAR DIARY

INTELLIGENCE SUMMARY

(Erase heading not required.)

Instructions regarding War Diaries and Intelligence Summaries are contained in F. S. Regs., Part II. and the Staff Manual respectively. Title Pages will be prepared in manuscript.

Place	Date	Hour	Summary of Events and Information	Remarks and references to Appendices
	30.5.16.		Casualties (Contd).	
			wounded O.R. 2, 19th Northd.Fus. wounded O.R. 1, 23rd Manch.R. wounded O.R. 2 (1 at duty) 17th R.Scots wounded O.R. 3, 17th W.Yorks killed O.R. 1 wounded 6.	
	31.5.16.		Casualties.	
			15th Sherwoods wounded 2/Lt. W.J.CRIDGE, 2/Lt.S.H.B.LESTER, 2/Lt. B.SNAPE (at duty), missing believed killed Lt. E.C. JACKSON, wounded and missing believed prisoner Capt. R.W.AINSWORTH, killed O.R. 8 wounded 17 (1 at duty) missing 21, 17th Lancs. Fus. wounded 2/Lt.F.R. DERWENT, O.R. 3, 20th Lancs. Fus. wounded O.R. 1, 23rd Manch.R. wounded O.R. 6 (1 at duty) 18th Lancs. Fus. killed O.R. 2 wounded 24 (3 at duty) 15th Cheshires killed O.R. 1 wounded 15 (7 at duty) 16th Cheshires wounded O.R. 2, 14th Closters killed O.R. 3 wounded 10 missing 6, 105th M.G. Coy wounded 2/Lt. R.W. ABBOTTS, 2/Lt. W.H. CANNING, 2/Lt. H.C. GRAHAM, killed O.R. 1 wounded 2, 17th R. Scots wounded 2/Lt. E.R. CRAIG, killed O.R. 1, 17th W.Yorks wounded O.R. 6, 204th Fd. Coy. R.E. killed O.R. 1, 157th F.A. Bde missing O.R. 1, 158th F.A. Bde wounded O.R. 3, 159th F.A. Bde wounded O.R. 2 missing 1, 106th F.Amb. killed O.R. 1, 19th Northd.Fus. wounded O.R. 2.	

WAR DIARY or **INTELLIGENCE SUMMARY**

Army Form C. 2118

Headquarters 35th Division

Date 30-6-16

JUNE 1916 Vol 4

A 59

Place	Date	Hour	Summary of Events and Information	Remarks and references to Appendices
IN THE FIELD	1-6-16		CASUALTIES. 19th. North Fus. killed 2ndLt. R.C.DAVIES: O.R. 1, wounded 5: 1/5 D.C.L.I. wounded O.R. 1: 17th. Royal Scots, killed O.R. 1, wounded 2: 17th. West Yorks, wounded O.R. 1: 18th. High L.I. wounded O.R. 1: 17th. Lan Fus, wounded O.R. 1: 15th. Cheshires, wounded O.R. 1: 205th. Field Coy, wounded O.R. 1.	
	2-6-16		CASUALTIES. 14th. Glosters, killed O.R. 1, wounded 3: 17th. West Yorks, wounded O.R. 1 at duty: 19th. Durh. L.I. wounded O.R. 1: 18th. High. L.I. wounded 2ndLt W. LAMBERT; 2/4th. Glosters, wounded O.R. 1: 23rd. Manch. Regt. wounded O.R. 1. 19th. North. Fus. wounded O.R. 1: (suppltmentary) 19th. North. Fus. wounded O.R. 1 1/5th. D.C.L.I. wounded O.R. 1:	
	3-6-16		CASUALTIES. 14th. Glosters, wounded O.R. 2: 2/8th. Worcesters, killed O.R. 1, wounded 1: 17th. Lan Fus, wounded O.R. 3, included 1 at duty: 18th. Lan Fus, wounded O.R. 1: 20th. Lan Fus, killed O.R. 1, wounded 1: 2/7th Worcesters wounded O.R. 1: 19th. Durh. L.I. killed O.R. 1: 18th. High. L.I. wounded O.R. 1: 1/3rd. Herts, wounded O.R. 1 (reported 8-6-16) :	
	4-6-16		CASUALTIES. 19th. Durh. L.I. wounded O.R. 2: 18th. High. L.I. wounded O.R. 2 : 8th. Worcesters, killed O.R. 2, wounded 1: 17th. Lan Fus, wounded O.R. 2,-1st duty: 14th. Glosters, killed O.R. 2, wounded 4 - includes 1 at duty:	
	5-6-16		CASUALTIES. 20th. Lan fus, wounded O.R. 3: 2/7th. Worcesters, wounded O.R. 1-accidentally at duty 23rd. Manchr. Regt. killed O.R. 1, wounded 2: 16th. Cheshires, killed O.R. 1 wounded 8: 14th. Glosters, wounded Lt H.C. KINRED, 2ndLt L.H.E. STENSON, O.R. 1: 2/8th. Worcesters, wounded O.R. 1: 17th. Royal Scots, killed O.R. 1: 17th. West Yorks, wounded O.R. 1.	

Army Form C. 2118

Headquarters
35th Division

No. ....
Date 30/6/16

WAR DIARY
or
INTELLIGENCE SUMMARY
(Erase heading not required.)

Instructions regarding War Diaries and Intelligence Summaries are contained in F.S. Regs., Part II. and the Staff Manual respectively. Title Pages will be prepared in manuscript.

Place	Date	Hour	Summary of Events and Information	Remarks and references to Appendices
IN THE FIELD	5-6-16. 31-5-16.		CASUALTIES. (supplementary) 19th. North Fus. killed O.R. 1, wounded 1; do. 14th. Glosters, missing O.R. 1;	
	6-6-16.		CASUALTIES. 17th. West Yorks, killed O.R. 1; 2/7th. Worcesters attached 18th. Lan Fus killed O.R.1 104th. Bde Machine Gun Coy, killed 2ndLt. D.W. SPANKIE; 2/4th. Glosters wounded O.R. 1 2/6th. Glosters, wounded O.R. 1.	
	7-6-16.		CASUALTIES. 18th. Lan. Fus, wounded 2ndLt. L. LOMAS, accidentally, bayonet wound. 2/7th. Worcesters, wounded O.R. 2, accidentally; 14th. Glosters, wounded O.R. 2 Accdly 2/4th. Glosters, killed O.R. 1, wounded 1; 17th. West Yorks, killed 2ndLt. S.L.HITCHEN. O.R. 2, wounded 2: D.A.C., wounded O.R. 1, (reported 8-6-16:	
	8-6-16.		CASUALTIES. 17th. Lan Fus, wounded O.R. 1: 18th. Lan Fus, wounded O.R. 1: 23rd Manchr. Regt, wounded O.R. 2: 2/8th. Worcesters, wounded O.R. 1: 17th. West Yorks, killed O.R. 1, wounded 1, at duty: 18th. High. L.I. killed O.R. 1; 2/4th. Glosters, killed O.R. 1, wounded 1:	
	9-6-16.		CASUALTIES. 18th. Lan Fus, wounded O.R. 5 (includes 2 at duty): 15th. Cheshires, wounded O.R. 1. accidentally, gun shot: 16th. Cheshires, wounded O.R. 1-attached 105/1 T.M. Battery 14th. Glosters, killed LT-COL. G.C. ROBERTS, CAPT. H.A. BUTT, wounded, 2ndLt. J.F.BROWN killed O.R. 3, wounded 14, missing 1: 15th. Sherwoods, wounded O.R. 1-attached 105/1 T.M. Battery (accidentally by bomb): 2/8th. Worcesters, wounded O.R. 2, includes 1 accidentally gun shot: 17th. West Yorks, killed O.R. 1: 203 Coy R.E. wounded O.R. 1 205 Coy R.E. wounded O.R. 1: B/163 Batty. R.F.A., wounded 2ndLt. W. CHAMBERS; O.R. 1 Z/35 T. M. Bty. wounded O.R. 1:	
	10-6-16.		CASUALTIES. 19th. North Fus., killed O.R. 1 (supplementary 9th): 14th. Glosters, missing O.R. 3 (supplementary 9th): 18th. Lan Fus wounded O.R. 2: 23rd. Manchr. R. wounded O.R. 1; 15th. Cheshires, wounded LIEUT. J.T.N. WILSON, accidental, at duty: O.R. 3, 2 accdtl, grenade explosion: 17th. Royal Scots, killed O.R. 1: 17th. West Yorks, wounded O.R1 19th. Durh. L.I., killed O.R.1:	
	8th-9th. June 16.		14th. Glosters raided German trenches during night of 8/9th, and captured one machine gun, and killed between 20 and 30 of the enemy.	

1875 Wt. W.533/826 1,000,000 4/15 J.B.C. & A. A.D.S.S./Forms/C.2118.

Army Form C. 2118

Headquarters
35th Division

No. ....
Date 30.6.16

WAR DIARY
or
INTELLIGENCE SUMMARY
(Erase heading not required.)

Instructions regarding War Diaries and Intelligence Summaries are contained in F.S. Regs., Part II. and the Staff Manual respectively. Title Pages will be prepared in manuscript.

Place	Date	Hour	Summary of Events and Information	Remarks and references to Appendices
IN THE FIELD	11-6-16.		CASUALTIES. 18th. Lan Fus, killed 2ndLt. J.V. STRONG, O.R. 2., wounded 2ndLt. E.M.STANSFIELD? O.R. 8, missing 1, (attempted raid): 23rd. Manchr. R, wounded 2ndLt, F.J. COOK, at duty: 20th. Lan Fus, wounded O.R. 1: X/35 T. M. Baty. wounded O.R. 1: 17th. Royal Scots, wounded O.R. 1: 17th. West Yorks, killed O.R. 1, wounded O.R. 2, (1 at duty): 19th. Durh L.I., killed O.R. 1: 15th. Sherwoods, wounded O.R. 2: (at duty)	
	12-6-16		CASUALTIES. 18th. Lan Fus, wounded 2ndLt. A.H. MARKWICK, O.R. 1: 23rd. Manch R, wounded O.R. 1: 15th. Cheshires, wounded O.R. 4 - (1 at duty): 15th. Sherwoods, killed O.R. 1: 17th. West Yorks, wounded O.R. 1:	
	13-6-16.		CASUALTIES. 17th. Lan Fus, killed O.R. 2 - (1 accidentally, rifle bullet): 20th. Lan Fus, wounded O.R. 3 - (1 at duty & 2 accidentally, rifle bullet): 15th. Cheshires, wounded O.R. 3:	
	14-6-16.		CASUALTIES. 15th. Cheshires, wounded 2ndLt. G.D. ALEXANDER, O.R. 5 - (includes 3 at duty): 15th. Sherwoods, wounded O.R. 1 - (accidentally, gun shot): 17th. West Yorks, wounded O.R. 1 - (accidentally by bomb): 17th. Lan Fus, wounded O.R. 3 - (includes 2 at duty): 20th Lan Fus, killed O.R. 1:	
	15-6-16.		CASUALTIES. 15th Cheshires, wounded O.R. 1: 15th Sherwoods, wounded O.R. 1: 20th Lan Fus, wounded O.R. 1: 17th West Yorks, wounded O.R. 1 - shell shock:	
	16-6-16.		CaSUALTIES. 17th. Lan Fus, killed O.R. 1, wounded O.R. 1: 20th Lan Fus, wounded O.R. 1:	
	17-6-16.		CASUALTIES. B/157 Bde R.F.A., killed 2ndLt. G.B. OLIVER,: 17th Lan Fus, wounded 2ndLt. G.E. CONDLIFFE, (at duty), O.R. 3, - includes 1 at duty: 105 Bde M.G. Coy, wounded O.R. 1: The Division was relieved on 17th. by the 39th. and 61st Divisions, and moved into Southern Corps Reserve Area with Divisional H.Q. at BUSNES.	
	18-6-16.		CASUALTIES. 106th Bde M.G. Coy., wounded O.R. 1:	

Army Form C. 2118

WAR DIARY
or
INTELLIGENCE SUMMARY
(Erase heading not required.)

Headquarters
35th Division
No..................
Date 30.6.16

Instructions regarding War Diaries and Intelligence Summaries are contained in F. S. Regs., Part II. and the Staff Manual respectively. Title Pages will be prepared in manuscript.

Place	Date	Hour	Summary of Events and Information	Remarks and references to Appendices
	20-6-16.		CASUALTIES. 163 Bde R.F.A., wounded O.R. 1, at duty, (supplementary to /9th): 106th Bde M.G. Coy., killed O.R. 1:	
	21-6-16.		CASUALTIES. 17th West Yorks, wounded O.R. 1 (accidentally by bomb):	
IN	22-6-16.		CASUALTIES. 106th Bde. M.G. Coy., killed O.R. 1., wounded 2:	
THE	24-6-16.		From noon on 24th. the Division became G.H.Q. Reserve and remained at BUSNES.	
FIELD.	25-6-16.		CASUALTIES. 15th Sherwoods, missing O.R. 1., (1 man more now reported missing from raid by enemy reported in casualty wire of 31st May):	
	27-6-16.		CASUALTIES. 104th Bde. M.G. Coy, wounded O.R. 1; 105th Bde M.G. Coy, wounded Lieut. J.J.LAING, (attached) from Artists Rifles:	
	30-6-16.		CASUALTIES. 167 Bde R. F. A., wounded 2ndLt. J.S.R. HUNTER, attached 39th. Division:	

A. & Q.

35th DIVISION.

JULY 1916

Army Form C. 2118

WAR DIARY
or
INTELLIGENCE SUMMARY
(Erase heading not required.)

Instructions regarding War Diaries and Intelligence Summaries are contained in F. S. Regs., Part II. and the Staff Manual respectively. Title Pages will be prepared in manuscript.

Headquarters
35th Division
No. A.B.
Date 11-8-16

Place	Date	Hour	Summary of Events and Information	Remarks and references to Appendices
IN THE FIELD.	1-7-16.		CASUALTIES. 16th. Cheshires, killed O.R. 1-(accidentally drowned): 17th. West Yorks, wounded O.R. 1:	
	2-7-16.		CASUALTIES. 157 Bde. R.F.A. killed 2ndLt. J.S.K.HUNTER - reported by 116 Inf. Bde:	
	8-7-16.		CASUALTIES. 19th. North. Fus. killed O.R. 3, wounded 14-(includes 6 at duty):	
	9-7-16.		CASUALTIES. 19th. North. Fus. wounded O.R. 5-(includes 2 at duty):	
	11-7-16.		CASUALTIES. 19th. North. Fus. killed O.R. 1, wounded 12-(includes 4 at duty): 204th. Field Coy. R.E. wounded O.R. 1: 203rd. Field Coy R.E. wounded O.R. 3-shell shock	
	12-7-16.		CASUALTIES. 19th. North. Fus. killed, CAPT. T.R.A.H. NOYES, O.R. 5, wounded CAPT. J.STORAR-(shell shock), O.R. 32-(includes 5 at duty & 17 shell shock), missing, beleived killed 3: 17th. Lan. Fus. killed O.R. 1, wounded 3: 17th. Royal Scots, wounded O.R. 1-(accidentally, bomb explosion): 204th. Field Coy, wounded O.R. 2: 205th. Field Coy, killed O.R. 1, wounded 4:	
	13-7-16.		CASUALTIES. 203rd. Field Coy, killed O.R. 2, wounded 2: 204th. Field Coy. wounded O.R. 1: 17th. Lan. Fus. wounded O.R. 1:	
	14-7-16.		CASUALTIES. 17th. Lan. Fus, wounded O.R. 12-(accidentally): 18th. Lan. Fus, killed O.R. 1: 19th. Durh. L.I. wounded O.R. 1: 18th. High. L.I. wounded O.R. 1: 1/1st. W. Hussars, wounded O.R. 1: 205th. Field Coy, wounded O.R. 1:	
	15-7-16.		CASUALTIES. 19th. Durh. L.I. wounded 2ndLt. S. CARROLL; 15th. Cheshires, wounded O.R. 1-(accidentally):	
	16-7-16.		CASUALTIES. 17th. West Yorks, wounded O.R. 4-(1 accidentally): 19th. Durh. L.I. wounded O.R. 9-(accidentally): 18th. High. L.I. killed O.R. 4, wounded 3: 106th. Mac Gun Coy, wounded O.R. 2: 15th. Cheshires, wounded O.R. 1:	

Army Form C. 2118

WAR DIARY
or
INTELLIGENCE SUMMARY

(Erase heading not required.)

Instructions regarding War Diaries and Intelligence Summaries are contained in F. S. Regs., Part II. and the Staff Manual respectively. Title Pages will be prepared in manuscript.

Place	Date	Hour	Summary of Events and Information	Remarks and references to Appendices
IN THE FIELD.	17-7-16.		CASUALTIES. 19th. Durh. L.I. wounded O.R. 4-(2 accidentally & 2 at duty): 18th. High. L.I. killed O.R. 4, wounded 22: 19th. North. Fus. wounded O.R. 2: 15th. Cheshires, wounded CAPT. WILLS. R.A.M.C., O.R. 1: 16th. Cheshires, wounded 2ndLt. R.MACLAREN, O.R. 3: 14th. Glosters, wounded O.R. 4-(1 at duty): 15th. Sherwoods, wounded CAPT. K.W. MORELL, O.R. 11-(4 at duty):	
	18-7-16.		CASUALTIES. 204th. Field Coy, wounded O.R. 1: 19th. North Fus, wounded O.R. 3: 15th. Cheshires killed O.R. 4, wounded XXX 6: 16th. Cheshires, killed O.R. 1, wounded 12: 14th. Glosters wounded O.R. 2: 15th. Sherwoods, killed O.R. 1, wounded 15: Mac. Gun Coy, wounded O.R. 1: 17th. West Yorks, wounded LT. A.H.COLBECK. O.R. 9: killed O.R. 4: 19th. Durh. L.I. killed O.R. 8, wounded LIEUT J.PHILLIPS, O.R. 17: 18th. High. L.I. killed O.R. 6, wounded 29:	
	19-7-16.		CASUALTIES. 15th.Cheshires, killed 2ndLt G.F.AUSTIN, O.R. 6, wounded CAPT H. JOHNSTON -(at duty) LT-COL. F.W.M.NEWELL, LT. C.S.ASHCROFT, O.R. 25: 14th. Glosters wounded O.R. 2: 15th. Sherwoods, killed O.R. 2: 105th. Mac. Gun. Coy, killed O.R. 2, wounded 3: 17th. Lan. Fus. killed O.R. 1, wounded 4: 20th. Lan Fus. wounded O.R. 1: 19th. Durh. L.I. wounded CAPT. R.C.TAYLOR, LT. J MUNDY, 2ndLT W.F.REEVE; 18th. High. L.I. killed O.R. 15, wounded, CAPT. W. KENNEDY-(at duty), Lieut. J. BARRIE; O.R. 42: 17th. Royal Scots, wounded, LT-COL. R.D.CHEALES, CAPT.R.C.BARRY, CAPT. E.E.RUDDELL,: 106th. Mac Gun Coy, wounded LT. G.G. DINEEN:	
	20-7-16.		CASUALTIES. 18th. Lan Fus, wounded O.R. 1: 20th. Lan Fus, wounded 2ndLt. N.G.MYERS, O.R. 7: 23rd. Manchr. Regt., killed, CAPT. J.E.ROTHBAND, CAPT. F.W.GOSLING, O.R. 22, wounded CAPT. A.W.COOPER, LT. J.WILSON, 2ndLt. R.A.HAMER, 2ndLt. A.EMPSON, 2ndLt. G.LYE, O.R. 111, missing, MAJOR E.L.MAXWELL, O.R. 19:	

WAR DIARY
or
INTELLIGENCE SUMMARY

(Erase heading not required.)

Army Form C. 2118

Instructions regarding War Diaries and Intelligence Summaries are contained in F.S. Regs., Part II. and the Staff Manual respectively. Title Pages will be prepared in manuscript.

Place	Date	Hour	Summary of Events and Information	Remarks and references to Appendices
IN THE FIELD.	20-7-15.		CASUALTIES. 19th. North Fus, wounded O.R. 7: 105th. Mac Gun Coy, killed O.R. 6, wounded 2ndLt R.W.ABBOTTS, 2ndLt S.GRIFFIN, 2ndLt H.WILLIAMS, O.R. 16: 15th. Cheshires, killed 2ndLt G.F.AUSTIN, O.R. 16, wounded LT-Col. F.W.M.NEWELL, 2ndLt. C.S. ASHCROFT. CAPT. H.JOHNSTON, O.R. 118: 16th. Cheshires, killed LT.A.C.STYLES, O.R. 32, wounded LT-COL. R.C.BROWNE CLAYTON, MAJOR. R. WORTHINGTON, LT. H.D.RYALLS, 2ndLt. J.A.BLAKE, - all at duty, CAPT. C JOHNSON, 2ndLts W.H.FINLAY, R.McLAREN, R.P. SCHOLEFIELD: O.R. 202: 15th. Sherwoods killed CAPT.T.B.CUTTS, LT.A.D.HODGSON, 2ndLTS. G.W.WINKLEY, F.L.REYNOLDS, F.J.DIXON, R.S.HOLLAM, G.B.KEATING, F.H.TALBOT, O.R. 59, wounded (MAJOR H.P.G.COCHRAN - at duty), CAPT. W.L.RENWICK, CAPT.J.N.MORRIS, 2ndLts M.N.HARVEY, J.W.P.MACKINTOSH, R.C.HOLMAN, S.L.WILSON, A.R.BUTLER, J.C.MACHUTCHEON, O.R. 234: 14th. Glosters, killed LT. E.C.STAGG, 2ndLt. P.B.LEES, O.R. 22, wounded CAPT. C.S.HILLER, 2ndLt A.G.LEGG, 2ndLt. G.W.REEVES, (2ndLt C.L.P.GILSHENAN, 2ndLt C.R.CHARSLEY - wounded at duty), O.R. 82: 17th. West Yorks, wounded CAPT. B.L. WILTSHIRE, O.R. 12: 19th. Durh. L.I. wounded 2ndLt. P.V.FRENCH, O.R. 116, killed O.R. 16, missing 28,: 18th. Hgh. L.I. wounded 2ndLt. T.CURR, O.R. 46, missing 13:	6 16 32 59 2 10
	21-7-16.		CASUALTIES. 17th. Royal Scots, killed O.R. 3, wounded 2ndLt. T.MILLER, O.R. 10,: 107th. Fld Amb. 17th. West Yorks, wounded O.R. 4,: 18th. Lan Fus, wounded O.R. 5: wounded O.R. 1: 19th. North Fus, wounded O.R. 1: 159 Bde. R.F.A. wounded O.R. 1, 158 Bde. R.F.A. wounded O.R. 1:	2 3
	22-7-15.		CASUALTIES. 17th. Royal Scots, wounded O.R. 1: 19th. Durh. L.I. killed O.R. 1, wounded 3: 107th. Field Amb. killed O.R. 1, wounded 1: 17th. Lan Fus, killed O.R. 2, wounded 2ndLt. S.N.OPENSHAW, O.R. 27: 18th. Lan Fus, killed LIEUT. E.H.S. EVANS, O.R. 4, wounded LIEUT J.WILLIAMS, LIEUT F. LINDSAY-JONES, CAPT H.R.WILCOX. 2ndLt. E.M.STANSFIELD, LIEUT J.P. MOUNSEY, LIEUT E.G. MATTINGLEY, 2ndLt. W.N. GREENHALGH, O.R. 59, missing 5: 20th. Lan Fus killed O.R. 3, wounded 5: 23rd. Manchr R. killed O.R. 1, wounded 7, missing 1: 104th. Mac Gun Coy. wounded O.R. 1: 157th. Bde R.F.A. killed O.R. 3, wounded 2ndLt. W. STUART, 2ndLt J.L.BARR: O.R. 15: 159th. Bde ½ R.F.A. wounded O.R. 1: 158th. Bde. R.F.A. wounded O.R. 1 :	3 4 3 3

Army Form C. 2118

WAR DIARY
or
INTELLIGENCE SUMMARY
(Erase heading not required.)

Instructions regarding War Diaries and Intelligence Summaries are contained in F. S. Regs., Part II. and the Staff Manual respectively. Title Pages will be prepared in manuscript.

Place	Date	Hour	Summary of Events and Information	Remarks and references to Appendices
IN THE FIELD.	22-7-16.		CASUALTIES. (Supplementary to 22nd) 19th. North Fus, wounded LIEUT. M.S. ANTHONY, O.R. 11 : 15th. Cheshires, wounded O.R. 1,: 16th. Cheshires, killed O.R. 1, wounded 5: 14th. Glosters, killed O.R. 1, wounded 8: 105th. Mac Gun Coy, wounded O.R. 4:	
	23-7-16.		CASUALTIES. 23rd. Manchr. Regt, wounded 2ndLt. H.L.WILLEY, O.R. 14: 104th. Mac Gun Coy, killed O.R. 1, wounded, 2ndLt. S.G.A.BROOKS, O.R. 3: 17th. Lan Fus, wounded LT-COL, A.M. MILLS, MAJOR SIR H.S.M. HAVELOCK ALLEN, O.R. 30: 17th. Royal Scots, killed O.R. 4, wounded 8: 17th. West Yorks, wounded O.R. 3: 203rd. Fld Co. R.E. wounded O.R. 5: 204th. Fld Co. R.E. wounded O.R. 1: 205th. Fld Co. R.E., wounded O.R. 2: 157th Bde. R.F.A. killed O.R. 2, wounded 3: 159th. Bde R.F.A. wounded CAPT. S.BROWN. R.A.M.C.(S.R.), O.R. 7, killed O.R. 2: 163rd. Bde R.F.A. wounded O.R. 1: (Supplementary) 104th. T.M. Battyery, wounded O.R. 2:	108
	24-7-16.		CASUALTIES. 19th. North Fus, wounded CAPT. A.W. MUIR, CAPT. W.S.GORDON. R.A.M.C.- at duty, O.R. 6: 18th. Lan Fus, killed O.R. 7, wounded 16, missing 3: 20th. Lan Fus, wounded LIEUT W.G.SHAND,(R.A.M.C.) 2ndLt. P.J. McKIVITT, O.R. 9, killed O.R. 3: 23rd. Manchr Regt, wounded lieut. W.E.A.BEARD (R.A.M.C); O.R. 19: 15th. Cheshires, killed O.R. 1, wounded 4: 16th. Cheshires, wounded 2ndLt. M.L.ABRAHAMS, O.R. 6: 14th. Glosters, killed O.R. 1: 15th. Sherwoods, wounded O.R.1: 205th, Fld Co. R.E.. killed O.R. 1, wounded 5: 203rd. Fld Coy R.E. wounded O.R. 3: 35th. Divl. Signal Co, wounded O.R. 1: 17th. Royal Scots, wounded O.R. 9: 17th West Yorks, killed O.R. 4, wounded 11: 19th. Durh. L.I., killed 2ndLt. W. BRAIDFORD, wounded 2ndLt. S.H.SMITH, O.R. 31: 18th. High. L.I., killed O.R. 2, wounded CAPT. A.C.BALFOUR (at Duty), O.R. 20: 106th. Mac Gun Coy, killed O.R. 1, wounded 6: 158th. Bde R.F.A. wounded CAPT. C.H.HUGHES-GIBB, O.R. 3: 157th. Bde. R.F.A. wounded O.R. 1: 163rd. Bde. R.F.A. wounded O.R. 2:	
	25-7-16.		CASUALTIES. 18th. Lan Fus, wounded O.R. 8: 17th. Lan Fus, killed O.R. 31, wounded, 2ndLt. S.R. CARTER, 2ndLt. H.MARSHALL, LIEUT. H.J. BIRNSTINGL, (LIEUT. W.D.CHESHIRE, 2ndLt. J.J.FLOWER, at duty), O.R. 141: 104th. Mac Gun Coy, killed O.R. 2, wounded 1: 15th. Cheshires, wounded O.R. 6: 14th. Glosters, wounded O.R. 1: 15th. Sherwoods, wounded 2ndLt. H. WHITWORTH, O.R. 3: 106th. Fld Amb. killed O.R. 2:	

1875 Wt. W593/826 1,000,000 4/15 J.B.C. & A. A.D.S.S./Forms/C. 2118.

Army Form C. 2118

WAR DIARY
or
INTELLIGENCE SUMMARY
(Erase heading not required.)

Instructions regarding War Diaries and Intelligence Summaries are contained in F.S. Regs., Part II. and the Staff Manual respectively. Title Pages will be prepared in manuscript.

Place	Date	Hour	Summary of Events and Information	Remarks and references to Appendices
IN THE FIELD.	25-7-16.		CASUALTIES. 17th. Royal Scots, killed O.R. 3, wounded 15, missing 3: 17th. West Yorks, killed O.R. 8, wounded 45: 19th. Durh. L.I. wounded, LIEUT. C.H.POLLOCK, O.R. 22, killed O.R. 1: 18th. High. L.I. killed O.R. 8, wounded LIEUT. H. MARTIN, O.R. 27: 106th. Mac Gun Coy, wounded O.R. 1: 19th. North Fus, wounded, 2ndLt. A.D.CARRICK, -(at duty O.R. 4: 107th. Fld. Amb, wounded O.R. 1: 157th. Bde. R.F.A. killed 2ndLt. R.G. BANNERMAN, O.R. 1, wounded 7: 163rd. Bde. R.F.A. wounded CAPT. J.KEITH - at duty, O.R. 1: Y. T.M.Battery, wounded O.R. 1: 159th. Bde. R.F.A. wounded O.R. 2:	(at duty
	26-7-16.		CASUALTIES. 203rd. Fld Ce. R.E., killed O.R. 1, wounded 9: 205th. Fld. Coy. R.E. wounded O.R. 4: 16th. Cheshires, wounded O.R. 2: 15th. Cheshires, wounded O.R. 1: 14th. Glosters wounded O.R. 4: 35th. Div Signal Coy., wounded LIEUT. S.B.MACLAREN, O.R. 1: 105th. Mac Gun Coy, wounded O.R. 1: 18th. Lan Fus, wounded O.R. 8: 23rd. Manchr. Regt. wounded 2ndLt. F.J. COOK, O.R. 1: 104th. Mac. Gun Coy, killed O.R. 1, wounded 1: 19th. North Fus, wounded, 2ndLt. A.P.JONES, O.R. 12: 17th. West Yorks, killed O.R. 1, wounded LIEUT. A.M. HAMILTON, O.R. 17: 19th. Durh. L.I., killed O.R. 6, wounded 5, missing 8: 106th. Fld Amb., wounded O.R. 1: 159th. Bde R.F.A., wounded, LIEUT. R?M. CAMPBELL, O.R. 1: Divl. Amm. Col, killed O.R. 1:	
	27-7-16.		CASUALTIES. 17th. Royal Scots, killed O.R. 1, wounded 2: 17th. West Yorks, wounded O.R. 1, missing, 1: 19th. North Fus, killed O.R. 1, wounded 5: 205th. Fld Coy, wounded O.R. 1: 15th. Cheshires, killed O.R. 5, wounded 25: 16th. Cheshires, wounded O.R. 3: 14th. Glosters, wounded O.R. 6: 15th. Sherwoods, killed O.R. 2 wounded 3: 105th. Mac Gun Coy, wounded 2ndLt. L.G.VERNER, O.R. 7: Divl. Train wounded O.R. 1: 18th. Lan Fus, killed O.R. 1, wounded 2ndLt. H.D.ALMON, 2nd. LT. F.D.SOWERBY, O.R. 10, missing 1:	
	24-7-16.) 27-7-16.)		CASUALTIES. 20th. Lan Fus, killed CAPT. L.R.C. DOUGLAS-HAMILTON, O.R. 25, wounded, CAPT. R.A.S. COKE - at duty, 2nd. Lieuts. R. HUGHES, W.E. ROTHWELL, W.D.CUMMINGS, L.G.MATTEWS, A.N.L.LAMBERT, LIEUT. R.M.MORLEY, missing 1, wounded O.R. 75, missing 13: 23rd. Manchr. Regt. killed O.R. 10, wounded 78, missing 2:	126
	27-7-16.		CASUALTIES. H.Q. 104th. Bde, wounded CAPT. B.L. MONTGOMERY - at duty: LIEUT. H?C.DAVIES (believed killed g)	

1875 Wt. W593/826 1,000,000 4/15 J.B.C. & A. A.D.S.S./Forms/C. 2118.

Army Form C. 2118

WAR DIARY
or
INTELLIGENCE SUMMARY
(Erase heading not required.)

Place	Date	Hour	Summary of Events and Information	Remarks and references to Appendices
IN THE FIELD.	27-7-16.		CASUALTIES. 159th. Bde. R.F.A., killed O.R. 3, wounded 1: 158th. Bde. R.F.A., wounded O.R. 4: 163rd. Bde. R.F.A., killed O.R. 1., WOUNDED 3: 157th. Bde. R.F.A., wounded O.R. 1:	
	28-7-16.		CASUALTIES. 15th. Cheshires, killed 2ndLt. G.H.DICKINSON, wounded 2ndLt. S. SCHOLEFIELD, 2ndLt. J.N. WATSON, killed O.R. 2, wounded 12: 14th. Glosters, killed O.R. 2; wounded 12: 15th. Sherwoods, missing O.R. 1: 106th. Fld Amb., wounded O.R. 1: 204th. Fld Coy R.E., wounded O.R. 1: 17th. Royal Scots, killed O.R. 4, wounded 7; missing 1: 17th. West Yorks, wounded O.R. 1: 18th. High. L.I. wounded O.R. 1: 19th. North. Fus., killed O.R. 2 wounded 13: 23rd. Manchr. Regt. wounded REV. J. DUFFIELD, C.F.: 159th. Bde. R.F.A., wounded O.R. 2: 163rd. Bde. R.F.A. killed O.R. 1; wounded 6:	
	29-7-16.		CASUALTIES. 15th. Cheshires, killed O.R. 9, wounded 15: 16th. Cheshires, killed O.R. 2, wounded 6: 14th. Glsoters, wounded O.R. 3: 15th. Sherwoods, killed O.R. 2; wounded 6: 105th. Fld. Amb. wounded O.R. 1: 19th. North Fus., wounded O.R. 16: 203rd. Fld Coy R.E. killed O.R.1 17th. West Yorks, wounded O.R. 2: 18th. High. L.I., wounded CAPT. W.KENNEDY - at duty: 163rd. Bde R.F.A. wounded LIEUT. C.A. MACLAREN, O.R. 4: 158th. Bde. R.F.A. wounded O.R. 1:	
	30-7-16.		CASUALTIES. 15th. Cheshires, wounded O.R. 3: 16th. Chesdires, killed O.R. 1, wounded 6, missing 1: 14th. Glosters, killed O.R. 2, wounded 8, missing 7: 15th. Sherwoods, wounded O.R. 3: 105th. Mac Gun Coy., wounded 2ndLt. W.M. WHITWORTH, O.R. 3: 107th. Fld Amb., wounded O.R. 2: 17th. Royal Scots, killed O.R. 4, wounded 6: 17th. West Yorks, killed O.R. 5, wounded LIEUT. E. FRICKER, 2ndLieuts. A.B.WESTON, E.F.LAWRENCE, S.A.O. THORNE, R. O'BRIEN, O.R. 65, missinh 10: 19th. Durh. L.I. killed O.R. 1: 18th. High. L.I. wounded O.R. 4: 106th. Mac Gun Coy., wounded O.R. 1: 18th. Lan Fus., wounded O.R. 5: Div. Amm Col., killed O.R. 1, wounded 2, missing 1: 159th. Bde. R.F.A., wounded LIEUT. T.W. MURRAY, 2ndLt. (at duty) F.L. UNDERWOOD, 2nd Lt. G.H. WINDER, O.R. 3: 157th. Bde. R.F.A. wounded 2ndLt. W.A. HENRICK, O.R. 5, killed O.R. 6: 35 T.M.Bty., killed O.R. 1: 163rd. Bde. R.F.A., wounded O.R. 4: 19th. North Fus., killed O.R. 1, wounded 4:	

Army Form C. 2118

WAR DIARY
or
INTELLIGENCE SUMMARY
(Erase heading not required.)

Instructions regarding War Diaries and Intelligence Summaries are contained in F.S. Regs., Part II. and the Staff Manual respectively. Title Pages will be prepared in manuscript.

Place	Date	Hour	Summary of Events and Information	Remarks and references to Appendices
IN THE FIELD.	31-7-16.		CASUALTIES. 17th. Lan Fus., killed 2ndLt. J.B. STRANG, O.R. 2, wounded CAPT. W.T. TAYLOR, 2ndLt. W.H. ROBINSON, O.R. 31, missing 7: 20th Lan Fus., wounded O.R. 13, missing 1: 23rd, Manchr Regt., wounded 2ndLt. E. HINES, 2ndLt. F. NORCROSS, O.R. 34, killed O.R. 5, missing 13: 104th. Mac Gun Coy., killed O.R. 1, wounded 1, missing 1: 19th. North Fus., killed O.R. 3, wounded 13: 107th. Fld Amb., wounded LIEUT. C.W. SHARRatt O.R. 1: A.B.C. (attchd. Fld Amb) wounded O.R. 1: 204th Field Coy R.E., wounded O.R. 5: 17th. Royal Scots, killed O.R. 2, wounded 11, missing 2: 19th. Durh. L.I., wounded O.R. 3: 18th. High. L.I., killed O.R. 1, wounded 3: 106th. Mac Gun Coy., killed O.R. 1, wounded 6: 17th. West Yorks., wounded 2ndLt. H.E. KEETON, O.R. 77, killed O.R. 19, missing 1: 14th. Glosters., wounded CAPT. F.H. TOOP, O.R. 10: 158th. Bde. R.F.A., killed CAPT. F.G. STEVENS, O.R. 1: 159th. Bde. R.F.A., wounded LIEUT. P.M. CAMPBELL, LIEUT. R.G. O'CONNOR, O.R. 4:	

A. & Q.

35th DIVISION

AUGUST 1 9 1 6

Army Form C. 2118

August Vol 6

WAR DIARY

INTELLIGENCE SUMMARY

Administrative Staff,
Headquarters,
35th Division.

(Erase heading not required.)

Instructions regarding War Diaries and Intelligence Summaries are contained in F.S. Regs., Part II. and the Staff Manual respectively. Title Pages will be prepared in manuscript.

Place	Date	Hour	Summary of Events and Information	Remarks and references to Appendices
	1.8.16.		Casualties. 17th W. Yorks Killed O.R. 1 wounded 7; 106th M.G. Coy. wounded O.R. 1; 20th Lancs. Fus. wounded O.R. 1; 107th Field Ambce. wounded O.R. 1.	
	2.8.16.		Casualties.19th D.L.I. missing O.R. 2;	
	3.8.16.		158th Bde R.F.A. Killed Capt. T. RILEY O.R. 2 wounded 4; 157th Bde R.F.A. wounded O.R. 2; 15th Sherwoods killed O.R. 1 accidental; 19th Northld. Fus. wounded O.R. 1 accidental	
	4.8.16.		159th Bde R.F.A. wounded 2/Lt. C.H. LANGTREE O.R. 3.	
	5.8.16.		157th Bde R.F.A. wounded O.R. 3; 163rd Bde R.F.A. wounded O.R.4; 159th Bde R.F.A. wounded O.R. 1.	
	6.8.16.		159th Bde R.F.A. wounded O.R. 1; 157th Bde R.F.A. wounded 2/Lt. A.G.S.GIBB, killed O.R. 3 wounded 5; 17th R. Scots wounded O.R. 1 accidentally.	
	7.8.16.		157th Bde R.F.A. killed O.R. 2 wounded 1; 163rd Bde R.F.A.wounded O.R. 1; 159th Bde R.F.A. wounded O.R. 1.	
	8.8.16.		157th Bde R.F.A. killed O.R. 1 wounded 1; 163rd Bde R.F.A. killed O.R./2 wounded 2; 158th Bde R.F.A. wounded 2/Lt. H.P. BENTON.	
	9.8.16.		158th Bde R.F.A. killed O.R.1; 157th Bde R.F.A.wounded O.R.2; 158th Bde R.F.A wounded O.R. 1.wounded 2/Lt. F.R. FORSTER	
	10.8.16.		159th Bde R.F.A.wounded O.R. 2.	
	11.8.16.		158th Bde R.F.A. wounded O.R. 1.	
	12.8.16.		Nil.	
	13.8.16.		15th Cheshires wounded Lt. R.FROST, killed O.R. 2 wounded 9.	
	14.8.16.		14th Glosters wounded O.R.	

WAR DIARY

INTELLIGENCE SUMMARY

(Erase heading not required.)

Army Form C. 2118

Place	Date	Hour	Summary of Events and Information	Remarks and references to Appendices
	15.8.16.		Casualties. 15th Cheshires wounded O.R.1; 16th Cheshires killed O.R. 1 wounded 11; 15th Sherwoods killed O.R. 1 wounded 3; 19th Northld. Fus. wounded O.R. 3; 17th W.Yorks wounded O.R. 1	
	16.8.16.		15th Cheshires wounded O.R.7; 204th Fld. Co. wounded O.R. 1; 23rd Manchesters wounded O.R. 2.	
	17.8.16.		14th Glosters wounded O.R. 8 ;	
	18.8.16.		20th Lancs. Fus. wounded O.R. 1; 19th Northld. Fus wounded O.R. 1; 158th Bde R.F.A. wounded 2/Lt. A.C.HOPKINS O.R. 1;	
	19.8.16.		16th Cheshires wounded O.R. 1; 19th Northld. Fus.wounded O.R. 1;	
	20.8.16.		158th Bde R.F.A. wounded O.R. 1; 16th Cheshires wounded O.R.1; 14th Glosters wounded O.R.2; 17th Lancs.Fus. killed O.R. 1; 23rd Manchesters Wounded 2/Lt. H.J.S.REYNOLDS at duty killed O.R. 7 wounded 3; 20th Lancs.Fus. killed O.R. 1 wounded 3.	
	21.8.16		15th Cheshires killed O.R. 1 wounded 2 missing 1; 16th Cheshires wounded 2/Lt. P.H.JONES killed O.R.1 wounded 36 missing 3; 14th Glosters wounded O.R. 4. 15th Sherwoods wounded O.R. 1; 105th M.G.Coy killed O.R.2 wounded 2; 17th Lancs.Fus. wounded O.R. 1; 23rd Manchesters wounded Lt. J.C. GUILLET killed O.R. 2 wounded 12; 20th Lancs.Fus wounded O.R.7; 104th T.M.B. wounded O.R. 2; 19th Northld.Fus. killed O.R. 1 wounded 1; 203rd Fld.Co.wounded O.R. 1; 14th Glosters wounded 2/Lt. E.P. MITCHELL.	
	22.8.16.		15th Cheshires killed O.R. 4 wounded 20 missing 3; 16th Cheshires wounded O.R. 1; 14th Glosters wounded Capt.T.RGRAWLEY BOEVEY 2/Lt.C.M.F. DEWDNEY wounded O.R.47 10; Rifles 4. 105th T.M.B. wounded Lt. A. GABRIEL; 19th Northld.Fus.wounded O.R. 5; 204th Fld. Co. wounded O.R.1; 205th Fld Co. wounded O.R. 3; 18th Lancs.Fus. killed O.R. 2 wounded 9; 20th Lancs Fus. killed 2/Lt. A.J. BERRY, wounded 2/Lt. A.N.L. LAMBERT, 2/Lt. J.H. GUEST(at duty) killed O.R. 9 wounded 37 missing 2; 23rd Manchesters wounded O.R.17; 104th M.G.Coy. killed O.R.2 wounded 4; 158th Bde R.F.A. wounded O.R.1; 15th Sherwoods wounded O.R. 10.	

WAR DIARY
INTELLIGENCE SUMMARY
(Erase heading not required.)

Army Form C. 2118

Place	Date	Hour	Summary of Events and Information	Remarks and references to Appendices
	23.8.16.	Casualties.	17th Lancs. Fus. wounded 2/Lt. G.D. CONDLIFFE (at duty) killed O.R.1 wounded 12; 18th Lancs. wounded O.R. 5; 20th Lancs. Fus. wounded O.R. 1; 23rd Manchesters killed O.R. 1 wounded 6; 19th Northld.Fus. wounded O.R. 2; 204th Fld. Co. R.E. wounded O.R.1; 203rd Fld Co. R.E. wounded O.R. 2; 163rd Bde R.F.A. wounded O.R.1; 17th R.Scots wounded O.R.2; 17th West Yorks wounded O.R. 1; 19th D.L.I. killed 2/Lt. J.C. CORRINGHAM O.R.1 wounded 13; 18th H.L.I. wounded O.R. 1; 14th Glosters wounded O.R. 15; 15th Sherwoods killed O.R. 10 wounded 21; 105th M.G.Co. wounded O.R.1.	
	24.8.16.		203rd Fld.Co. R.E. wounded Lt. G.V. COLCHESTER O.R.6; 19th Northld.Fus. killed O.R1 wounded O.R. 20 missing 2; 17th R. Scots wounded O.R. 2 missing 3; 17th W.Yorks killed O.R. 1 wounded 5; 19th D.L.I. wounded 2/Lt. R.A. WILSON killed O.R. 15 wounded 66 missing 2; 18th H.L.I. killed O.R. 4 wounded 10; 106th M.G.Coy. killed O.R. 3 wounded 10; 163rd Bde R.F.A. wounded O.R. 1; 15th Cheshires wounded O.R. 2; 16th Cheshires wounded O.R. 4; 14th Glosters killed O.R. 3 wounded 34 missing 11; 15th Sherwoods killed O.R. 3 wounded 16 missing 6; 23rd Manchesters wounded Lt. M.H. ROSE O.R.1; 104th M.G.Co.wounded 2/Lt. P.H.HIGHT (at duty) wounded O.R. 6; 18th Lancs. Fus. killed O.F. 10 wounded 29;	
	25.8.16.		17th West Yorks killed O.R.9 wounded 46 missing 1; 19th D.L.I. killed O.R.1 wounded 28 missing 1; 18th H.L.I. killed O.R.3 wounded 13; 106th M.G.Coy. wounded 2/Lt. H. GRABHAM killed O.R. 1 wounded 5; 106th T.M.B. wounded O.R.2; 18th Lancs. Fus wounded Lt. G.C. MC.LAUGHLIN 2/Lt. W.D. RUSHTON (at duty) 2/Lt. R.W. BRIGGS killed O.R. 4 wounded 9; 23rd Manchesters killed 2/Lt. L.H. BARNARD O.R. 2 wounded 9; 104 M.G.Coy Killed O.R. 1, wounder 8, missing 1; 19th Northld. Fus. Killed O.R.1, wounded 8; 204th. Field Coy. R.E. Killed Lt. F.G.D. Stoney, O.R. 1, wounder 1; 203rd. Field Coy. R.E. wounded O.R. 1; 17th. Royal Scots, Killed 2/Lt. H.R. FRASER, wounded Capt. A.G. SCOUGAL, O.R. 8 missing 1.	
	26.8.16.		203rd. Field Coy. R.E. wounded O.R. 2; 204th. Field Coy R.E. wounded O.R. 1; 205th. Field Coy. R.E. wounded Lt. G. BAXTER 2/Lt. A.M. WYLIE, killed O.R. 3 wounded 3; 15th. Cheshires wounded O.R. 2; 19th. D.L.I. wounded 2/Lt.xxxRxxxxxI,Lt.HCV HALL 18th. H.L.I. killed O.R. 5 wounded 5; 106th M.G.Coy. missing 2/Lt. R. WAIT, killed O.R. 1 wounded 1; 17th. West Yorks. Killed Lt. W.W.STEAD, wounded 2/Lt. W.REDMAN	

Army Form C. 2118

WAR DIARY
INTELLIGENCE SUMMARY
(Erase heading not required.)

Instructions regarding War Diaries and Intelligence Summaries are contained in F.S. Regs., Part II. and the Staff Manual respectively. Title Pages will be prepared in manuscript.

Place	Date	Hour	Summary of Events and Information	Remarks and references to Appendices
	26.8.16			
		Casualties	17th. West Yorks. (contd.) wounded 2/Lt. G.S.FORSHAW killed O.R. 2 wounded 58 missing 8.	
	27.8.16		17th. Royal Scots Killed Capt. W.A.DOUGLAS; 35th. Divs. Sig. Coy. wounded O.R. 1; 17th. Lancs. Fus. wounded Lt. E.N. SCHILL, 2/Lt. J.J. FLOWER, 2/Lt. R.N.RAWLINSON, Lt. W.E.N. CURNOCK, missing Cpt. J.N. COWAN, 2/Lt. J.E. SAUNDERS, killed O.R. 10, wounded 105, missing 31; 20th. Lancs. Fus. wounded Cpt. R.A.S. SOKE, O.R. 1; 23rd. Manchrs. killed O.R. 7, wounded 11; 104th. M.G.Coy wounded 2/Lt. A.D.C. BURRELL, missing O.R. 6; 204th. Field Coy. R.E. wounded O.R. 1; 23rd. Manchrs. wounded Lt. G.G. YEANDLE, Killed O.R. 1, wounded 1; 104th. M.G.Coy. wounded Lt. G.H. CROSSE; 17th. Royal Scots. wounded Lt. W.S. EDIE, O.R. 5; 18th. H.L.I. killed O.R. 1 wounded 2.	
	3.9.16			

G. Staff

Position of Divisional H.Q. and Units 35th Division in New Area (No 3.)

```
Div. H.Q .............................
Div Signal Coy......................CAVILLON.
Div Pioneers (19th N.F.)............CAVILLON.
Div Arty H.Q.  )                    RIENCOURT.
4 Bdes R.F.A.  )    ...........     HANGESTE
               )                    CROUY
Div Amm Col.........................ST PIERRE.
104th Inf Bde H.Q...................CROUY.
2 Battalions.......................CAMPS-IN-AMIENOIS.  MOLLIENS
1   -do-  .........................CAMPS.
1   -do-  .........................MONTAGNE.
Bde M.G. Coy. )                    RIENCOURT.
T.M. Battery. )    ..............  MONTAGNE.
203rd Fd Coy R.E....................
105th Fd Ambl.......................DREUIL.
105th Inf Bde H.Q...................CAMPS.
3 Battalions.......................MOLLIENS.    OISSY
1 Battalion........................MOLLIENS.
Bde M.G. Coy.)                     OISSY.
T.M. Battery.)    ..............   OISSY.
204th Fd. Coy R.E)                 MOLLIENS.
106th Fd. Amb.   )    ..........
106th Inf Bde. H.Q..................
2 Battalions.......................FOUDRINOY.
1 Battalion........................FOUDRINOY.
1   -do-  .........................SAISSEVAL-SAISSEMENT.
Bde M.G. Coy.......................LES MESGES.
T.M. Battery.......................LES MESGES.
205th Fd. Coy......................SAISSEVAL.
107th Fd. Ambce....................LES MESGES.
Div Train H.Q....)                 SAISSEMENT.
No 1,2,3,4 Coys..)    ..........   SOUES.
Sanitary Sect......................
Div Supply Col.....................RIENCOURT.
Div Amm Sub Park...................SCUFS.
Mob Vet Sect.......................RIENCOURT.
Supply Railhead....................ST PIERRE.
                                   VIGNACOURT.
```

4-8-16.

Lt-Col,
A.A. & Q.M.G., 35th Divn.

DISTRIBUTION OF BILLETS 35th DIVISION.

```
D.H.Q.                    CORBIE.
Div.Signal Coy.             "
HdQrs R.A.                  "
C.R.E.                      "
Hdqrs.Div.Train           VAUX
A.D.M.S.                  CORBIE.
D.A.D.O.S.                MORLANCOURT.
A.D.V.S.                  CORBIE.
Mob.Vet.Sect.             MORLANCOURT.
San.Sect.                 CORBIE.
H.Qrs 104th Inf.Bde.      SAILLY LE SEC.
17th Lancs.Fus.           VAUX
18th    do                CORBIE.
20th    do.                 "
23rd Manchesters          SAILLY LE SEC.
H.Q.105th Inf.Bde.        CITADEL.
15th Cheshires              "
16th    do.                 "
14th Glosters               "
15th Sherwoods              "
H.Q. 106th Inf. Bde       MORLANCOURT.
17th Royal Scots.           "
17th W.Yorks                "
19th D.L.I.                 "
18th H.L.I.                 "
19th Northld. Fus.        CITADEL.
    (Pioneers)
203rd Fd.Coy. R.E.        VAUX.
204th   do.               CITADEL.
205th   do.               MORLANCOURT.
105th Fld. Ambce.         SAILLY.
106th   do.               CITADEL.
107th   do.               MORLANCOURT.
Hd.Qrs Coy.Train          CROVETOWN
2   "   "   "              do
3   "   "   "             CORBIE VAUX ROAD
4   "   "   "               "    "    "
104th M.G.Cpy.            CORBIE.
105th   "   "             CITADEL.
106th   "   "             MORLANCOURT.
Supply Col.               J.22.a.
Sub.Park.                 DOUARS.
157th Bde R.F.A.          Bois des Tailles.
158th    "   "              "
159th    "   "              "
163rd    "   "              "
D.A.C.                    F.26.a.
```

11. 8. 16.

17.8.16.

DISTRIBUTION OF BILLETS 35TH DIVISION.

```
D.H.Q...............................................CITADEL.
Div Signal Coy......................................CITADEL.
H.Q.,R.A............................................CORBIE.
C.R.E...............................................CITADEL.
Headquarters 35th Div Train.........................MORLANCOURT.
A.D.M.S.............................................CITADEL.
D.A.D.O.S...........................................CITADEL.
A.D.V.S.............................................CITADEL.
75th Sanitary Section...............................CITADEL.
H.Qrs 104th Inf Bde.................................HAPPY VALLEY.
17th Lancs Fusiliers................................  DO.
18th   "      "   ..................................  DO.
20th   "      "   ..................................  DO.
23rd Manchesters....................................  DO.
H.Qrs 105th Inf Bde.................................CITADEL.
15th Cheshires......................................  Do.
16th    "   ........................................  Do.
14th Glosters.......................................  Do.
15th Sherwoods......................................  Do.
H.Qrs 106th Inf Bde.................................SANDPIT VALLEY.
17th Royal Scots....................................  Do.
17th West Yorks.....................................  Do.
19th D.L.I..........................................  Do.
18th H.L.I..........................................  Do.
19th Northumberland Fusiliers (Pioneers)CITADEL.
203rd Field Coy R.E.................................HAPPY VALLEY.
204th Field Coy R.E.................................CITADEL.
205th Field Coy R.E.................................SANDPIT VALLEY.
105th Field Ambulance...............................HAPPY VALLEY.
106th Field Ambulance...............................CITADEL.
107th Field Ambulance...............................SANDPIT VALLEY.
Hd.Qr Coy 35th Div Train............................GROVETOWN.
2 Coy 35th Div Train................................  Do.
3. "    "    "    "  ...............................  Do.
4. "    "    "    "  ...............................  Do.
104th M.G.Coy.......................................HAPPY VALLEY.
105th M.G.Coy.......................................CITADEL.
106th M.G.Coy.......................................SANDPIT VALLEY.
35th Div Supply Col.................................J.22.a.
35th Div Sub Park...................................DAOURS.
157th Bde R.F.A.....................................BUIRE.
158th Bde R.F.A.....................................BUIRE.
159th Bde R.F.A.....................................E.27.a.
163rd Bde R.F.A.....................................A.22.b.(Attd 3rd D.A.)
D.A.C.  ............................................E.21.c.
```

WAR DIARY
INTELLIGENCE SUMMARY

(Erase heading not required.)

Army Form C. 2118

3rd Army September A60 Vol 7. 642

Place	Date	Hour	Summary of Events and Information	Remarks and references to Appendices
	3/9/16		Casualties. 16th. Cheshires. 3 O.R. wounded.	
	4/9/16		15th. Sherwoods. 3 O.R. wounded.	
	5/9/16		16th. Cheshires wounded O.R. 3; 105th. M.G.Coy wounded O.R. 1; 18th. H.L.I. wounded 2/Lt. H.W. TAYLOR.	
	6/9/16		18th. H.L.I. wounded O.R. 1; 16th. Cheshires killed O.R. 1 wounded 5; 20th. Lancs. Fus. wounded O.R. 1.	
	7/9/16		17th. West Yorks. wounded O.R. 1; 16th. Cheshires killed O.R. 1 wounded 9; 14th. Glosters killed O.R. 1; 15th. Sherwoods wounded O.R. 2.	
	8/9/16		18th. H.L.I. wounded O.R. 4; 16th. Cheshires killed O.R. 1 wounded 4; 14th. Glosters killed O.R. 5 wounded 2.	
	9/9/16		18th. Lancs. Fus. wounded O.R. 1; 20th. Lancs. Fus. wounded O.R. 1; 18th. H.L.I. killed O.R. 2 wounded 10; 17th. Royal Scots wounded O.R. 1 missing 1; 203rd. Field Coy. R.E. killed O.R. 1.	
	10/9/16		20th. Lancs Fus. wounded O.R. 2; 15th. Sherwoods wounded O.R. 1; 17th. West Yorks wounded O.R. 1; 19th. D.L.I. killed O.R. 1 wounded 1; 18th. H.L.I. wounded O.R. 1.	
	11/9/16		104th. T.M.B. wounded O.R. 1; 17th. West Yorks wounded 2/Lt. A. MARTIN O.R. 4; 19th. D.L.I. wounded O.R. 1	
	12/9/16		16th. Cheshires killed O.R. 1 wounded 3; 17th. West Yorks wounded O.R. 1 19th. D.L.I. killed O.R. 2 wounded 4; 23rd. Manchrs. wounded O.R. 1	
	13/9/16		16th. Cheshires wounded O.R. 1; 17th. West Yorks wounded O.R. 2; 19th. D.L.I. killed O.R. 1; 106th. M.G.Coy. wounded O.R. 1; 23rd. Manchrs. wounded O.R. 1	

Army Form C. 2118

WAR DIARY
~~INTELLIGENCE SUMMARY~~

(Erase heading not required.)

Instructions regarding War Diaries and Intelligence Summaries are contained in F. S. Regs., Part II. and the Staff Manual respectively. Title Pages will be prepared in manuscript.

Place	Date	Hour	Summary of Events and Information	Remarks and references to Appendices
		Casualties.	Cheshires	
	14/9/16		15th. ~~Sherwoods~~ wounded 2/Lt. J.B. JONES, killed O.R. 2 wounded 27 missing 2; 16th. Cheshires wounded O.R. 1; 15th. Sherwoods wounded O.R. 1; 23rd. Manchrs. wounded O.R. 2; 17th. West Yorks; killed O.R. 1 wounded 12	
	15/9/16		23rd. Manchrs. killed O.R. 1 wounded 1; 17th. Lancs. Fus. wounded O.R. 1; 16th. Cheshires wounded O.R. 2; 17th. West Yorks wounded O.R. 1; 19th. D.L.I. killed O.R. 2 wounded 4; 18th. H.L.I. wounded O.R. 3	
	16/9/16		17th. West Yorks killed O.R. 1 wounded 3; 18th. H.L.I. killed O.R. 1; 18th. Lancs. Fus. killed O.R. 3 wounded 6; 23rd. Manchrs. wounded O.R. 3; 15th. Cheshires wounded O.R. 5; 15th. Sherwoods killed O.R. 3 wounded 17.	
	17/9/16		20th. Lancs. Fus. wounded O.R. 4; 17th. Royal Scots wounded O.R. 1	
	18/9/16		18th. H.L.I. wounded O.R. 1; 20th. Lancs. Fus. wounded O.R. 1; 158 Bds R.F.A. wounded Cpt. H. SANDERSON.	
	19/9/16		17th. Royal Scots. killed O.R. 1 wounded 1; 17th. West Yorks killed 1; 18th. H.L.I. wounded O.R. 2.	
	20/9/16		16th. Cheshires wounded O.R. 1; 18th. H.L.I. wounded O.R. 1.	
	21/9/16		14th. Glasters wounded O.R. 1; 15th. Sherwoods wounded O.R. 1; 20th. Lancs. Fus. wounded O.R. 1	
	22/9/16		17th.Lancs. Fus. wounded 2/Lt. R.S. HEAPE (at duty); 16th. Cheshires wounded O.R. 1; 17th. West Yorks wounded O.R. 1; 18th. H.L.I. wounded O.R. 2	
	24/9/16		17th. West Yorks wounded O.R. 2	
	25/9/16		158 Bds R.F.A. wounded 2/Lt. R. JACKSON (at duty); 15th. Cheshires wounded O.R. 1; 17th. Lancs. wounded O.R. 1; 23rd. Manchrs. wounded O.R. 2	

Army Form C. 2118

WAR DIARY
INTELLIGENCE SUMMARY
(Erase heading not required.)

Instructions regarding War Diaries and Intelligence Summaries are contained in F. S. Regs., Part II. and the Staff Manual respectively. Title Pages will be prepared in manuscript.

Place	Date	Hour	Summary of Events and Information	Remarks and references to Appendices
	26/9/16		Casualties. 15th. Cheshires wounded O.R. 1; 19th. D.L.I. wounded O.R. 2; 23rd. Manchrs. wounded O.R. 2	
	27/9/16		23rd. Manchester wounded O.R. 2; 17th. West Yorks wounded O.R. 2	
	28/9/16		23rd. Manchester killed 1 wounded 2; 17th. West Yorks wounded O.R. 1	
	29/9/16		18th. H.L.I. wounded O.R. 2; 16th. Cheshires wounded O.R. 1	
	30/9/16		23rd. Manchrs. Killed O.R. 1 wounded 1; 17th. Royal Scots wounded O.R. 3; 16th. Cheshires wounded O.R. 9	

Army Form C. 2118

Vol 8

WAR DIARY
Headquarters 35th Division, Administrative Staff.

~~INTELLIGENCE SUMMARY~~

(Erase heading not required.)

Instructions regarding War Diaries and Intelligence Summaries are contained in F.S. Regs., Part II. and the Staff Manual respectively. Title Pages will be prepared in manuscript.

Place	Date	Hour	Summary of Events and Information	Remarks and references to Appendices
	1/10/16.		CASUALTIES. 16th Cheshires wounded O.R.1. 20th Lancs Fus wounded 2/Lt.J.LENNOX.killed O.R.1. 104 T.M.B. killed O.R.1. 17th Royal Scots wounded O.R.2. 17th West Yorks wounded O.R.1.	
	2/10/16.		CASUALTIES. 18th Lancs.Fus. wounded 2/Lt.H.C.WARD. wounded O.R.4 missing O.R.1. 20th Lancs. Fus. missing 2/Lt.H.BAKER. wounded O.R.1 missing O.R.2. 19th Northld. Fus. O.R. wounded 1.	
	3/10/16.		CASUALTIES. 15th Cheshires killed 2/Lt. G.H.CHAMBERLAIN. killed O.R. 2 wounded O.R. 3. 20th Lancs.Fus. wounded O.R.3.	
	4/10/16.		CASUALTIES. 17th Royal Scots wounded O.R. 3. 18th High. L.I. killed 2/Lt. T.CURR. killed O.R. 4 wounded 1. 16th Cheshires wounded O.R1 14th Glosters wounded O.R. 1. 18th Lancs Fus. wounded O.R.1.	
	5/10/16.		CASUALTIES. 17th Lancs. Fus. wounded O.R. 4. 19th Durh. L.I. O.R. wounded 1. 15th Cheshires wounded O.R. 1. 14th Glosters wounded O.R.1.	
	6/10/16.		CASUALTIES. 23rd Manchesters killed O.R. 1. wounded O.R. 2. 16th Cheshires wounded O.R. 1. 18th High.L.I. wounded O.R. 2.	
	7/10/16.		CASUALTIES. 17th Lancs. FUS. wounded O.R. 2. 18th Lancs. Fus. wounded O.R. 2. 23rd Manchesters wounded O.R. 11. 17th West Yorks wounded O.R. 1. 15th Cheshires wounded O.R. 7. 23rd Manchesters killed O.R. 1. wounded O.R. 16. 17th West Yorks killed O.R.1. wounded 9. 19th Durh. L.I. killed 2/Lt. F.G.SMITH. O.R. 1. wounded 5. 15th Cheshires	
	8/10/16.		CASUALTIES. killed O.R.1 wounded O.R.1. 16th Cheshires wounded O.R.1. 6th D.C.L.I. attd 184th Tunnelling Coy wounded O.R.1. 104th T.M.B. wounded O.R.1. 16th Cheshires killed O.R.1 wounded O.R.3. 15th Sherwoods	
	9/10/16.		CASUALTIES. wounded O.R.2.	
	10/10/16.		CASUALTIES. 17th West Yorks killed O.R. 4 wounded O.R. 2. 19th Durh.L.I. wounded 2/Lt. R.H. MEACOCK. wounded O.R. 7. 18th High. wounded O.R. 1. 19th Northld.Fus. killed O.R. 2 wounded O.R. 6. 15th Cheshires wounded O.R.1. 14th Glosters wounded O.R. 2. 18th Lancs. Fus. wounded 2/Lt. J.PAGET. wounded O.R. 3. 23rd Manchesters wounded O.R. 7. 6th D.C.L.I. attd 184th Tunnelling Coy killed O.R.1.	
	11/10/16.		CASUALTIES. 15th Cheshires wounded Lt.C.B.KIDD. 14th Glosters wounded O.R.2 20th Lancs.Fus. killed O.R. 1. 23rd Manchesters wounded O.R.1. 17th West Yorks killed O.R.1. 19th Durh.L.I. wounded O.R.1. 18th High.L.I. wounded O.R.2.	
	12/10/16.		CASUALTIES. 15th Cheshires wounded O.R.2. 17th Royal Scots wounded O.R.2. 18th High.L.I. killed O.R.1 wounded O.R.5.	

WAR DIARY

Army Form C. 2118

Headquarters 35th Division, Administrative Staff.

INTELLIGENCE SUMMARY

(Erase heading not required.)

Instructions regarding War Diaries and Intelligence Summaries are contained in F.S. Regs, Part II. and the Staff Manual respectively. Title Pages will be prepared in manuscript.

Place	Date	Hour	Summary of Events and Information	Remarks and references to Appendices
	13/10/16.		CASUALTIES. 15th Cheshires wounded O.R.1. 14th Glosters killed O.R.1. wounded O.R. 11.	
	14/10/16.		CASUALTIES. 157th Bde.R.F.A.wounded O.R.2. 17th Royal Scots killed O.R.2. 17th West Yorks wounded O.R.2. 18th High.L.I. wounded O.R.2. D.A.C. attd T.M.B. wounded 2/Lt. J.S.BUTCHART.	
	15/10/16.		CASUALTIES. X/35 T.M.B.wounded O.R.1. 15th Cheshires wounded O.R.4. 184th Tunnelling Coy R.E. wounded O.R.1. 16th Cheshires wounded O.R.1. 15th Sherwoods killed O.R.2.	
	16/10/16.		CASUALTIES. 17th Royal Scots killed O.R.1. wounded O.R.1.	
	17/10/16.		CASUALTIES. 15th Sherwoods wounded O.R.2. 18th Lancs.Fus.wounded O.R.2. 20th Lancs.Fus. wounded O.R.4. 23rd Manchesters wounded O.R.2.	
			15th Cheshires wounded O.R.1. 15th Sherwoods wounded O.P.1. 17th West Yorks wounded O.R.3. 19th Durh.L.I. wounded O.R.4. 18th High.L.I. wounded O.R.2. 106th M.G.Coy wounded O.R.1. 17th LancsFus .wounded O.R.2. 23rd Manchesters wounded O.R.2.	
	18th/10/16. 19th/10/16.		CASUALTIES. 17th West Yorks wounded O.R.2. 17th Lancs.Fus. wounded O.R.1.	
			CASUALTIES. 16th Cheshires wounded O.R.1. 17th West Yorks wounded O.R.2. 19th Durh.L.I. killed O.R.1. 17th Lancs.Fus. killed O.R.1. wounded O.R.2.	
	20/10/16.		CASUALTIES. 23rd Manchesters wounded 2/Lt. A.BROADHEAD X killed O.R. 2 wounded O.R 1. 17th West Yorks wounded O.R.1.	✗ 2/Lt.E.HINES
			missing O.R.1. 104th T.M.B. wounded O.R.1. 17th Royal Scots wounded O.R.1. 15th Cheshires 19th Durh.L.I. wounded O.R. 2.	
	21/10/16.		CASUALTIES. 20th Lancs.Fus. wounded O.R.2. 16th Cheshires wounded O.R.1.	
			killed O.R.1. 23rd Manchesters wounded O.R.2. 16th Cheshires killed O.R.1. 17th West Yorks	
			killed O.R.1. wounded O.R.2.	
	22/10/16.		CASUALTIES. 17th Lancs. Fus. wounded Captain L.W.WHITTY (at duty) O.R.1. 23rd Manchesters wounded O.R.3. 15th Cheshires wounded O.R.9. 16th Cheshires wounded O.R.1.	
			14th Glosters killed O.R.1. wounded O.R.3. 15th Sherwoods killed O.R.1.	
			17th West Yorks wounded Captain C.W.BANKS. killed O.R. 2 wounded O.R.1.	
			19th Durh.L.I. killed O.R.3.	
	23/10/16.		CASUALTIES. 16th Cheshires wounded O.R.1. 14th Glosters wounded O.R.1. 15th Sherwoods wounded O.R.2. 17th West Yorks wounded O.R.3. 18th High.L.I. killed O.R. 1. wounded O.R.1. 158th Bde. R.F.A. attd R.E. wounded O.R.1.	
	24/10/16.		CASUALTIES. 20th LancsFus. wounded O.R1. 16th Cheshires wounded O.R.2. 14th Glosters wounded O.R.2. 15th Sherwoods wounded O.R.1. 17th Royal Scots killed O.R.1 wounded	2.

Army Form C. 2118

WAR DIARY

Headquarters 35th Division.
Administrative Staff.

INTELLIGENCE SUMMARY

(Erase heading not required.)

Instructions regarding War Diaries and Intelligence Summaries are contained in F.S. Regs., Part II. and the Staff Manual respectively. Title Pages will be prepared in manuscript.

Place	Date	Hour	Summary of Events and Information	Remarks and references to Appendices
	25/10/16.		CASUALTIES. 20th Lancs.Fus. wounded O.R.1. 17th R.Scots killed O.R.4 wounded O.R.9. 18th High.L.I. wounded O.R.3. Z/35 T.M.Battery wounded O.R.1. 16th Cheshires wounded O.R.1. 14th Glosters killed Lt.A.B.COLTHURST. wounded O.R.1. 15th Sherwoods killed 2/Lt.G.E.F.HOLMES. wounded 2/Lt.J.C.DUNN. 2/Lt.J.K.SWALLOW. missing 2/Lt.E.WARBURTON. killed O.R.2 wounded O.R.21. missing O.R.1.	
	26/10/16.		CASUALTIES. 15th Cheshires O.R. wounded 2. 16th Cheshires wounded 2/Lt.P.B.SILCOCK. O.R.3 missing O.R.1. 17th R.Scots killed O.R.1 wounded O.R.2. 19th Borthld.Fus. wounded O.R.1.	
	27/10/16.		CASUALTIES. 35th Divl. Signal Coy wounded O.R.1. 17th West Yorks wounded O.R.1. 23rd Manchesters wounded O.R.1.	
	28/10/16.		CASUALTIES. 16th Cheshires wounded O.R.2. 18th Lancs.Fus.wounded O.R.2 23rd Manchesters killed O.R.1. wounded O.R.1. 17th R.Scots wounded O.R.1. 18th High.L.I. wounded O.R.2.	
	30/10/16.		CASUALTIES. 17th West Yorks wounded O.R.1. 19th Durh.L.I. wounded O.R.1.	

Army Form C. 2118

WAR DIARY
INTELLIGENCE SUMMARY

ADMINISTRATIVE STAFF.

H.Q. 35th DIVISION.

(Erase heading not required.)

A+Q

Vol 9

Place	Date	Hour	Summary of Events and Information	Remarks and references to Appendices
			CASUALTIES.	
	1/11/16		17th W. Yorks, killed O.R.2: wounded O.R.4:; 15th Cheshires, wounded O.R.2: 14th Glosters, wounded O.R.1: 15th Sherwoods, killed O.R.1: wounded O.R.2: N.Z.T.C., wounded O.R.1:	
	2/11/16		15th Cheshires, killed O.R.8: wounded 10: missing 1; 16th Cheshires, wounded O.R.1: 15th Sherwoods, killed Capt.J.P.HODGKINSON: wounded 2/Lt. J.Y.POTTER: wounded O.R.8: missing 5:, 17th Lancs.Fus. killed O.R.1:, 20th Lancs.Fus. killed O.R.1: wounded O.R.3 (1 accidentally cleaning rifle):, 104th M.G.Coy, wounded O.R.2:, 17th Royal Scots wounded O.R.1:; 17th W.Yorks, killed O.R.1: wounded O.R.2:, 19th D.L.I. killed O.R.1: wounded O.R.3:, 157th Bde R.F.A. wounded O.R.1 Reported as accidental:,	
	3/11/16		17th Lancs.Fus. wounded Lt. J.E.LAPES:, 20th Lancs.Fus. wounded O.R.1; 104th M.G.Coy, wounded O.R.1accidentally cleaning revolver:, 15th Cheshires, wounded O.R.7: missing O.R.4:, 15th Sherwoods, missing 2:, 17th Royal Scots, wounded O.R.2:, 17th W.Yorks, wounded O.R.3:, V/35 T.M.B. wounded 2/Lt C.R.HARPER:, 19th D.L.I. wounded O.R.3 (1 accidental Lewis Gun):, 205th Fd. Coy R.E. wounded O.R.1:, 203rd Fd.Coy R.E. wounded O.R.1:;	
	4/11/16		18th Lancs.Fus. killed O.R.1: wounded O.R.1:, 20th Lancs.Fus. missing Lt B.H.HARTLEY: wounded O.R.3:, 17th Royal Scots, killed O.R.1: wounded O.R.1:, 17th W.Yorks, wounded O.R.1 Self-inflicted rifle bullet:, 19th D.L.I. killed O.R.1: wounded O.R.2 (1 Accidental rifle bullet):, 184th Tunn.Coy.R.E. wounded O.R.1:;	
	5/11/16		17th Royal Scots, wounded O.R.1:, 19th D.L.I. killed O.R.1:, 18th H.L.I. wounded O.R. 4 (1accidentally comrade cleaning rifle):, 15th Cheshires, wounded O.R.1:, 16th Cheshires, killed O.R.1::	
	6/11/16		18th Lancs.Fus. wounded O.R.5:, 23rd Manchesters, wounded O.R.1:, 15th Cheshires, wounded O.R.1:, 16th Cheshires, wounded O.R.3 accidentally by own grenades:, 14th Glosters, wounded O.R.2:, 17th W.Yorks, wounded O.R.1:accidentally, cleaning patients rifles at Divl.Rest Stn::	

Army Form C. 2118

WAR DIARY

INTELLIGENCE SUMMARY

(Erase heading not required.)

ADMINISTRATIVE STAFF

H.Q. 35th DIVISION.

Instructions regarding War Diaries and Intelligence Summaries are contained in F.S. Regs., Part II. and the Staff Manual respectively. Title Pages will be prepared in manuscript.

Place	Date	Hour	Summary of Events and Information	Remarks and references to Appendices
	7/11/16		CASUALTIES. 23rd Manchesters, wounded O.R.1 (accidental "Very light"); 18th H.L.I. wounded Lt. J.N.FERGUSON: wounded O.R.1; 19th N.F. wounded O.R.1:;	
	8/11/16		23rd Manchesters, killed O.R.1: wounded O.R.1; 15th Cheshires, wounded O.R.1 (accidentally comrade cleaning rifle):, 18th W.Yorks, wounded O.R.1 accidentally comrade cleaning rifle:, 18th H.L.I. killed O.R.5:.	
			(Supplementary 1/9/16) 18th H.L.I. wounded O.R.1 accidentally particulars unobtainable)	
	9/11/16		17th Lancs.Fus. wounded O.R.1; 18th Lancs.Fus. wounded O.R.1; 23rd Manchesters wounded O.R.2:; 19th D.L.I. wounded O.R.1; 184th Tunn.Coy.R.E. wounded O.R.1:;	
	10/11/16		18th H.L.I. killed O.R.1; 9th K.R.R. attd 184th Tunn.Coy.R.E. wounded O.R.1:.	
	11/11/16		17th Lancs.Fus. wounded O.R.1; 20th Lancs.Fus. wounded O.R.2:; 23rd Manchesters, killed O.R.1; 17th W.Yorks, wounded O.R.1; 19th D.L.I. killed O.R.1: wounded O.R.1:.	
	12/11/16		New Z.T.Coy. killed Lt W.McLEISH DURANT: 16th Cheshires, wounded O.R.1 accidentally comrade leading rifle:, 14th Glosters, wounded O.R.1; 17th W.Yorks, wounded O.R.1:, 19th D.L.I. wounded O.R.1 accidentally comrade cleaning rifle:;	
	13/11/16		20th Lancs.Fus. wounded O.R.2:, 23rd Manchesters, wounded O.R.1; 15th Cheshires, wounded O.R.2; suffering from being buried and crushed front line:, 16th Cheshires, wounded 2/Lt R.N.BASKETT: 15th Sherwoods, wounded O.R.1; 19th D.L.I. wounded O.R.1:, 9th Seaforth Highlanders, 9th Div.Pioneers, wounded O.R.2:;	
	14/11/16		20th Lancs.Fus, attd 104th T.M.B. wounded O.R.1;accidentally explosion of shell whilst loading Stokes gun:, 203rd Fd.Coy R.E. wounded O.R.1; N.Z.Tunn.Coy. wounded O.R.1:;	
	15/11/16		15th Cheshires, wounded O.R.1;accidentally Lewis Gun stoppage:, 14th Glosters, killed O.R.1: wounded O.R.2:;	
	16/11/16		203rd Fd.Coy R.E. killed O.R.1; 20th Lancs.Fus, wounded O.R.1:.	

Army Form C. 2118

WAR DIARY
or
INTELLIGENCE SUMMARY

ADMINISTRATIVE STAFF.

H.Q. 35th DIVISION.

(Erase heading not required.)

Instructions regarding War Diaries and Intelligence Summaries are contained in F. S. Regs., Part II. and the Staff Manual respectively. Title Pages will be prepared in manuscript.

Place	Date	Hour	Summary of Events and Information	Remarks and references to Appendices
			CASUALTIES.	
	17/11/16		17th Royal Scots, wounded Lt. W.A.WELLS, Lt. S.McKNIGHT: wounded O.R.3; 19th D.L.I. wounded O.R.1; 18th Lancs.Fus, wounded O.R.3; 15th Sherwoods, wounded O.R.1; 15th Cheshires, wounded Lt. J.T.N.WILSON:.	
	18/11/16		15th Cheshires, wounded O.R.1:.	
	19/11/16		17th W.Yorks, wounded O.R.1; 14th Glosters, wounded O.R.2; 15th Sherwoods, wounded O.R.1 Accidentally shot by sentry when returning from patrol; 159th Bde R.F.A. wounded O.R.2;.	
	20/11/16		16th Cheshires, wounded O.R.1; 17th Lancs.Fus, wounded O.R.2; 23rd Manchesters, wounded O.R.1; 205th Fd.Coy R.E. wounded O.R.1; 17th Royal Scots, wounded O.R.2 (1 accidentally cleaning revolver):.	
	21/11/16		17th Royal Scots, killed O.R.1; 18th H.L.I. wounded O.R.1; 15th Cheshires, wounded O.R.1; 23rd Manchesters, wounded O.R.2:.	
	22/11/16		17th Lancs.Fus, killed O.R.6; wounded O.R.2; 18th Lancs.Fus, wounded O.R.1 Accidentally rifle grenade blank cartridge burst among shavings;, 15th Cheshires, wounded O.R.1 Accidentally slipped whilst firing Very light; 16th Cheshires, wounded O.R.1; 14th Glosters, wounded O.R.1 Accidentally, explosion at bomb practice Bomb School; 15th Sherwoods, wounded Lt. E.J.WRIGHT, Accidentally, explosion at Bomb practice, Bomb School; 17th Royal S cots, wounded O.R.1; 17th W.Yorks, killed O.R.1; wounded O.R.3; 18th H.L.I. wounded O.R.1; 19th N.F. wounded O.R.1; 1st Cheshires attd 184th Tunn.Coy, wounded O.R.1:.	
	23/11/16		19th D.L.I.wounded O.R.1 Accidental; 17th Lancs.Fus, wounded O.R.1 Accidental, premature burst Hales rifle grenade:, 23rd Manchesters, killed O.R.1; 15th Sherwoods, killed O.R.2: wounded O.R.2;;	

WAR DIARY

INTELLIGENCE SUMMARY

Army Form C. 2118

ADMINISTRATIVE STAFF.

H.Q. 35th DIVISION.

Place	Date	Hour	Summary of Events and Information	Remarks and references to Appendices
	24/11/16		CASUALTIES. 205th Fd.Coy R.E. wounded O.R.1; 7th Rifle Bde attd 184th Tunn.Coy. wounded O.R.1; 15th Cheshires, wounded O.R.1; 15th Sherwoods killed 2/Lt. R.WHEATLEY: wounded 2/Lt. R.T.WRIGHT; killed O.R.1; wounded O.R.5; 14th Glosters attd T.M.B. wounded O.R.1; 15th Sherwoods attd T.M.B. wounded O.R.- 2/Lt. F.P.STUBBS; 17th Lancs.Fus. killed O.R.4; wounded O.R.2; 20th Lancs.Fus, wounded O.R.4; 19th N.F. killed O.R.1;	
	25/11/16		20th Lancs.Fus, wounded O.R.1; 16th Cheshires, killed O.R.1; 15th Sherwoods, wounded Lt. E.F.MILLAR & 2/Lt. T.S.McINTYRE; killed O.R.5; wounded O.R.8; missing 3 (buried) believed killed; 17th W.Yorks, wounded O.R.2; 19th D.L.I. killed O.R.2; wounded O.R.1; 19th N.F. killed O.R.5; 184th Tunn.Coy R.E. wounded O.R.1;	27
	26/11/16		17th Lancs.Fus, killed O.R.2; wounded O.R.2; missing O.R. 24 (enemy raid); 17th W.Yorks, wounded O.R.2; 19th D.L.I. wounded Lt. T.MUNDY, 2/Lts. W.E.HARDING & E.WELBOURNE; killed O.R.2; wounded O.R.11; missing O.R.1; 16th Lancs.attd 16th Cheshires wounded 2/Lt. H.N.HALLAM (at duty); 16th Cheshires, wounded O.R.5; 105th M.G.Coy, killed O.R.1 Accidentally, comrade cleaning revolver;	
	27/11/16		18th H.L.I. wounded O.R.1:Premature burst of Stokes shell in gun; 19th N.F. wounded O.R.1;	
	28/11/16		17th Royal Scots, wounded O.R.1 Accidentally wounded cleaning rifle; 18th H.L.I. killed O.R.7; wounded O.R.6; 17th W.Yorks, wounded O.R.1; 18th Lancs.Fus. wounded O.R.2 Accidentally, Newton Pippen; 20th Lancs.Fus, wounded O.R.1; 15th Cheshires, killed Capt. R.F.WOLSTENHOLME; wounded 2/Lt. H.E.FITZGERALD; 16th Cheshires, wounded O.R.1 Accidental comrade cleaning rifle; 14th Glosters, wounded O.R.2; 159th Bde R.F.A. killed 2/Lt. G.N.SLINGER;	
	29/11/16		18th Lancs.Fus, wounded O.R.1 Accidentally, faulty Very Light Pistol; 20th Lancs. Fus, wounded O.R.1; 15th Cheshires, killed O.R.1;	
	30/11/16		17th Lancs.Fus, wounded O.R.1 Accidentally, explosion of detonator; 15th Cheshires, O.R. wounded 1; 16th Cheshires, wounded O.R.2; 17th W.Yorks, wounded O.R.1 Accidentally (explosion in fire)	

Army Form C. 2118

WAR DIARY
INTELLIGENCE SUMMARY
(Erase heading not required.)

35 Division. A.
Vol 10

Place	Date	Hour	Summary of Events and Information	Remarks and references to Appendices
	1/12/16.		CASUALTIES. 1/12/16. 15th Cheshires wounded O.R.1 16th Cheshires wounded O.R.1 17th Royal Scots killed O.R.1.	
	2/12/16.		CASUALTIES. 23rd Manchesters wounded O.R.1.	
	3/12/16.		CASUALTIES. 17th Lancs. Fus.½ wounded O.R. 4. 20th Lancs. Fus. wounded O.R.2.	
	4/12/16.		CASUALTIES. NIL.	
	5/12/16.		CASUALTIES. 20th Lancs. Fus. wounded O.R.2. 23rd Manchesters wounded O.R.1. 18th Lancs. Fus. wounded O.R.1.	
	6/12/16.		CASUALTIES. NIL.	
	7/12/16.		CASUALTIES. NIL.	
	8/12/16.		CASUALTIES. NIL.	
	9/12/16.		CASUALTIES. 159th Brigade R.F.A. wounded O.R.1.	
	10/12/16.		CASUALTIES. NIL.	
	11/12/16.		CASUALTIES. NIL.	
	12/12/16.		CASUALTIES. NIL.	
	13/12/16.		CASUALTIES. NIL.	
	14/14/16.		CASUALTIES. NIL.	
	15/12/16.		CASUALTIES. 35th D.A.C. killed O.R.1. wounded 1. 17th West Yorks wounded O.R.2.	

Army Form C. 2118

WAR DIARY
or
INTELLIGENCE SUMMARY

(Erase heading not required.)

Instructions regarding War Diaries and Intelligence Summaries are contained in F. S. Regs., Part II. and the Staff Manual respectively. Title Pages will be prepared in manuscript.

Place	Date	Hour	Summary of Events and Information	Remarks and references to Appendices
	16/12/16.		CASUALTIES. 18th Lancs. Fus. wounded O.R.1.	
	17/12/16.		CASUALTIES. NIL.	
	18/12/16.		CASUALTIES. NIL.	
	19/12/16.		CASUALTIES. X/35 T.M.B. wounded O.R.1.	
	20/12/16.		CASUALTIES. X/35 T.M.B. wounded O.R.1.	
	21/12/16.		CASUALTIES. NIL.	
	22/12/16.		CASUALTIES. 17th West Yorks wounded O.R.1.	
	23/12/16.		CASUALTIES. Z/35 T.M.B. wounded O.R. 3.	
	24/12/16.		CASUALTIES. 17th West Yorks wounded O.R.1.	
	25/12/16.		CASUALTIES. NIL.	
	26/12/16.		CASUALTIES. NIL.	
	27/12/16.		CASUALTIES. 51st Brigade R.F.A. killed O.R.1. wounded O.R.2.	
	28/12/16.		CASUALTIES. NIL.	
	29/12/16.		CASUALTIES. NIL.	
	30/12/16.		CASUALTIES. 16th Cheshires wounded O.R.1. (accidentally.) 18th Highland L.I. wounded O.R.1.	
	31/12/16.		CASUALTIES. NIL.	

1875 Wt: W593/826 1,000,000 4/15 J.B.C. & A. A.D.S.S./Forms/C. 2118.

WAR DIARY
INTELLIGENCE SUMMARY

Army Form C. 2118

A + Q 35

Place	Date	Hour	Summary of Events and Information	Remarks and references to Appendices
			35th DIVISION	
	1/1/17.		CASUALTIES 1/1/17.	
			20th Lancs.Fusiliers killed O.R. 1, wounded 2, missing 7.	
	2/1/17.		CASUALTIES. 2nd.Lt. E.C.Helmore 15th Sherwoods wounded, (Accidentally, since died), wounded O.R.1., 19th D.L.I. wounded O.R.1.	
	3/1/17.		CASUALTIES. NIL.	
	4/1/17.		CASUALTIES. 205 Fd.Coy. R.E. wounded O.R.1., 15th Sherwoods wounded O.R.2., 19th D.L.I. wounded O.R.1.	
	5/1/17.		CASUALTIES. 17th West Yorks killed O.R.1., wounded 1.	
	6/1/17.		CASUALTIES. NIL.	
	7/1/17.		CASUALTIES. 14th Gloucesters wounded O.R.1.	
	8/1/17.		CASUALTIES. NIL.	
	9/1/17.		CASUALTIES. NIL.	
	10/1/17.		CASUALTIES. NIL.	
	11/1/17.		CASUALTIES. NIL.	
	12/1/17.		CASUALTIES. NIL.	
	13/1/17.		CASUALTIES. NIL.	
	14/1/17.		CASUALTIES. 17th Lancs. Fus. wounded O.R.1.	
	15/1/17.		CASUALTIES. 18th H. L. I. wounded O.R.1.	

Army Form C. 2118

WAR DIARY

INTELLIGENCE SUMMARY

(Erase heading not required.)

Instructions regarding War Diaries and Intelligence Summaries are contained in F. S. Regs., Part II. and the Staff Manual respectively. Title Pages will be prepared in manuscript.

Place	Date	Hour	Summary of Events and Information	Remarks and references to Appendices
	16/1/17.		CASUALTIES. NIL.	
	17/1/17.		CASUALTIES. 159 Bde. R.F.A. wounded O.R.1.	
	18/1/17.		CASUALTIES. NIL.	
	19/1/17.		CASUALTIES. NIL.	
	20/1/17.		CASUALTIES. NIL.	
	21/1/17.		CASUALTIES. NIL.	
	22/1/17.		CASUALTIES. NIL.	
	23/1/17.		CASUALTIES. 14th Gloucesters wounded O.R.1.	
	24/1/17.		CASUALTIES. 23rd Manchesters wounded O.R.1.	
	25/1/17.		CASUALTIES. NIL.	
	26/1/17.		CASUALTIES. NIL.	
	27/1/17.		CASUALTIES. NIL.	
	28/1/17.		CASUALTIES. 157 Bde. R.F.A. killed O.R.1., wounded 5.	
	29/1/17.		CASUALTIES. 104 M.G.Coy. wounded O.R.1., 35 Div. Sig. Coy. R.E. wounded O.R.4.	
	30/1/17.		CASUALTIES. NIL.	
	31/1/17.		CASUALTIES. 17th R.Scots. wounded O.R.1., V/35 T.M.B. wounded O.R.1.	

1875 W: W.93/826 1,000,000 4/15 J.B.C. & A. A.D.S.S./Forms/C. 2118.

Army Form C. 2118.

35th Division Administrative Staff.

WAR DIARY

INTELLIGENCE SUMMARY.

(Erase heading not required.)

Headquarters
35th Division.

No. A.H.26.
Date 3-4-17

Instructions regarding War Diaries and Intelligence Summaries are contained in F.S. Regs., Part II. and the Staff Manual respectively. Title pages will be prepared in manuscript.

Place	Date	Hour	Summary of Events and Information	Remarks and references to Appendices
MARCH.	1st.		CASUALTIES: 15th Cheshires Killed O.R. 1., 15th Sherwoods Wounded O.R.1., 17th West Yorks Wounded O.R.1. 18th Highland L.I. Killed O.R.1. Wounded O.R.1.	
	2nd.		16th Cheshires Wounded O.R.1., 15th Sherwoods Wounded O.R.1., 17th West Yorks Wounded O.R.2. 19th Durham L.I. Wounded O.R.1., 18th Highland L.I. Wounded O.R.1.	
	3rd.		157 Bde. R.F.A. Wounded O.R. 3., 204 Fd.Coy.R.E. Wounded O.R.1., 16th Cheshires Wounded Officers 2/Lt. H.S.BAXTER. 2/Lt. H.E.MARROW. 2/Lt. H.C.HORSFALL. 2/Lt. W. PICKFORD.,Killed O.R. 5, Wounded O.R.11., Missing O.R.20., 15th Sherwoods Killed O.R.1. Wounded 2., 105 T.M.B. Wounded O.R.3., 17th Royal Scots Killed O.R.2., Wounded 2., 17th West Yorks Wounded O.R.2., 19th Durham L.I. Killed O.R.2; Wounded O.R.4. (2accidental), 19th North'd Fus. Wounded O.R.2.	
	4th.		157 Bde. R.F.A. Killed O.R.1., 16th Cheshires Wounded O.R. 4. (accidental).14th Glosters Wounded O.R. 2., 15th Sherwoods Killed O.R.1. Wounded 3., 17th Royal Scots, Killed O.R.1. Wounded 1. 19th Durham L.I. Wounded O.R.4., 18th Highland L.I. Killed O.R.2. Wounded O.R.1. (all accidental).	
*5th.			106 M.G.Coy Wounded O.R.1. 105 Fd. Ambce. Wounded O.R.1.,*16th Cheshires Wounded Officers 2/Lt. J.P.FLYNN (at duty) Killed O.R.1. *19th Durham L.I. Wounded O.R.3.	
	6th.		16th Cheshires Wounded Officers 2/Lt. R.A.McKNIGHT. Wounded O.R.2., 15th Sherwoods Wounded0.R.1. 17th Royal Scots Killed O.R.1. Wounded 4., 19th Durham L.I. Wounded O.R.1., 106 M.G.Coy Wounded O.R.2.	
	7th.		157 Bde. R.F.A. Wounded Officers 2/Lt.(A/Capt) D.F.GOODWIN. (Since Died), Wounded O.R.5., 18th Lanc. Fus. Wounded O.R.2., 20th Lan. Fus. Wounded O.R.1., 23rd Manchesters Wounded O.R.1., 14th Glosters Wounded O.R. 2 (accidental)., 16th Cheshires Wounded O.R.2., 17th Royal Scots Wounded O.R.1. 18th Highland L.I. Wounded O.R.1., 19th North'd Fus. Killed O.R.1.	
	8th.		17th Royal Scots Wounded O.R.1., 17th West Yorks, Killed O.R.1 Wounded 1 Missing 5., 19th Durham L.I. Wounded O.R.1., 13th Highland L.I. Killed O.R.1. Wounded 2., 106 M.G.Coy Killed O.R. 1 Wounded 4.	
	9th.		17th Lancs.Fus. Wounded Officers 2/Lt. W.W.SPROSEN. Wounded O.R. 2., 23rd Manchesters Wounded O.R.7. 17th Royal Scots. Wounded O.R.2. Missing O.R.1., 17th West Yorks, Killed O.R.1, Wounded O.R.1 Accidental.	

Army Form C. 2118.

WAR DIARY

INTELLIGENCE SUMMARY.

(Erase heading not required.)

Instructions regarding War Diaries and Intelligence Summaries are contained in F.S. Regs., Part II. and the Staff Manual respectively. Title pages will be prepared in manuscript.

Place	Date	Hour	Summary of Events and Information	Remarks and references to Appendices
MARCH.			CASUALTIES. Cont'd.	
	10th.		17th Lan.Fus. Killed O.R.1. Wounded 1., 23rd Manchesters Wounded Officers 2/Lt. C.R.CHAFFEY. The grave of this officer has since been found behind the lately occupied ground at HALLU. 17th West Yorks Killed Officers Capt. J.A.ROSE, Wounded O.R.2. 106 M.G.Coy Wounded O.R.1.	
	11th.		159 Bde R.F.A. Wounded Officers 2/Lt. H.T.BURT. (at duty). 20th Lan. Fus. Wounded O.R.2.(1 accidental). 17th West Yorks Killed Officers Wounded O.R.1. 17th Royal Scots Wounded O.R.1.	
	12th.		17th Royal Scots Killed O.R.1. Wounded O.R.3. 17th Lan.Fus. Wounded Accidental O.R.2., 20th Lan. Fus. Wounded O.R.2. 18th Highland L.I. Wounded O.R.1. 19th North'd Fus. Wounded O.R.1. 17th West Yorks Wounded O.R.1. (attd 106 T.M.B.), 19th D.L.I. (Attd 106 T.M.B.) Wounded O.R.3.	
	13th.		18th Lan. Fus. Killed O.R.1. Wounded O.R. 1., 20th Lan.Fus. Wounded O.R.1., 17th Royal Scots, Wounded O.R.5., 19th Durham L.I. Wounded O.R.2. 106 M.G.C. Wounded O.R.3.	
	14th.		159 Bde. R.F.A. Wounded O.R. 10. (5 at duty), 17th Lancs. Fus. Wounded O.R.1., 20th Lancs. Fus. Wounded O.R.2. 17th Royal Scots. Wounded O.R. 2, 19th Durham L.I. Wounded O.R.2. 19th North'd Fus. Wounded O.R.1.	
	15th.		23rd Manchesters. Wounded O.R.1.	
	16th.	XX	17th Lancs.Fus. Wounded O.R.4.,18th Lancs.Fus. Wounded O.R.1.,20th Lancs.Fus. Wounded O.R.1.(S.I.) 15th Cheshires Wounded O.R.1. 17th Royal Scots Wounded O.R.1.	
	17th.		18th Lancs. Fus. Wounded O.R.1.,23rd Manchesters Killed O.R.1.Wounded O.R.1,15th Cheshires Wounded O.R.2.,14th Glosters Wounded O.R.1. 19th North'd Fus. Wounded O.R.2. X/35 T.M.B. Wounded Officers 2/Lt. P.M.LECKIE Killed O.R.2. Wounded O.R.1., Y/35 T.M.B. Wounded O.R.1.	
	18th.		NIL.	
	19th.		17th West Yorks Wounded O.R.1. Accidental.	
	20th.		18th Lancs.Fus. Wounded O.R.1.	

Army Form C. 2118.

WAR DIARY

(Erase heading not required.)

Place	Date	Hour	Summary of Events and Information	Remarks and references to Appendices
			CASUALTIES. Cont'd.	
	MARCH. 21st.		157 Bde. R.F.A. Wounded. O.R. 4. Accidental.	
	22nd.		NIL.	
	23rd.		17th Royal Scots Wounded O.R. 1. Accidental.	
	24th.		NIL.	
	25th.		NIL.	
	26th.		NIL.	
	27th.		159nBde. R.F.A. Wounded Officers 2/Lt. H.T.BURT. Accidentally.	
	28th.		NIL.	
	29th.		NIL.	
	30th.		16th Cheshires Died O.R.L.	
	31st.		NIL.	

Major-General,
Commanding 35th Division.

WAR DIARY

35th Divl. Administrative Staff.

Army Form C. 2118

(Erase heading not required.)

Place	Date	Hour	Summary of Events and Information	Remarks and references to Appendices
	1-4-17.		**CASUALTIES.** 17th West Yorks. Wounded O.R.1.	
	2-4-17.		NIL.	
	3-4-17.		18th Highland L.I. Wounded Accidentally O.R.3., 15th Cheshires Wounded S.I. O.R.1.	
	4-4-17.		NIL.	
	5-4-17.		NIL.	
	6-4-17.		NIL.	
	7-4-17.		159 Bde. R.F.A. Killed 2/Lt. G.M.WOOLNOUGH, O.R.2.	
	8-4-17.		104 Machine Gun Coy. Wounded O.M.PARKER. (at duty).	
	9-4-17.		NIL.	
	10-4-17.		NIL.	
	11-4-17.		NIL.	
	12-4-17.		17th Lan. Fus. Wounded Lt. HG.LEAVER. O.R.3., Missing O.R.2. 23rd Manchesters Wounded O.R.1.	
	"		19th D.L.I. Missing O.R.2.; 106 M.G.Coy Wounded O.R.1.	
	13-4-17.		17th Lan. Fus. Wounded 2/Lt. H.H.VALE. 2/Lt. A. BELL. O.R. 9. 104 M.G.C. Wounded O.R.1.	
	"		17th Royal Scots. Wounded Capt. E.E.RUDDELL. O.R.12, Missing O.R.5. 19th D.L.I.Killed O.R.1. Wounded O.R.2.	
	14-4-17.		17th Lan. Fus. Killed O.R.2. Wounded O.R.10. 18th Lan.Fus. Wounded O.R.1. 20th Lan. Fus. Killed O.R.1. Wounded O.R.5. 23rd Manchesters Wounded Lt. M.H.ROSE.M.C., O.R.3. 17th Royal Scots Killed O.R.1. Wounded O.R.6. 19th D.L.I. Wounded 2/Lt. P.W.DAY. 2/Lt. G.B.CHESTER. Killed O.R.1. Wounded O.R.1., 157 Bde. R.F.A. Wounded O.R.1.	
	15-4-17.		17th Royal Scots. Wounded 2/Lt. I.C.FALCONER. Killed O.R.29, Wounded O.R.54, Missing believed killed O.R.16. 19th D.L.I. Killed O.R.1. 169 Bde. R.F.A. wounded Major R.D.HARRISSON (at duty), 2/Lt. V.L.HAYES. O.R.4. 157 Bde. R.F.A. wounded O.R.1. 17th Lan. Fus. Wounded 2/Lt. J.H.KIRBY. Killed O.R.9. Wounded O.R.27. 18th Lan. Fus. Wounded Capt. H.R.WILCOX, 2/Lt. F.V.COSLETT. 2/Lt. W.HODKIN. Killed O.R. 5. Wounded 39. 23rd Manchesters Wounded O.R.1.	
	"		20th Lan. Fus. Wounded Lt. R.M.MORLEY, 2/Lt. A.MILLAR. 2/Lt. R.R.ADAMS. Killed O.R.5. Wounded 21.	
	"		18th Lan. Fus. Wounded 2/Lt. R.J.PRESCOTT. (Now reported missing, believed killed). Killed O.R.3.	
	16-4-17.		Wounded 15. 20th Lan. Fus. Killed O.R.11. Wounded 14. Missing 2. 23rd Manchesters Killed O.R.1. Wounded 7. 104 M.G.C. Wounded O.R.1. 105 M.G.C. Wounded O.R.1. 17th West Yorks Wounded 2/Lt. E.G. ADDINGTON. Killed O.R.2. Wounded 2. 105 Fd. Ambce. Killed O.R.1. A.S.C.Attd 105 F.A. Killed O.R.1. 17th Royal Scots. Killed O.R.2. Wounded 9.	

Major-General
Commanding 35th Division.

WAR DIARY
INTELLIGENCE SUMMARY

(Erase heading not required.)

Army Form C.2118

Instructions regarding War Diaries and Intelligence Summaries are contained in F.S. Regs, Part II. and the Staff Manual respectively. Title Pages will be prepared in manuscript.

Place	Date	Hour	Summary of Events and Information	Remarks and references to Appendices
	17-4-17.		23rd Manchesters Wounded 2/Lt. A.H.BRAMLEY. Killed O.R.2. Wounded 8. 15th Cheshires Wounded O.R.5. 16th Cheshires Killed O.R.1. Wounded 1. 17th Royal Scots. Wounded O.R.1. 17th West Yorks. Wounded O.R.8. Missing 10. 18th H.L.I. Wounded O.R.1. 106 M.G.C. Wounded O.R.1. 159 Bde. R.F.A. Wounded 2/Lt. D.MARSHALL.	
	18-4-17.		20th Lan. Fus. Killed O.R.1. Wounded 8. 15th Cheshires. Killed O.R.2. wounded 1. 16th Cheshires Killed O.R.1. Wounded 1. 18th H.L.I. Killed O.R.1. X	
	19-4-17.		15th Cheshires. Killed O.R.3. Wounded 3. 14th Gloucesters Wounded O.R.1. 18th H.L.I. Killed O.R.1. Wounded 1. 106 M.G.C. Wounded O.R.1. 157 Bde. R.F.A. Wounded O.R.1.	
	20-4-17.		15th Cheshires wounded O.R.1. Accidentally. 19th D.L.I. Killed O.R.1. 18th H.L.I. Wounded O.R.2. 159 Bde. R.F.A. Wounded O.R.2.	
	21-4-17.		15th Cheshires Wounded O.R.1. 17th Royal Scots. Wounded O.R.1.	
	22-4-17.		15th Cheshires Wounded O.R.1. 16th Cheshires Wounded Capt. G.STURLA. 2/Lt. R.J.MORRIS. Killed O.R.3. Missing 1. 14th Gloucesters. wounded Lt. J.YOUNG,R.A.M.C. 15th Sherwoods Killed Major F.VICKERS. Wounded Lt. A.G.HAINES. 2/Lt. E.J.MOONEY. 2/Lt. W.G.WOOD. 17th Royal Scots Wounded O.R.1. 19th D.L.I. Wounded 2/Lt. J.R. OZZARD, Killed O.R.1. Wounded 1. 306th Bde. R.F.A. Wounded O.R.2.	
	23-4-17.		16th Cheshires Wounded O.R.1. 105 M.G.C. Wounded O.R.1. 17th Royal Scots, Wounded O.R.3. 157 Bde. R.F.A. Wounded O.R.1. 159 Bde. R.F.A. Wounded O.R.1.	
	24-4-17.		15th Sherwoods Wounded O.R.1. 17th Royal Scots Killed O.R.1. Wounded 2. 19th D.L.I. Wounded O.R.1. R.A.M.C. attd 107 F.A. Wounded O.R.1. (at duty).	
	25-4-17.		16th Cheshires Wounded Lt. C.E.E.HEYWOOD. Killed O.R.1. 19th D.L.I. Killed O.R.1. 157 Bde. R.F.A. Killed O.R.1. Wounded 1. 17th Royal Scots. Wounded O.R.1. 19th D.L.I. Killed O.R.1. 157 Bde. R.F.A. Killed O.R.1.	
	26-4-17.		14th Gloucesters Wounded O.R.1. 15th Sherwoods Killed O.R.1. wounded 3.	
	27-4-17.		23rd Manchester Wounded O.R. 7. Missing 2. (believed killed). 15th Cheshires Killed O.R. 2 Wounded 2. 15th Sherwoods Wounded O.R. 2.	
	28-4-17.		15th Cheshires wounded O.R. 1. Missing 1. 14th Gloucesters wounded O.R.1. 306th Bde. R.F.A. Wounded O.R.1.	
	29-4-17.		20th Lan. Fus. wounded 2/Lt. T.LYNCH Wounded O.R.14. 15th Cheshires Wounded 2/Lt. E.H.HODSON. O.R.2. 16th Cheshires Wounded 2/Lt. T.L.WOOD. Killed O.R.1. Wounded 26. Missing 2. 105 M.G.C. Killed O.R.3. Wounded 1. 157 Bde. R.F.A. Killed O.R.1. wounded 1.	
	30-4-17.		20th Lan. Fus. Wounded 2/Lt. E.I.GIBBONS (Missing, believed prisoner). Killed O.R.1. wounded 2. 15th Cheshires Wounded O.R.1. Missing 1. 306th Bde. R.F.A. Wounded O.R.2. 35th D.A.C. Wounded 2/Lt. D.HAWKIN. Accidentally and at duty).	

Major-General.
Commanding 3 5th Division.

WAR DIARY

35th Divisional Administrative Staff.

INTELLIGENCE SUMMARY

(Erase heading not required.)

Army Form C. 2118

Place	Date	Hour	Summary of Events and Information	Remarks and references to Appendices
			CASUALTIES.	
	1-5-17.		20th Lancs.Fus. Wounded O.R.1. Missing 2., 14th Glosters killed O.R.1, 18th H.L.I. wounded O.R.2. missing 2., 19th D.L.I. attd 106 T.M.B. wounded accidentally (at duty) 2/Lt. A.S.CARROLL.	
	2-5-17.		17th Royal Scots attd T.M.B. killed O.R.3., 17th W.Yorks attd T.M.B. killed O.R.3., 19th D.L.I. attd T.M.B. killed O.R.1., 18th H.L.I. wounded O.R.6, 18th H.L.I attd T.M.B. killed O.R.1. wounded 1., 106 M.G.C. wounded O.R.1., 203rd Coy R.E. wounded O.R.1.	
	3-5-17.		D.A.C.attd 157 Bde. R.F.A. wounded O.R.2., 18th Lancs. Fus. wounded O.R.3., 17th W.Yorks wounded O.R.1., 18th H.L.I. killed O.R.1. wounded 1., 106 M.G.C. wounded O.R.1.	
	4-5-17.		157 Bde. R.F.A. wounded O.R.1., 18th H.L.I. wounded O.R.1.,	
	5-5-17.		23rd Manchesters wounded O.R.8. (includes 3 at duty)., 17th West Yorks wounded O.R.10. missing 1., 106 M.G.C. wounded O.R.2., 205th Fd. Coy. R.E. killed O.R.1.	
	6-5-17.		17th Lancs. Fus. killed O.R.1. wounded O.R.5., 16th Cheshires wounded O.R.1., 17th Ryl. Scots. killed O.R.2. wounded 7., 17th W. Yorks wounded O.R.3. (2 at duty)., 19th D.L.I. killed 2/Lt. G.F.GOLIGHTLY (died of wounds 7-5-17 at 21st C.C.S.)., wounded 2/Lt. W.GRAY (6-5-17). missing believed killed 2/Lt. F.BLENKINSOP. O.R. killed 8, wounded 39, missing believed killed 9.	
	7-5-17.		17th Lancs. Fus. wounded O.R.1. missing 2., 20th Lancs. Fus. killed O.R.1.	
	8-5-17.		19th D.L.I. wounded O.R.3.	
	9-5-17.		15th Cheshires wounded O.R.2., 16th Cheshires wounded O.R.1., 15th Sherwood wounded O.R.1.	
	10-5-17.		15th Cheshires wounded Capt. H.F.A. LE MESURIER (10-5-17), 16th Cheshires wounded O.R.2., 15th Sherwoods wounded (at duty) 2/Lt. W.DUNS (9-5-17), O.R. killed 4, wounded 13, missing 2. 157 Bde. R.F.A. wounded O.R.1.	
	11-5-17.		15th Cheshires killed O.R.1. wounded 2., 16th Cheshires wounded O.R.1., 15th Sherwoods wounded O.R.2, 15th Sherwoods attd T.M.B. missing 1.	

Army Form C. 2118

WAR DIARY
INTELLIGENCE SUMMARY

(Erase heading not required.)

Instructions regarding War Diaries and Intelligence Summaries are contained in F. S. Regs., Part II. and the Staff Manual respectively. Title Pages will be prepared in manuscript.

Place	Date	Hour	Summary of Events and Information	Remarks and references to Appendices
	12-5-17.		23rd Manchesters wounded 2/Lt. R.A.FISHER, 14th Glosters wounded O.R.1., 19th North'd Fus. wounded O.R.1.	
	13-5-17.		20th Lancs. Fus. wounded O.R.3., 23rd Manchesters wounded O.R.6., 104 T.M.B. wounded O.R.1., 15th Sherwoods killed O.R.2., wounded 2.	
	14-5-17.		17th Lancs. Fus. wounded O.R.2. (1 at duty).	
	15-5-17.		23rd Manchesters killed O.R.1.	
	16-5-17.		16th Cheshires wounded O.R.1., 14th Glosters wounded O.R.2., 15th Sherwoods wounded 2/Lt. J.B.FARMER. killed O.R.2. wounded 23, missing 11, (2 believed killed, 1 wounded)., 19th D.L.I. wounded O.R.1. (Self-inflicted)., 18th H.L.I. attd T.M.B. wounded O.R.1., 204 Fd. Coy. R.E. killed O.R.1., wounded 1 (at duty).	
	17-5-17.		Royal Canadian Dragoons wounded O.R.1., 15th Sherwoods, wounded O.R.1. (Self-inflicted).	
	18-5-17.		15th Cheshires wounded O.R.9., 16th Cheshires killed Major R.WORTHINGTON, Lord Strathcona's Horse wounded O.R.1., Fort Garry Horse wounded O.R.1., 8th Hussars wounded O.R.1.	
	19-5-17.		157 Bde. R.F.A. wounded O.R.1., 14th Glosters killed 2/Lt. W.E.COX, wounded O.R.1.	
	20-5-17.		16th Cheshires wounded O.R.8., missing 3., 14th Glosters wounded O.R.2.	
	21-5-17.		157 Bde. R.F.A. wounded 2/Lt. E.B.WOODROW, O.R.6. (2 at duty).	
	22-5-17.		NIL.	
	23-5-17.		NIL.	
	24-5-17.		18th H.L.I. killed Capt. W.S.BARR (Self-inflicted) Wounded O.R.1.,	
	25-5-17.		106 M.G.C. wounded O.R.1.	
	26-5-17.		17th West Yorks wounded 2/Lt. W.J.MOORE., 18th H.L.I. wounded 2/Lt. W.A.STUART, O.R.1.	

Army Form C. 2118

WAR DIARY
INTELLIGENCE SUMMARY
(Erase heading not required.)

Instructions regarding War Diaries and Intelligence Summaries are contained in F. S. Regs., Part II. and the Staff Manual respectively. Title Pages will be prepared in manuscript.

Place	Date	Hour	Summary of Events and Information	Remarks and references to Appendices
	27-5-17.		17th Lancs. Fus. wounded O.R.1., 18th H.L.I. wounded O.R.1.	
	28-5-17.		17th West Yorks wounded O.R.6., missing 1., 19th D.L.I. wounded 2/Lt. K.SMITH (at duty).	
	29-5-17.		17th Lancs. Fus. wounded O.R.3. (1 at duty) & (2accidental)., 18th Lancs. Fus. wounded O.R.1. accidentally., 17th West Yorks, killed Capt. E.G.HADOW, 35th D.A.C. wounded O.R.1. accidentally.	
	30-5-17.		17th West Yorks wounded O.R.1. (at duty).	
	31-5-17.		17th Lancs. Fus. wounded 2/Lt. W.M.HOLDEN, O.R.1., 14th Glosters wounded O.R.1., 17th Ryl. Scots. Killed O.R.1. wounded 1., 17th West Yorks wounded O.R.1., 19th D.L.I. killed O.R.1. 19th North'd Fus. wounded O.R.1.	
			On May 19th the left sector of the line was taken over by the 5th Cavalry Division. On May 20th the right sector of the line was taken over by the G.O.C. 87th French Division. All S.A.A. and Grenades were taken over by the 5th Cavalry Division. All trench and area stores such as tents, shelters etc. with the exception of two Nissen Huts and half a dozen tents which were loaned to the French were taken over by the 5th Cavalry Division. On the 19th and following days, Division moved from the IVth Corps to the XVth Corps into the PERONNE area. The move was carried out without incident and the arrangements made for handing over billets, supplies and transport as detailed in Administrative orders 7 and 8 (App A. & B.) were found to work well. The method of directing units to dump all stores that they could not carry with D.A.D.O.S. and the subsequent weeding out of illegitimate stores by the D.A.D.O.S has been found to be a good way of withdrawing from units the surplus stores which are invariably collected by them, and the subsequent returning of them to the Base tends towards economy. On going into the new area the transport lines and Quarter-masters stores at HEUDECOURT were taken over from the 40th Division. It was subsequently found necessary to alter the dispositions for the purposes of Administration and to divide HEUDECOURT into two areas, the Southern one to the right sector and the Northern one to the left sector.	

1875 Wt. W593/826 1,000,000 4/15 J.B.C. & A. A.D.S.S./Forms/C. 2118.

Army Form C. 2118

WAR DIARY
INTELLIGENCE SUMMARY
(Erase heading not required.)

Place	Date	Hour	Summary of Events and Information	Remarks and references to Appendices
			Some difficulty was experienced during the month in obtaining clean clothing owing to the length of time it took to get back clothing sent to the laundry. This difficulty, however, was overcome by obtaining an extra 5,000 sets of clothing from Ordnance. On the 27th May 1 Officer and 105 O.R. arrived as the nucleus of the Divisional Employment Company. These were originally intended to be "B" men, but on inspection were found to be "C" men. The Company is formed with the object of releasing category "A" men from their employment, and substituting men from the Employment Company in their place. The scheme is, as yet, in its infancy, and it is difficult to know how it will work out. The general principle is that employed men classed as "B" by a medical board shall be transferred to the Employment Company and struck off the strength of their units. Employed men classed as "A" will be gradually replaced by men of the Employment Company, and when so replaced returned to their units. Difficulties are anticipated in being able to find men to take over the various employments from the men who were sent up with the draft.	
1-6-17. PH.				

[signature]

Major-General.
Commanding 35th Division.

App. A

35th DIVISION.

ADMINISTRATIVE ORDER No. 7.

TENTS AND SHELTERS.

The whole of the Tents and Shelters in the Divisional Area (except those on Mobilization Establishment) will be handed over to the 5th Cavalry Division, and receipts obtained and forwarded to D.H.Q.

Dumps will be formed at

(1) Ammunition Dump MERAUCOURT;

(2) Mausoleum, CAULAINCOURT;

(3) Town Major's Office, VERMAND.

For (1) The D.A.C. will detail an officer to take over these tents etc.

For (2) Captain F.L. WAINWRIGHT, 17th Lancashire Fusiliers, will take over tents etc.

For (3) Captain WARMINGTON will take over and remain until all are handed in.

104th Brigade Group.

Will return all tents and shelters to No. 2 Dump (CAULAINCOURT) except the Battalion at MONCHY, which will return tents etc. to No. 1 Dump (MERAUCOURT).

105th Brigade Group

Will take over all tents and shelters from 106th Brigade Group, and will hand over all the tents and shelters it vacates prior to this move to No. 3 Dump (VERMAND).   105th Brigade will hand over all tents and shelters taken from 106th Brigade to the nearest Dumps.

It is suggested that the blanket lorries be used for this before moving to new area.

R.A. will take tents and shelters with them until vacating the Divisional area, when all tents and shelters will be handed over to the nearest Dump.

All other units will hand over their tents and shelters to the most convenient Dump before vacating the area.

LORRIES.

Five lorries will report at each Brigade Headquarters at 6 p.m. on the day before each move.   On completion of each day's march they will return to Corps Park.

Four lorries will report at Headquarters, R.A. at 6 p.m. on 22nd.

/Baggage

Baggage wagons will move with units.

Orders regarding Refilling, Medical and Billeting arrangements will be issued later.

The Divisional Bomb Store at R 31.b.3.8. will be taken over by the 5th Cavalry Division on the 18th instant. 105th Brigade will arrange to transfer its ammunition, bombs, etc. and Bomb Store to the Divisional Bomb Store on relief by the French.

M. Hare

Lieut-Colonel,
A.A. & Q.M.G. 35th Division.

16-5-17.
RCF

App. B.

35th DIVISION.
ADMINISTRATIVE ORDER No. 8.

1. REFILLING.

      Until they leave the present area, units will refil as at present along the TERTRY - BEAUVOIS Road.

      Refilling point for units in PERONNE will be PERONNE.

      Refilling point for units in the forward area will be TEMPLEUX LA FOSSE.

      Railhead will change from NESLE to PERONNE on the 21st inst.

2. BILLETING.

      The billeting areas for Brigades before going into the line will be as under :-

    (A) Brigade H.Q.   )
           2 Battalions   ) W. 19 b & d.
           M.G. Co. & T.M.B.   )

    (B) 2 Battalions   ) D. 28 b.
           Field Co. R.E.   )

3. Tents for this Brigade Group will be dumped as under :-

    (A) Town Major, SOREL LE GRAND.

    (B) TEMPLEUX LA FOSSE Cross Roads near Church D.28.d.6.2.

4. The 8th Division have kindly lent 2 G.S. Wagons to be at each of these places at 12 noon on May 20th. to take the tents to the spot selected by the Brigade representatives for the camps. The 106th Brigade will send an advanced party to each place on 20th. May, of sufficient size to take over and pitch the camp for the Brigade.

5. WATERING POINTS.

      Camp 'A' - W.14.a. central

      Camp 'B' - D.29.c.2.7.

6. The Train will billet in and near TEMPLEUX LA FOSSE.

7. The D.A.D.O.S. will set up his establishment on the roadside near the farm in D.15.a.

8. The Divisional Bomb Store will be located at W.14.b.5.4.

9. Reference Administrative Order No. 7, the Dump ordered to be formed at the Mausoleum CAULAINCOURT will now be formed at the old R.E. dump CAULAINCOURT, W.5.a.1.3.

P.T.O.

10. **MEDICAL ARRANGEMENTS.**

106th Field Ambulance will be located at HEUDECOURT and collect from the forward Brigades.

107th Field Ambulance will be located at TEMPLEUX LA FOSSE and collect from units in the back area.

105th Field Ambulance will take over duties of Corps Rest Station South of FINS.

11. **BAGGAGE WAGONS.**

With reference to Administrative Order No. 7, Baggage Wagons will march with their Train Companies and not with their units as therein stated.

M Hare
Lieut-Colonel,
A.A. & Q.M.G. 35th Division.

17-5-17.
RCF

WAR DIARY 35th Division Administrative Staff.

Army Form C. 2118

INTELLIGENCE SUMMARY

H.Q., 35TH DIVISION, "A" BRANCH.

A.H.146.   2.7.17.

95/16

Place	Date	Hour	Summary of Events and Information	Remarks and references to Appendices
			CASUALTIES.	
	1-6-17.		17th West Yorks wounded O.R.1, Missing O.R.1.	
	2-6-17.		17th Lancs. Fus. wounded O.R.1.	
	3-6-17.		23rd Manchesters wounded O.R.1, 16th Cheshires killed (accidental) 2/Lt. R.M.HAMILTON, 14th Glosters killed O.R.2., 19th D.L.I. wounded O.R.1, 204th Field Coy R.E. wounded O.R.1., 157 Bde. R.F.A. wounded O.R.4.	
	4-6-17.		23rd Manchesters wounded O.R.1., 15th Cheshires wounded O.R.1., 14th Glosters killed O.R.1., 3rd Troop 'A' Squadron Royal Wiltshire Yeomanry wounded O.R.1., 2nd N.F. attd 19th North'd Fus. wounded Lieut. C.W.SCOTT.	
	5-6-17.		NIL.	
	6-6-17.		14th Glosters wounded 2/Lt. L.H.E.STENSON, killed O.R.2. wounded 1, (accidental).	
	7-6-17.		19th D.L.I. wounded Capt. C.E.S.NOAKES, 2/Lt. J.ROBERTSON, O.R.3. (all accidental)., 18th H.L.I. wounded O.R.2. (accidental, 1 at duty).	
	8-6-17.		23rd Manchesters killed O.R.1., 14th Glosters killed O.R.1., 15th Sherwoods killed O.R.1.	
	9-6-17.		18th Lancs. Fus. wounded O.R.1. (at duty).	
	10-6-17.		14th Glosters killed O.R.1. wounded 5.	
	11-6-17.		16th Cheshires wounded O.R.1., (accidental)., 159 Bde. R.F.A. wounded O.R.1.	
	12-6-17.		17th West Yorks wounded 2/Lt. E.S.RAWSON, O.R.3., 18th H.L.I. wounded O.R.5.	
	13-6-17.		14th Glosters wounded 2/Lt. F.C.MILLER, O.R.1., 157 Bde. R.F.A. killed O.R.1.	
	14-6-17.		15th Cheshires wounded O.R.1. (at duty)., 17th Royal Scots wounded O.R.4. (at duty). 18th H.L.I. wounded 2/Lt. S.McGUFFIE, O.R.1, 19th North'd Fus. killed O.R.1., 159 Bde. R.F.A. wounded O.R.1.	

Army Form C. 2118

WAR DIARY
INTELLIGENCE SUMMARY

(Erase heading not required.)

Place	Date	Hour	Summary of Events and Information	Remarks and references to Appendices
	15-6-17.		CASUALTIES: Cont'd. 203rd Field Coy. R.E. wounded O.R.1., 15th Sherwoods killed O.R.1., 18th H.L.I. killed O.R.2.	
	16-6-17.		15th Sherwoods wounded O.R.1., 18th H.L.I. wounded O.R.1.	
	17-6-17.		15th Cheshires wounded O.R.1., 19th D.L.I. wounded O.R.1. (accidental), 18th H.L.I. wounded O.R.1.	
	18-6-17.		16th Cheshires wounded 2/Lt. W.G.HASLER (at duty),O.R.4. (2 at duty)., 15th Sherwoods wounded O.R.1., 18th H.L.I. wounded O.R.1.	
	19-6-17.		18th Lancs. Fus. wounded O.R.4., 17th Royal Scots killed O.R.3., 18th H.L.I. wounded O.R.1. 159 Bde. R.F.A. wounded 2/Lt. L.A.HEARN, 35th Divl. Train wounded O.R.1 (self-inflicted).	
	20-6-17.		18th Lancs. Fus. wounded O.R.2. (1 at duty)., 20th Lancs. Fus. wounded O.R.2., 17th Royal Scots wounded O.R.3. 19th D.L.I. wounded O.R.1.	
	21-6-17.		17th Lancs. Fus. wounded O.R.2., 17th Royal Scots wounded O.R.4 (1 accidental, 2 at duty).	
	22-6-17.		18th H.L.I. wounded O.R.1. (accidental)., 35th D.A.C. wounded O.R.2. (1 accidentally), X/35 T.M.B. killed 2/Lt. C.W.BACKWELL, O.R.2. wounded O.R.2.	
	23-6-17.		19th D.L.I. wounded O.R.1., 17th West Yorks wounded O.R.1. (accidental).	
	24-6-17.		18th Lancs. Fus. wounded O.R.5. (1 at duty)., 159 Bde. R.F.A. wounded O.R.1.	
	25-6-17.		18th Lancs. Fus. killed O.R.2. wounded 5., 8th Hussars attd. 18th Lancs. Fus. on probation killed O.R.1., 17th Lancs. Fus. wounded O.R.2., 17th Royal Scots killed O.R.1., 19th North'd Fus. wounded O.R.1.	
	26-6-17.		17th Lancs. Fus. wounded O.R.1., 17th Royal Scots wounded O.R., killed 1., 17th West Yorks killed O.R.1.	
	27-6-17.		203rd Field Coy. R.E. wounded O.R.1. (accidental)., 17th Lancs. Fus. wounded O.R.2., (1 at duty). 23rd Manchesters killed O.R.4. wounded 5.	

-3-

Army Form C. 2118

Instructions regarding War Diaries and Intelligence
Summaries are contained in F. S. Regs., Part II.
and the Staff Manual respectively. Title Pages
will be prepared in manuscript.

WAR DIARY
INTELLIGENCE SUMMARY
(Erase heading not required.)

Place	Date	Hour	Summary of Events and Information	Remarks and references to Appendices
	28-6-17.		CASUALTIES. Cont'd.	
			20th Lancs. Fus. wounded O.R.1. (at duty).	
	29-6-17.		15th Cheshires wounded O.R.2. (1st duty)., 14th Glosters wounded O.R.2.	
	30-6-17.		23rd Manchesters missing O.R.1 (believed prisoner)., 15th Cheshires wounded O.R.1., 14th Glosters wounded O.R.10.	
			EXTRA CAMP ACCOMMODATION IN DIVISIONAL AREA.	
			During the month sites for the camps for an Infantry Division plus the Artillery of two Divisions, and 4 Heavy Battery Wagon Lines and less the Infantry of two Brigades were selected in the Area occupied by the Division. These camps were marked out with notice boards and latrines were dug.	
			In addition to this, sites in the villages of HEUDICOURT and SOREL were cleared for the erection of NISSEN HUTS, to accommodate two battalions from each place. The greater part of the work which chiefly consisted in digging latrines and marking out camps was completed. Some of the camps however, after they had been finished, had the sites altered by the Corps and had to be done over again. This has delayed matters somewhat.	
			Standard types of latrines, incinerators, cookhouses, officer's messes. etc. etc. are being provided by the Corps Engineers, and, as they arrive, will be put up on the sites selected.	
			HAYMAKING.	
			During the month, two parties of Haymakers were sent out, one under Lieut. HURLEY. A.S.C. into the LIERAMONT and forward area, and the other under Lieut. FENTON. A.S.C. into the BUSSU or back area.	
			Each party consisted of 3 officers and some 60 O.R., their duties being to collect and cut the most suitable grass, lucerne, clover etc.; make it into hay and stack when done. It is anticipated that the amount collected will largely diminish freightage as far as hay is concerned in the future.	
			Up to the end of the month, about 200 acres have been cut. The crops average about 1 ton per acre. Twelve stacks have been erected by the sides of roads.	

1875 Wt. W593/826 1,000,000 4/15 J.B.C. & A. A.D.S.S./Forms/C. 2118.

Army Form C. 2118

WAR DIARY
INTELLIGENCE SUMMARY
(Erase heading not required.)

Place	Date	Hour	Summary of Events and Information	Remarks and references to Appendices
			LEAVE. The number of men with over nine months service in the country without leave is 6701. The leave allotment for the month of June was 28 per diem. This was increased on the 27th to 43 per diem. **SAIL BATHS.** Sail baths made out of tarpaulins were constructed for each battalion in the reserve Bde. area. This number was increased to a total of 12, throughout the Divisional area up to the end of the month. The pattern found most suitable was to dig a pit 12 feet x 12 feet and 3 ft. deep. These sail baths were all sited within 20 yards of the men's tents or bivouacs. Ablution benches were made close to the sail baths. In only one case was it found possible to connect the bath by means of a pipe, with the existing water supply. In the other cases, the baths had to be filled either by water lorry, or the units own water carts. **P.B.OFFICERS** Two P.B. officers joined the Division. Major DAVIDSON was appointed Divisional Reinforcement and Disbursing Officer and took over these duties from Lieut. WHARTON, 15th Sherwood Foresters who re-joined his battalion. Colonel CLARKE was temporarily appointed Salvage Officer. He has now been detailed for duty as Town Major, TINCOURT. **CATERING.** The Fourth Army Instructor in Catering visited the Division between the 26th and 28th of the month. He expressed himself much satisfied and said that the cooking arrangements in the Division were far above the average. This is attributed to the fact that the Division has had a School of Cookery in being for the last six months, which trains, on an average, 20 to 30 men per month. The N.C.O. in charge, Sergeant HENDERSON, 19th North'd Fuslrs. went through a course at the Third Army School, and has since carried out his duties as Instructor of the Divisional Cookery School in a most satisfactory manner. **EMPLOYMENT COMPANY.** The Employment Company which was started last month is now a going concern. **COURTS MARTIAL.** Courts Martial for last month - 17. Courts Martial for this month - 11.	

2-7-17.

H.J.S. Lawson
Major-General.
Commanding 35th Division.

SECRET.

WAR DIARY 35th DIVISION ADMINISTRATIVE STAFF. Army Form C. 2118.

INTELLIGENCE SUMMARY

No 17

Place	Date	Hour	Summary of Events and Information	Remarks and references to Appendices
			CASUALTIES.	
	1-7-17.		18th Lancs. Fus wounded 2/Lieut A.S.CORMACK, (at duty) O.R. 1. 14th Glosters killed O.R. 2 wounded 8. 19th N.Fus. wounded 4 (includes 1 at duty) (1 accidental).	
	2-7-17.		17th Lancs. Fus. killed O.R. 1 wounded 5. 23rd Manchesters wounded O.R. 2. (1 accidentally).	
	3-7-17.		NIL.	
	4-7-17.		23rd Manchesters wounded O.R. 1 accidentally. 18th H.L.I. attached T.M.B. wounded O.R. 1 at duty.	
	5-7-17.		19th Northld Fus.wounded 2/Lieut W. MILLER, killed O.R. 1 wounded 4.	
	6-7-17.		204th Field Coy R.E. wounded O.R. 2 (includes 1 at duty).	
	7-7-17.		17th West Yorks wounded O.R. 1. 19th Durh.L.I. wounded O.R. 1. 203rd Field Coy R.E. killed O.R. 1.	
	8-7-17.		15th Cheshires.wounded O.R. 1. 16th Cheshires wounded O.R. 1 15th Sherwoods wounded O.R. 2. 18th High.L.I. wounded O.R. 2. 4th Hussars wounded O.R. 3.	
	9-7-17.		15th Sherwoods wounded O.R. 1. 18th High.L.I. wounded 2/lieut J.T.McINTYRE, wounded O.R.12. (includes 11 gas).	
	10-7-17.		15th Sherwoods wounded O.R. 2 (at duty) 17th West Yorks wounded O.R. 2. 203rd Field Coy R.E. wounded Lieut H.S.SEMPLE (accidentally).	
	11-7-17.		17th Lancs. Fus. wounded O.R. 1. 16th Cheshires wounded O.R. 1. 14th Glosters killed O.R.1. attached T.M.B. wounded O.R.1. 15th Sherwoods wounded Lieut G.L.WHARTON, killed O.R. 2 (includes 1 attached T.M.B.).	
	12-7-17.		14th Glosters wounded O.R. 4 (includes 1 at duty.) 17th West Yorks wounded 2/Lieut A.A.SOWRY, (at duty).	

WAR DIARY 35th DIVISION ADMINISTRATIVE STAFF. Army Form C. 2118.

INTELLIGENCE SUMMARY.

(Erase heading not required.)

Place	Date	Hour	Summary of Events and Information	Remarks and references to Appendices
	13-7-17.		15th Cheshires killed Lieut I.GLESDALE, O.R. 1. wounded 3. 16th Cheshires killed O.R. 2 wounded 5. 14th Glosters killed O.R. 1. 15th Sherwoods wounded Captain A.S.JOHNSON (at duty). killed O.R. 7 wounded 16. 105th M.G.Coy wounded O.R. 1. 17th Royal Scots wounded O.R. 2. 17th West Yorks wounded O.R. 1. 19th Durh.L.I. wounded O.R. 1. 18th High.L.I. killed O.R. 1. wounded 7. 19th N.Fus. killed O.R. 6 wounded 36. (Includes 11 at duty.)	
	14-7-17.		16th Cheshires wounded O.R. 3. 17th West Yorks killed O.R. 3 wounded 7. 19th Durh.L.I. wounded Lieut. L. BROTHERTON, wounded O.R. 1. 18th High.L.I. wounded 2/Lieut W.SMITH. wounded O.R. 9. 106th M.G.Coy wounded O.R. 1.	
	15-7-17.		15th Cheshires wounded O.R. 1 (accidental) 17th Royal Scots wounded O.R.1.(accidental) 17th West Yorks killed O.R. 3 wounded 2.	
	16-7-17.		23rd Manchesters killed O.R.1. (accidental) 17th Royal Scots wounded O.R.1. 17th West Yorks wounded Lieut A.B.COHEN, 18th High.L.I. killed O.R. 1. 19th Norhtld Fus. wounded O.R.1.	
	17-7-17		18th Lancs. Fus. killed O.R. 1 wounded 2. 17th Royal Scots killed O.R.1 18th High.L.I. wounded O.R.1. 19th Norhld. Fus. wounded O.R.1.	
	18-7-17.		17th Lancs. Fus. wounded O.R.1. 19th Durh.L.I. wounded O.R.1.(self-inflicted).	
	19-7-17.		105th M.G.Coy wounded O.R. 1 (accidental) 19th Durh.L.I. killed O.R. 2 wounded 1.	
	20-7-17.		23rd Manchesters wounded O.R. 1. 17th Royal Scots killed O.R. 1. wounded 4.19th Durh.L.I. killed O.R. 6 wounded 20. 18th High.L.I. killed O.R. 1. wounded 1. (shock).	
	21-7-17.		18th Lancs.Fus. wounded 2/Lieut J.PAGET, 20th Lancs. Fus. wounded O.R.1 (accidental). 23rd Manchesters attached 104th T.M.B, wounded O.R.1. 17th West Yorks wounded O.R.1. 19th Durh.L.I. killed O.R. 3 wounded 1. 18th High.L.I. killed O.R.1.	
	22-7-17.		157th Bde. R.F.A. wounded O.R. 2. 19th Durh.L.I. wounded O.R. 3. (includes 1 accidental). 19th Northld.Fus. wounded O.R. 1.	

WAR DIARY 35th DIVISION ADMINISTRATIVE STAFF. Army Form C. 2118.

INTELLIGENCE SUMMARY.

(Erase heading not required.)

Place	Date	Hour	Summary of Events and Information	Remarks and references to Appendices
	23-7-17.		17th Royal Scots wounded O.R. 2.	
	24-7-17.		D.A.C. wounded O.R. 1. 17th Lancs. Fus. wounded O.R. 1. 15th Cheshires wounded O.R.1. 17th Royal Scots wounded O.R.1 (accidental).	
	25-7-17.		18th Lancs. Fus wounded O.R. 1. 15th Cheshires wounded O.R. 3. 16th Cheshires wounded 2/Lieut G.E.WALTHO (accidental). "D" Battery 210th Bde. R.F.A. attached 35th D.Arty. wounded 2/Lieut H.S.SMALLMAN, O.R. 2. (at duty.)	
	26-7-17.		159th Bde. R.F.A. wounded Captain S.BROWN (gassed). wounded O.R. 1. 17th Lancs. Fus. wounded Lieut R.S.HEAPE, 2/Lieut G.M.THOMPSON, killed O.R. 4. wounded 38. 18th Lancs. Fus. killed O.R. 4. wounded 19 (includes 1 at duty.) 20th Lancs. Fus wounded O.R. 4 (includes 1 at duty.) 18th Lancs. Fus. attached 104th T.M.Battery.) wounded O.R. 1. 15th Cheshires wounded O.R. 1 (at duty) 19th Northld. Fus. wounded O.R. 9. (includes 1 at duty).	
	27-7-17.		17th Lancs. Fus. wounded Captain S.A.BULL R.A.M.C. wounded O.R. 4. 18th Lancs. Fus wounded O.R. 1. 15th Sherwoods wounded O.R. 4. (includes 2 at duty.) 19th N.Fus. wounded O.R. 4. 157th Bde. R.F.A. wounded Major J.WEBSTER, R.A.M.C. wounded O.R. 1. 204th Field Coy R.E. wounded O.R.1.	
	28-7-17.		18th Lancs. Fus wounded O.R. 2. 15th Cheshires wounded O.R.1. 16th Cheshires wounded O.R.1. 15th Sherwoods wounded O.R.3. 157th Bde R.F.A. wounded Major J.KEITH, O.R.1.	
	29-7-17.		18th Lancs. Fus. killed O.R.1.(accidental) wounded O.R. 4. 23rd Manchesters wounded O.R.9 missing O.R.1 (believed killed) 104th T.M.Battery wounded O.R. 4. – units of these men as follows:- 1 of 18th Lancs. Fus,1 of 23rd Manchesters, 2 of 17th Lancs. Fus.	
	30-7-17.		17th Lancs. Fus. wounded O.R. 5. 18th Lancs. Fus. wounded O.R. 1. 20th Lancs. Fus wounded O.R. 1.15th Cheshires wounded O.R. 1. (accidental).	
	31-7-17.		14th Glosters wounded O.R. 1. (accidental.)	

WAR DIARY 35th DIVISION ADMINISTRATIVE STAFF. Army Form C. 2118.

INTELLIGENCE SUMMARY.

(Erase heading not required.)

Place	Date	Hour	Summary of Events and Information	Remarks and references to Appendices
			COMMAND.	

COMMAND.

Major-General G.M.FRANKS, C.B. took over command of the Division on the 9/7/17 from Major-General H.J.S.LANDON, C.B. to England 9/7/17.

MOVE.

Divisional Headquarters moved from GURLU WOOD to VILLERS FAUCON on 9th July, 1917.

COOKERY SCHOOL.

On the 9th July, 1917 the Divisional Cookery School took over cooking for the personnel of D.H.Q. The result was satisfactory. Excellent practice was obtained for cooks. The messing has been on the restaurant system and very good.

M.G.Coy.

The 241st Machine Gun Company arrived on the 18th July, 1917.

COURTS-MARTIAL.

Courts-Martial for last month:- 12.
" for this month:- 8.

HONOURS & REWARDS.
The undermentioned honours & rewards have been granted during the month of July:-
Military Medals....... 13. Distinguished Conduct Medals.... 2.

WAR DIARY 35th DIVISION ADMINISTRATIVE STAFF.

INTELLIGENCE SUMMARY.

(Erase heading not required.)

Army Form C. 2118.

Place	Date	Hour	Summary of Events and Information	Remarks and references to Appendices
			HAYMAKING. Haymaking has been continued throughout the month. 27 stacks have been completed in the LIERAMONT area and 11 in the BUSSU area, totalling about 700 tons of hay. Cutting in the areas round VILLERS FAUCON and ROISEL taken over from the Cavalry Corps, has gone on under officers left behind by the 2nd Cavalry Division; labour and wagons being provided by this Division. 3-8-17. G. H. Franks Major-General, Commanding 35th Division.	

SECRET.

WAR DIARY 35th Divl. Administrative Staff.

INTELLIGENCE SUMMARY

Army Form C. 2118.

H.Q., 35TH DIVISION "A" BRANCH.
No. A.H.176.
Date 10-9-17.

Place	Date	Hour	Summary of Events and Information	Remarks and references to Appendices
			CASUALTIES.	
	1-8-17.		23rd Manchester Regt. Wounded 2/Lt. H.R.HUGHES (Accidental).	
	2-8-17.		NIL.	
	3-8-17.		17th West Yorks killed O.R.1.	
	4-8-17.		17th Royal Scots. wounded O.R.1., 106th M.G.Coy. wounded O.R.1. (Self-Inflicted).	
	5-8-17.		17th Royal Scots. wounded O.R.1.	
	6-8-17.		17th Royal Scots wounded 2/Lt. H.GLADSTONE (at duty) killed O.R.1. wounded 16 (included 1 S.I. and 1 at duty), Missing O.R.2., 19th D.L.I. wounded 2/Lt. T.A.HOLDEN., 17th Royal Scots. attd. 106 T.M.B. wounded O.R.3. (at duty).	
	7-8-17.		19th D.L.I. killed O.R.1. wounded 4 (includes 1 S.I)., No. 1 Sect. 59th D.A.C. attd. 35th Div. Artillery, wounded O.R.1. (Accidental).	
	8-8-17.		19th D.L.I. killed O.R.1., wounded 4., 29th Lancers wounded O.R.2. (Indian).	
	9-8-17.		17th Royal Scots. killed O.R.1., 19th D.L.I. wounded O.R.1., III Corps Cyclists wounded O.R.1., Kings Dragoon Guards killed O.R.1., wounded 5., 17th Lancers killed O.R.1. wounded 2., 19th Lancers wounded O.R. 4 (Indian).	
	10-8-17.		17th Royal Scots. wounded O.R.2.,	
	11-8-17.		14th Glosters, wounded O.R.1. (accidental), 17th Royal Scots wounded O.R.2., 36th Jacob's Horse wounded O.R.1. (Indian)., 29th Lancers wounded O.R.1. (Indian), 19th Lancers wounded O.R.1.	
	12-8-17.		NIL.	
	13-8-17.		16th Cheshires wounded O.R.4., (2 accidental & 2 at duty), 17th Royal Scots, wounded O.R.1., Kings Dragoon Guards wounded O.R.1.,	

P.T.O.

Army Form C. 2118.

WAR DIARY
INTELLIGENCE SUMMARY.

(Erase heading not required.)

Place	Date	Hour	Summary of Events and Information	Remarks and references to Appendices
			CASUALTIES. (Cont'd).	
	14-8-17.		16th Cheshires wounded O.R.2 (attd. T.M.B), 17th Royal Scots wounded O.R.1 (S.I)., III Corps Cyclists wounded O.R.1, 157 Bde. R.F.A. wounded Major J.A. CROMBIE.	
	15-8-17.		16th Cheshires wounded O.R.3., includes 1 at duty & 1 accidental, 18th H.L.I. killed O.R.1., 29th Lancers wounded O.R.1. (Indian), III Corps Cyclists wounded Capt. E.O.N. HOGBEN (at duty). A/296 Bde. R.F.A. wounded O.R.1.	
	16-8-17.		14th Glosters wounded O.R.1. (accidental), 17th West Yorks killed O.R.1. wounded 2., 16th Cheshires wounded Lieut. R.F. LAWRENSON. O.R.2.	
	17-8-17.		17th West Yorks wounded O.R.1. (at duty), 18th H.L.I. wounded O.R.5 (accidental)., 29th Lancers killed O.R.2. wounded O.R.1. (Indian).	
	18-8-17.		16th Cheshires wounded O.R.1. (at duty)., Jodhpur Lancers wounded O.R.1. (Indian), 19th Lancers wounded O.R.7 (Indian), III Corps Cyclists wounded O.R.1. 29th Lancers wounded O.R.1. (accidental, Indian).	
	19-8-17.		17th Royal Scots wounded O.R.12 (1 at duty), 17th West Yorks killed O.R.5. wounded 9., 18th H.L.I. wounded 2/Lt. V.A. LYONS killed O.R.1. (accidental), wounded 30., 19th D.L.I. attd T.M.B. killed O.R.1., wounded O.R.1., 17th Lancers wounded O.R.1. (accidental), 157 Bde. R.F.A. wounded O.R.2., 241 M.G. Coy. killed O.R.1. xiikxx 15th Cheshires killed Capt. G.E. SCHULTZ. 2/Lt. J. GRACE, wounded 2/Lt. C.F. TISSINGTON, killed O.R.20. wounded 87, includes 5 at duty and 2 accidental, missing O.R.6., 16th Cheshires wounded Capt. R.S. BACON, 2/Lt. E. JOHNSTON, 2/Lt. J. MILLER, killed O.R.4., wounded 17 (includes 1 at duty and 2 attached T.M.B.), 15th Sherwoods wounded 2/Lt. W.E.D. SCHULER, 2/Lt. J.G. STARKEY Attd. T.M.B., Killed O.R.17, wounded 32, includes 3 at duty), missing 6., 14th Glosters, wounded Capt. B.A. RUSSELL (at duty), killed O.R.1. wounded 8.	
	20-8-17.		17th Royal Scots. killed O.R.1. wounded 11 (includes 2 at duty), 17th West Yorks killed O.R.4., wounded 6 (includes 1 at duty), 18th H.L.I. wounded 2/Lt. J. BRYCE (at duty), Capt. J. BARRIE. O.R.35 (Includes 1 gassed & 1 at duty), missing 5., 106 M.G. Coy. wounded O.R.1. (at duty). 35th D.A.C. wounded Lt. B.W. INGRAM (accidental), 159 R.F.A. Bde. killed O.R.1. wounded 1., 19th North'd Fuslrs. wounded O.R.1.	

P.T.O.

Army Form C. 2118.

WAR DIARY
or
INTELLIGENCE SUMMARY.
(Erase heading not required.)

Place	Date	Hour	Summary of Events and Information	Remarks and references to Appendices
	21-8-17.		CASUALTIES. (Cont'd). 17th Lancs. Fus. wounded 2/Lt. G. MACKERETH, M.C. 2/Lt. W.B.K.GLASS, 2/Lt. J.R.HAMILTON killed O.R.6., wounded 53 (Includes 2 at duty), 23rd Manchesters wounded Major J.S.FOULKES, Capt. A.McKENZIE, Lieut. J.L.M.MORTON, 2/Lt. F.HAMMOND., killed O.R.3. (includes 1 accidental), wounded O.R.42. (2 at duty) & (1 accidental)., missing 4., 17th Royal Scots wounded O.R.3. (Includes 1 N.Y.D).; 18th H.L.I. killed O.R.1, 19th D.L.I. wounded O.R.5. (includes 1 N.Y.D).; 18th H.L.I. killed O.R.2, wounded 24, missing 2 (believed killed). 106th M.G.Coy. wounded O.R.2., 203rd Field Coy. R.E. wounded O.R.4. (Includes 2 at duty), 19th North'd Fus. killed O.R.2., wounded 2 (at duty)., A/296 Bde.R.F.A. killed Lt. E.ALCOCK, wounded O.R.1. (at duty)., 106th Fd. Ambulance, R.A.M.C., wounded O.R.2., 17th Lancers killed O.R.2., 10th M.G. Squadron, wounded O.R.1.	
	22-8-17.		20th Lancs. Fus. wounded 2/Lt. W.D.CAMPBELL, killed O.R.1. wounded 21., 104 M.G.Coy. wounded O.R.1. (at duty)., 15th Cheshires wounded O.R.1., 16th Cheshires killed O.R.2., wounded 11, 14th Glosters killed 2/Lt. H.F.PARSONS, wounded 2/Lt. C.L.P.GILSHENAN, killed O.R.4. wounded 24.(includes 1 at duty)., 15th Sherwoods killed 2/Lt. H.T.ORCHARD, O.R.7., wounded 23 (includes 1 at duty).,17th Royal Scots. wounded O.R.5., (includes 1 attd. No.4 Coy. Div. Train), 17th West Yorks wounded O.R.4.(includes 1 at duty), 19th D.L.I. killed O.R.2., wounded 11. 18th H.L.I. killed O.R.2., wounded 1, missing 1 (Believed killed)., 157 Bde. R.F.A. wounded 2/Lt. W.SLADE, Lieut. W.A.REID, killed O.R.1. wounded 2 (includes 1 at duty)., H.Q. 296 Bde.R.F.A. killed O.R.1., 19th North'd Fus. wounded O.R.4. (includes 2 at duty), 204th Field Cpy. R.E. wounded O.R.2., 11th M.G.Squadron killed O.R.1. wounded 1., III Corps Cyclists wounded 2/Lt. D.J.HUTSON, Lieut. G.W.ARNOLD, O.R.1.,	
	23-8-17.		20th Lancs. Fus. wounded O.R.1., 23rd Manchesters wounded O.R.1., 15th Cheshires wounded O.R.4., 16th Cheshires wounded O.R.1., 14th Glosters killed O.R.1., wounded 4 (includes 1 at duty), 15th Sherwoods wounded Major A.S.JOHNSON (At duty), Rev. G.SMISSEN C.F. (At duty), (Attd)., 17th Royal Scots, killed O.R.1., wounded 3 (includes 1 at duty), 19th D.L.I. wounded O.R.4., (includes 1 N.Y.D)., 19th North'd Fus. killed O.R.1. wounded 8 (includes 1 at duty), 204th Field Coy. R.E., 205th Field Coy. R.E. wounded O.R.1., A.S.C.,M.T.,attd.107th Field Ambulance wounded O.R.1.	

P.T.O.

Army Form C. 2118.

WAR DIARY
INTELLIGENCE SUMMARY

(Erase heading not required.)

Place	Date	Hour	Summary of Events and Information	Remarks and references to Appendices
			CASUALTIES. (Cont'd).	
	24-8-17.		18th Lancs. Fus. wounded O.R.1. (at duty), missing 1., 15th Cheshires wounded O.R.2., 17th Royal Scots killed O.R.3., wounded 13, (includes 4 at duty)., 17th West Yorks wounded O.R.1., 19th D.L.I. wounded O.R.2., 205 Field Coy. R.E. wounded O.R.1. (at duty), 157 Bde. R.F.A. wounded O.R.1., 159 Bde.R.F.A. wounded O.R.1 (at duty)., 296 Bde. R.F.A. wounded O.R. III Corps Cyclists wounded O.R.1 (at duty).	
	25-8-17.		18th H.L.I. killed Capt. G.JACKSON, wounded Lieut. J.K.THOMSON, 2/Lt. A.W.MARTIN, 2/Lt. H. FLEMING, wounded & missing 2/Lt. J.T.MACINTYRE, killed O.R.15. wounded 77, (includes 2 at duty) missing 38,(Believed Killed)., 17th West Yorks, killed O.R.1. wounded O.R. 3, 19th D.L.I. killed O.R.2., wounded 13, (Includes 2 N.Y.D), 106th M.G. Coy. wounded O.R.2., 19th D.L.I. attd. T.M.B. killed O.R.2., 35th Div. Signal Coy. wounded O.R.2 (at duty), 159 Bde.R.F.A. wounded O.R.1., 104 M.G.Coy. wounded O.R.1. (accidental), 15th Cheshires killed O.R.3., wounded 4., 16th Cheshires attd. T.M.B. wounded O.R.1., 14th Glosters killed 2/Lt. F.V.TRATMAN, wounded O.R.5., 105th M.G.Coy. wounded O.R.1., 19th North'd Fus. wounded O.R.1., 15th Sherwoods, wounded 2/Lt. H.E.LEADER, 2/Lt. F.DELVES (at duty), 2/Lt. W.DUNS (at duty), 2/Lt. C.E.BLURTON (at duty), 2/Lt. F.G.MOTTERSHAW (N.Y.D)., killed O.R.19, wounded 74, (Includes 30 N.Y.D).,	
	26-8-17.		157 Bde.R.F.A. wounded O.R.1., 159 Bde. R.F.A. wounded O.R.2., 203 Field Coy. R.E. wounded O.R.1. (at duty), 17th Lancs. Fus. wounded O.R.3., 18th Lancs. Fus. wounded 2/Lt. E.F.A. GOODWIN (at duty), killed O.R.1., wounded 6, 16th Cheshires wounded O.R. 5 (includes 1 at duty), 14th Glosters killed O.R.3., 107th Field Ambulance. R.A.M.C. wounded O.R.3. (includes 1 gassed), 18th H.L.I. killed O.R.4. wounded 9., 17th Royal Scots, wounded O.R.5. (includes 1 at duty), missing 9 (Believed buried or prisoners). 19th North'd Fus. wounded O.R.1., 17th West Yorks wounded O.R.1., 19th D.L.I. killed Lt. (A/Capt). G.R. FORSTER, 2/Lt. G.W.BERRY, O.R.9., wounded 38.	
	27-8-17.		157 Bde. R.F.A. wounded O.R.1., 18th Lancs. Fus. wounded O.R.1. (at duty), 20th Lancs Fus. wounded O.R.1. (at duty), 104 T.M.B. wounded O.R.1. (at duty), 16th Cheshires wounded O.R 1. (accidental), 19th D.L.I. killed O.R.2. wounded 1.	
	28-8-17.		157 Bde.R.F.A. wounded O.R.1. (at duty), 17th Royal Scots wounded O.R.4. includes 1 accidental), 17th West Yorks wounded O.R.1., 19th D.L.I. wounded 2/Lt. G.E.BROWN O.R.2.	

P.T.O.

Army Form C. 2118.

WAR DIARY

INTELLIGENCE SUMMARY.

(Erase heading not required.)

Instructions regarding War Diaries and Intelligence Summaries are contained in F. S. Regs., Part II. and the Staff Manual respectively. Title pages will be prepared in manuscript.

Place	Date	Hour	Summary of Events and Information	Remarks and references to Appendices
	29-8-17.		CASUALTIES. (Cont'd.)	
			17th Lancs. Fus wounded O.R. 1 at duty. 17th Durh.L.I. killed O.R. 1 19th Durh.L.I. killed O.R. 5 wounded 4.	
	30-8-17.		159th Bde. R.F.A. wounded O.R. 1 at duty. 17th Lancs. Fus. wounded O.R. 1 accidental. 17th Royal Scots wounded O.R. 2 17th West Yorks killed O.R. 1 wounded 11 (includes 1 at duty and 1 possibly accidental.)	
	31-8-17.		157th Bde. R.F.A. wounded O.R. 1 gassed. 159th Bde. R.F.A. wounded 2/Lieut F.R.FORSTER, O.R.1. (at duty.) 105th M.G.Coy wounded O.R. 2. 17th Royal Scots wounded O.R. 4. 19th Durh.L.I. killed O.R.2 wounded 3. 106th M.G.Coy killed O.R. 3 17th West Yorks attached T.M.B. wounded O.R. 1. 19th Durh.L.I. attached T.M.B. wounded O.R. 1. 17th West Yorks killed 2/Lieut. C.G.LACHLAN, 2/Lieut A.A.SOWRY, wounded Captain R. BEST, 2/Lieut. B.C.BLAMIRES, 2/Lieut. F. BURBRIDGE, Captain A.J.A.POIGNANT (at duty) Captain S.L.BELL (at duty) missing Lieut. G.J.ACHESON, 2/Lieut N. ODDY, 2/Lieut A.D.ROSE? M.C., 2/Lieut O.DAY. killed O.R. 7. wounded 50. missing 53.	
			REFILLING POINTS.	
			3 Refilling Points were completed on the Decauville Railway System at MARQUAIX, VILLERS FAUCON, and just South of LIERAMONT. Refilling by First Line Transport direto from Decauville was commenced on the 6th August. This system has been found to work excellently and has released a considerable number of wagons for other purposes.	
			OPERATIONS FOR THE ATTACK ON GILLEMONT FARM AND THE KNOLL.	
			These operations were a complete success, and the Administrative arrangements in conjunction with them proved entirely successful. The chief difficulty experienced was the removal of the dead back to the cemeteries in rear. However, by the aid of G.S. wagons, this was effected. The G.R.U. expressed entire satisfaction of the system adopted and its results. The arrangements for the supply of ammunition and rations worked smoothly and were entirely satisfactory. The total casualties in killed wounded and missing during these operations were just below 1000.	

P.T.O.

Army Form C. 2118.

WAR DIARY
of
INTELLIGENCE SUMMARY
(Erase heading not required.)

COURTS-MARTIAL.

Courts-Martial for last month :— 8.
Courts-Martial for this month :— 16.

HONOURS AND REWARDS.

The undermentioned Honours and Rewards have been granted during the month of Aug:—

Distinguished Service Order. 1. Military Cross. 13.
Distinguished Conduct Medal. 5. Military Medal. 77.
Decoration Militaire. 1.

WINTER HUTTING.

A scheme for Winter Quarters was made out. Owing to the shortage of personnel in the Division and the extra work required for the operations little or no work was possible on erecting huts etc, but as much as possible in this line was done at the new Transport and Wagon Lines.

HAYMAKING.

The haymaking parties ceased work and rejoined their units on the 7th inst. After completing 29 stacks in "A" Area and 12 in "B" Area.
The tonnage of the stacks by measurement after settling down is "A" Area 491½ tons, "B" Area 232½ tons.

Brig-General,
Commanding 35th Division.

SECRET.

ORIGINAL.

WAR DIARY 35th Divisional Administrative Staff. Army Form C. 2118.

INTELLIGENCE SUMMARY. September 1917.

(Erase heading not required.)

Place	Date	Hour	Summary of Events and Information	Remarks and references to Appendices
			CASUALTIES.	
	1.9.17.		17th West Yorks. Wounded, Major J.H.GILL (at duty). 17th Royal Scots wounded 1 O.R. (accidental) 17th West Yorks. Wounded, O.R. 6. 18th H.L.I. Wounded O.R.3.	
	2.9.17.		20th Lancashire Fusrs. O.R. 1 killed, 1 wounded (accidental). 14th Glosters. O.R. 1 wounded. 17th West Yorks. O.R. 1 wounded (accidental).	
	3.9.17.		14th Glosters. O.R. 2 killed, 4 wounded (1 at duty). 15th Sherwood Foresters O.R. 1 killed. 19th Nothd. Fusrs. 1 killed O.R. 12 wounded (1 since died, 2 at duty). 18th Lancs. Fusrs. O.R. 2 wounded (accidental, 1 at duty).	
	4.9.17.		15th Sherwood Foresters O.R. 2 wounded.	
	5.9.17.		159 Bde. R.F.A. O.R. 4 wounded (gassed at duty). 20th Lancs. Fus. O.R.1 wounded. 15th Sherwood Foresters O.R. 4 wounded (shell gas) 1 wounded (at duty). 106 M.G.Coy O.R. 1 wounded (at duty)	
	6.9.17.		20th Lancashire Fus. O.R. 1 wounded (Self inflicted). 17th West Yorks. O.R. 1 wounded (accidental) 203rd Field Coy. killed Lt. (A/Major) H.S.SEMPLE, M.G., 2/Lt. G.S. BLAKE, 2/Lt. F.L.GEE, wounded 2/Lt. (A/Capt) R.K.UHTHOFF, O.R. 2 wounded.	
	9 7.11.17.		18th Lancs. Fus. wounded O.R.1, 15th Cheshires wounded O.R.3 (includes 1 at duty). 16th Cheshires wounded O.R.1, 14th Glosters attd. T.M.B. wounded O.R.1, 15th Sherwoods wounded O.R. 1 (at duty) 19th D.L.I. wounded O.R.1.	
	8.9.17.		15th Sherwoods, missing O.R.1., 15th Cheshires wounded O.R. 2 (includes 1 Self inflicted), 16th Cheshires wounded 2/Lt. N.K.BARBAR (at duty) wounded O.R.1 (at duty) 17th R.Scots wounded O.R. 1, 17th West Yorks wounded O.R. 1 (accidental) 18th H.L.I. wounded O.R. 1 (accidental)	
	9.9.17.		16th Cheshires killed O.R. 8, wounded 4. (includes 1 at duty) 16th Cheshires wounded 2/Lt. N.K. BARBAR,	
	10.9.17.		15th Sherwoods wounded O.R.1, 17th R.Scots wounded O.R.2, 18th H.L.I. wounded O.R.2 (1 accidental and 1 Self inflicted).	

SECRET.   ORIGINAL.   WAR DIARY   Headquarters (Administrative Staff)   Army Form C. 2118.
                                      INTELLIGENCE SUMMARY.
                                            35th Division.
                                            September 1917.

Instructions regarding War Diaries and Intelligence
Summaries are contained in F.S. Regs., Part II.
and the Staff Manual respectively. Title pages
will be prepared in manuscript.

(Erase heading not required.)

Place	Date	Hour	CASUALTIES.	Summary of Events and Information	Remarks and references to Appendices
	11.9.17.		23rd Manchesters wounded O.R.1 (at duty), 16th Cheshires killed O.R.1, wounded 3, 241 M.G.Coy. wounded O.R.1.		
	12.9.17.		NIL.		
	13.9.17.		18th H.L.I. wounded 2/Lt. M.C.CALL.		
	14.9.17.		17th Lancs. Fusrs. wounded O.R.1, 18th Lancs.Fusrs. killed O.R.1, wounded 5 (includes 1 at duty), 17th West Yorks. wounded Lt. J.L.JENKINSON, killed O.R.4, wounded O.R.11 (includes 1 at duty). 19th D.L.I. 2/Lt. J.J.CARNEY (accidental). 106 M.G.Coy. wounded O.R.1. 19th Nortd. Fus. wounded O.R.1. (at duty)		
	15.9.17.		NIL.		
	16.9.17.		17th Lancs. Fus. wounded O.R.1, 18th H.L.I. wounded O.R.1, 19th Nortd. Fus. wounded O.R.1 (at duty). Divnl. Employment Coy. wounded O.R.1 (accidental). 203rd Field Coy. R.E. wounded 2/Lt. G.THOMPSON (gassed). X		
	17.9.17.		17th Lancs. Fus. wounded O.R.1, 23rd Manchesters wounded O.R.1, 17th R.Scots killed 2/Lt. J.S. STRUTH, wounded Capt. W.SIMPSON, 2/Lt. M.S.BARCLAY, O.R.4.; 17th West Yorks. killed O.R.4, wounded 6.; 18th H.L.I. wounded O.R.2 (includes 1 at duty) 106 M.G.COY. wounded O.R.1, 159 Bde. R.F.A. killed Major R.D.HARRISSON, D.S.O.		
	18.9.17.		NIL.		
	19.9.17.		NIL.		
	20.9.17.		106 M.G.Coy, wounded O.R.1 (at duty).		
	21.9.17.		23rd Manchesters, wounded O.R.1 (self inflicted).		
	22.9.17.		20th Lancs. Fus. wounded O.R.1. 15th Sherwoods killed,O.R.1, wounded 3 (includes 1 self inflicted)		
	23.9.17.		23rd Manchesters, wounded O.R.1. 16th Cheshires, killed O.R.1, 35th Div. Signal Coy, wounded O.R.1.		

SECRET. ORIGINAL. WAR DIARY Headquarters (Administrative Staff)
INTELLIGENCE SUMMARY
35th Division.
September 1917.

Army Form C. 2118.

Instructions regarding War Diaries and Intelligence Summaries are contained in F. S. Regs., Part II. and the Staff Manual respectively. Title pages will be prepared in manuscript.

(Erase heading not required.)

Place	Date	Hour	Summary of Events and Information	Remarks and references to Appendices
			CASUALTIES.	
	24.9.17.		20th Lancs. Fus. wounded, O.R. 1, 15th Sherwoods, wounded, O.R.2.	
	25.9.17.		17th Lancs., wounded, LT. J.A.WALLIS, O.R.1 (at duty). 18th Lancs.Fus. wounded, O.R.7 (includes 2 at duty), 23rd Manchesters, wounded, 2/Lt. E.TATTERSALL, O.R.2, 19th Northd. Fus. wounded, O.R. 1 (accidental).	
	26.9.17.		20th Lancs.Fus. wounded, O.R.1.	
	27.9.17.		18th H.L.I., wounded O.R.2, Missing O.R.1 (enemy raid).	
	28.9.17.		14th Glosters, wounded O.R.1, 17th R.Scots, wounded O.R.1.	
	29.9.17.		14th Glosters, wounded, 2/LT. J.G.GOLDICOTT, O.R.4, 18th H.L.I., killed O.R.1.	
	30.9.17.		NIL.	

H. Farmar Lieut Colonel
for Major-General.
Commanding 35th Division.

SECRET.

ORIGINAL.

WAR DIARY
of
INTELLIGENCE SUMMARY

Headquarters (Administrative Staff) Army Form C. 2118.

35th Division. October 1917.

(Erase heading not required.)

Instructions regarding War Diaries and Intelligence Summaries are contained in F.S. Regs., Part II. and the Staff Manual respectively. Title pages will be prepared in manuscript.

Place	Date	Hour	Summary of Events and Information	Remarks and references to Appendices
			CASUALTIES.	
	1.10.17.		NIL.	
	2.10.17.		205 Field Coy. R.E. wounded O.R.3.	
	3.10.17.		17th R.Scots, wounded O.R.4.	
	4.10.17.		Nil.	
	5.10.17.		18th H.L.I., wounded O.R.1 (accidental).	
	6.10.17.		NIL.	
	7.10.17.		NIL.	
	8.10.17.		NIL.	
	9.10.17.		NIL.	
	10.10.17.		NIL.	
	11.10.17.		Nil.	
	12.10.17.		NIL.	
	13.10.17.		NIL.	
	14.10.17.		NIL.	
	15.10.17.		NIL.	
	16.10.17.		NIL.	
	17.10.17.		17th Lancs. Fus., wounded O.R.3, 18th Lancs. Fus., killed O.R.1, wounded 1., 20th Lancs. Fus. wounded O.R.4, 23rd Manchesters, wounded 2/Lt. E.McKENZIE - McMURTRIE, killed O.R.4, wounded 14.	

SECRET.

ORIGINAL.

Army Form C. 2118.

WAR DIARY ~~OR~~ INTELLIGENCE SUMMARY.

Headquarters (Administrative Staff)
35th Division.   October 1917.

(Erase heading not required.)

Instructions regarding War Diaries and Intelligence Summaries are contained in F.S. Regs., Part II and the Staff Manual respectively. Title pages will be prepared in manuscript.

Place	Date	Hour	Summary of Events and Information	Remarks and references to Appendices
	18.10.17.		CASUALTIES:- 20th Lancs., wounded O.R.10, 23rd Manchesters, wounded O.R.3, missing 2, 104 M.G.Coy., wounded O.R.2, 17th Lancs., wounded O.R.3.	
	19.10.17.		17th Lancs., killed O.R.2, wounded 7 (includes 4 at duty), 18th Lancs., killed O.R.1, wounded 6 (includes 1 at duty), ~~20th Lancs.,~~ ~~xxntssingx&Rxx~~ 23rd Manchesters, wounded O.R.4 (includes 1 at duty), 15th Cheshires, wounded 2/LT. W.N.DUNN, 19th O.R., 14th Glosters, wounded O.R.2 (includes 1 at duty), 19th Northd. Fus. wounded O.R.6, 157 Bde. R.F.A. wounded O.R.1, 159 Bde. R.F.A. wounded O.R.5, (includes two at duty), 35th D.A.C. wounded LT/J.F.KING. 35th Div. Sigs. attd. Bde. H.Q. killed O.R.1, wounded 6, 17th R.Scots, ~~woundedxx~~O.R.2 killed, wounded 2/Lt. D.G. EDNIE, Lt. W.D.SIMM, 2/Lt. C.T. THORNTON (latter 2 gassed). wounded O.R.29 (1 at duty, 13 gassed) 17th West Yorks, killed O.R.1, wounded 12 (includes 1 at duty and 7 gassed). 19th D.L.I. wounded, O.R.6 (includes 1 at duty, 1 gassed) N.Y.D.N. O.R.1. 18th H.L.I. killed O.R.1, wounded 5, 17th West Yorks. attd. 106 T.M.B. wounded O.R.1.	
	20.10.17.		15th Cheshires, wounded O.R.6 (includes 5 gassed), 15th Sherwoods, wounded O.R.1, 17th Lancs. attd. Traffic Control, wounded O.R.1, R.A.M.C. attd. 19th D.L.I. wounded, Capt. S.R.GLEED (gassed), R.A.M.C., 106 Field Ambulance, wounded O.R.2 (gassed), Royal Engineers, killed O.R.1, wounded 6. 157th Bde. R.F.A., wounded O.R.1, 159th Bde. R.F.A., wounded Lt.H.F.R.ADAMS, O.R.3, 106 M.G.Coy. wounded 2/Lt. H.H.BUCKLEY, killed O.R.3, wounded 4., 17th R.Scots, killed O.R.2, wounded 41. 17th West Yorks, killed O.R.3, wounded 20, (includes 5 at duty) Missing 1. 19th D.L.I. wounded O.R.5, 18th H.L.I. killed O.R.2, wounded 2.	
	21.10.17.		18th Lancs. wounded O.R.8 (includes 1 at duty), 20th Lancs. wounded O.R.2, (1 accidentally and 1 self inflicted), 23rd Manchesters, wounded O.R.4, 17th R.Scots, killed O.R.2, wounded 5, 19th D.L.I., killed O.R.2, wounded 6, 18th H.L.I., wounded 2/Lt. I. MACFARLANE, O.R.3. 19th Northd. Fus. wounded O.R.1, 35th Div. Sigs. wounded O.R.1 (gassed) 15th Sherwoods, wounded O.R.2, 14th Glosters, wounded O.R.1 (at duty) Missing 1, 15th Cheshires, wounded O.R.2, 17th West Yorks, killed O.R.1, wounded O.R.5 (at duty), 15th Cheshires attd. Traffic Control, killed O.R.1 35th Div. M.M.P., wounded M.M.P., wounded O.R.1, 159th Bde. R.F.A. wounded 2/Lt. A.R.JOHNSTONE, killed O.R.1, wounded 3, Z/3 5 T.M.B. wounded O.R.2, 35th D.A.C. wounded O.R.2, 106 M.G.Coy. wounded O.R.9, 15th Cheshires, wounded O.R.1, 14th Glosters, killed O.R.10, wounded 4, 15th Sherwoods, wounded O.R.7, 105 M.G.Coy, killed O.R.7, wounded 2/Lt. W.B.JONES, O.R.18.	

SECRET.

Army Form C. 2118.

Instructions regarding War Diaries and Intelligence Summaries are contained in F.S. Regs., Part II. and the Staff Manual respectively. Title pages will be prepared in manuscript.

WAR DIARY

ORIGINAL. ~~INTELLIGENCE~~ SUMMARY ~~Headquarters~~ (Administrative Staff)

(Erase heading not required.)

35th Division.   October 1917.

Place	Date	Hour	Summary of Events and Information	Remarks and references to Appendices
	22.10.17.		CASUALTIES. 17th West Yorks., wounded O.R.6, 106 M.G.Coy., killed O.R.4, wounded 19, 35th Div.Sigs. wounded O.R.1, 19th Northd. Fus. wounded O.R.2, R.A.M.C., 106 Field Amb. wounded O.R.7, 35th D.A.C. killed O.R.1, wounded 2, xx (includes 1 at duty), 205 Field Coy. R.E. wounded O.R.1, 157th Bde. R.F.A.. wounded Lt. (A/Major) W.J.LUCK, killed O.R. 4, wounded 6.	
	23.10.17.		X/35 T.M.B., killed O.R.1, R.A.M.C. 106 F.Amb., killed OR.1, wounded 1, 105 F.Amb. wounded O.R.3, 107 F.Amb. killed O.R.1, 19th Northd. Fusrs., wounded O.R.3 (includes 2 at duty), 241st M.G.Coy., wounded O.R.1, 17th R.Scots, wounded O.R.8, Missing 1. 19th D.L.I., killed O.R.3, wounded 13.	
	24.10.17.		159 Bde. R.F.A., killed O.R.5, wounded 5, 35th D.A.C., wounded O.R.2 (includes 1 at duty). R.A.M.C. 105 F.Amb. killed O.R.1, wounded 1, 106 F.Amb. wounded O.R.3, 107 F.Amb. wounded O.R.9, 203rd Field Coy., R.E., wounded O.R.6 (includes 1 at duty). 204 Field Coy. R.E., wounded O.R.3.	
	25.10.17.		17th R.Scots, killed Lt. H.HOUSTON, wounded Capt. J.H.MITCHELL, 2/Lt. W.E.COATS, killed O.R.8, wounded 14 (includes two at duty). 17th West Yorks. wounded Lt. W.E.RAMSDEN, 2/Lt. H. SHARP, killed O.R.4, wounded 45, 19th D.L.I., wounded 2/Lt. B.L.H.JONES, killed O.R.1, wounded 13. 18th H.L.I., killed O.R.1, wounded O.R.2, 241 M.G.Coy., killed O.R. 3, wounded 3 (includes 1 N.Y.D.N.), 159 Bde. R.F.A. killed O.R.6, wounded 7, 35th D.A.C. wounded O.R.3 (includes 1 at duty)	
	26.10.17.		17th Lancs., killed O.R.31, wounded 141, missing 6, 18th Lancs. killed Capt. M.R.WOOD M.C., Lieut. S.G.WOLFE, Lt. W.DOBINSON, M.C., wounded Captain C.A.J.BONNER, Captain E.V.FINCH M.C., 2/Lt. W.M. GREENHALGH, 2/Lt. J.WHITE, 2/Lt. P.SOUTHERN, 2/Lt. E. MITCHELL, 2/Lt. G.M.GRIME, Lt. A.P.DRAPER (R.A.M.C. attd.) Missing 2/Lt.P.TORRANCE (believed killed). Killed O.R.33, wounded 128, missing 76 (believed killed). 23rd Manchesters killed O.R.19, missing 171 (includes 113 wounded and missing). 23rd Manc.attd. 104 T.M.B. killed O.R.3, wounded 1, 18th Lancs. attd. 104 T.M.B. wounded O.R.1, 20th Lancs. attd. 104 T.M.B. wounded O.R.1, 104 M.G.Coy. wounded O.R.3. 17th West Yorks. wounded O.R.4, 19th D.L.I., killed O.R.2, wounded 11, 157 Bde. R.F.A. killed O.R.1, wounded 1, 159 Bde. R.F.A., wounded Lt. G.A.PILCHER, 35th D.A.C. wounded O.R.2, 19th Northd. Fus. killed O.R.1, wounded 1 (at duty) R.A.M.C. 106 F.Amb. wounded O.R.2, 106 F.Amb. wounded O.R.4. 17th R.Scots, killed O.R.1, wounded 4, missing 1.	

SECRET. ORIGINAL. Army Form C. 2118.

WAR DIARY
~~or~~ INTELLIGENCE ~~SUMMARY~~

Headquarters (Administrative Staff)

35th Division.   October 1917.

(Erase heading not required.)

Instructions regarding War Diaries and Intelligence
Summaries are contained in F.S. Regs., Part II.
and the Staff Manual respectively. Title pages
will be prepared in manuscript.

Place	Date	Hour	Summary of Events and Information	Remarks and references to Appendices
			CASUALTIES.	
	27.10.17.		17th Lancashire Fus. killed 2/Lt. H.A.ALLIN, 2/Lt. H.N.LEWIS, 2/Lt. H.CRANE, 2/Lt. J.R.HAMILTON. wounded 2/Lt. J.D.YOUNG (gassed) Captain R.S.HEAPE, M.C., 2/Lt. J.A.SHEARSTONE, 2/Lt. A.C.ESSON, 2/Lt. P.FORMAN, Lt. J.GOODIER, Capt. L.KITCHEN, Lt. H.C.LEAVER (~~missing~~ 20th Lancashire Fus. wounded 2/Lt. J.W.HOLLOWS, 2/Lt. H.A.HARRIS, 2/Lt. R.S.PARRY (died of wounds) Capt. F.J.TOMS, (at duty) Capt W.A.SWARBRICK (at duty) 2/Lt. W.W.COTTON (at duty) killed O.R. 26, wounded 161, (includes 2 accidental and 5 N.Y.D.N) Missing 13. 23rd Manchesters killed Capt. G.E.SSIMPSON Capt. J.L.M.MORTON, Lt. H.W.WILLEY, Lt. A.A.MOORE, Lt. W.L.WEIR, 2/Lt. C.H.COOK, 2/Lt. J.W.DIXON, 2/Lt. H.A.WILSON, wounded Capt. W.P.GIBBONS, Capt. A.T.ABRAHAM M.C., 2/Lt. F.F.FRIPP, 2/Lt. H.S. GROOM, 2/Lt. H.T.STYLES, missing 2/Lt. A.W.BELLAMY. 104 M.G.Co. killed O.R.2, wounded Lt. N.H.A. RICHARDSON, 2/Lt. T.BOWKER. O.R. 23. 157 Bde. R.F.A. wounded O.R.1. 17th Lancs. attached Div. Traffic Control wounded O.R.1. 15th Cheshires attd. Div. Traffic Control wounded O.R.1, 19th D.L.I. wounded O.R.1. 20th Lancs. killed O.R.1. 15th Sherwoods killed O.R.1, 241st M.G.Co. wounded O.R.7. R.A.M.C. 105 Field Ambulance killed O.R.1, wounded 3..	
	28.10.17.		20th Lancs. wounded O.R.6, (includes 1 at duty) 157 Bde. R.F.A. wounded O.R.2.	
	29.10.17.		17th Lancs. wounded O.R.1., 17th R.Scots. killed O.R.1 (accidentally), 17th W.Yorks. wounded 2/Lt. H.WHITE (gassed), Lt. and Adj. A.S.TADMAN, Lt. J.A.C.GREEN, M.C. (R.A.M.C. attached)	
	30.10.17.		17th Lancs. wounded Lt. C.P.JOHNSTONE, 20th Lancs. wounded O.R.2, 104 M.G.Co. killed O.R.1. wounded 1. 19th Northumberland Fus. killed O.R.1., 14th Glosters wounded O.R.3, 15th Sherwoods killed 2/Lt. C.BELL, O.R.8. wounded Capt. A.McK.FORSYTH, O.R.21, 205 Field Coy. R.E. wounded O.R.4 (includes 1 gassed) 241st M.G.Co. wounded O.R. 1(N.Y.D.N.) 17th R. Scots. wounded O.R.1. 35th Div. Train, wounded 2/Lt. J.B.CLARK, Royal Engineers wounded Lt.Col. J.W.SKIPWITH (at duty) 15th Cheshires killed O.R.21, wounded 2/Lt. A.T.HODGES, O.R. 125 (includes 8 at duty) Missing 4. 16th Cheshires killed 2/Lt. R.J.McCULLOUGH, O.R.41, wounded Capt. H.R.MAKIN, Capt. E.W.BIGLAND, 2/Lt. A.C.WOOD, 2/Lt. C.KENYON, 2/Lt. J.R.P.MILLAR, 2/Lt. J.HOPWOOD, Capt. L.MILLINGTON (at duty) 2/Lt. C.D.HOWELLS (at duty) 2/Lt. J.FINCH (at duty) O.R.173 (includes 4 at duty and one S.I.) Missing 114 (includes 31 wounded and missing) 14th Glosters killed Lt. T.H.W.WALLER, O.R.64 wounded Capt. W.BAKER, Capt. B.A.RUSSELL, 2/Lt. I.A.CROMACK, 2/Lt. F.J.S.DRAPER, 2/Lt. H.BARRETT, 2/Lt. N.P.HARRISON, 2/Lt. A.E.PERRY, O.R. 165, Missing 2/Lt. F.WOMAR, O.R.33 (includes 1 wounded and missing). 16th Cheshires, Missing 2/Lt. J.D.ELLIOTT, 15th Sherwoods, killed 2/Lt. B.H.PENFOLD, O.R.15, wounded 2/Lt. K.J.ROE, 2/Lt. H.MAXWELL (N.Y.D.N.) O.R.180 (includes 8 at duty and 15 NYDN0 Missing 2/Lt. C.E.BLURTON, O.R.30. 105 M.G.Co. killed O.R.3, wounded 9, missing 3.	

SECRET.

Army Form C. 2118.

WAR DIARY
INTELLIGENCE SUMMARY
Headquarters (Administrative Staff)
35th Division. October 1917.

ORIGINAL.

(Erase heading not required.)

Instructions regarding War Diaries and Intelligence Summaries are contained in F. S. Regs., Part II. and the Staff Manual respectively. Title pages will be prepared in manuscript.

Place	Date	Hour	Summary of Events and Information	Remarks and references to Appendices
	31.10.17		**CASUALTIES.** 18th Lancs. wounded 2/Lt. G.S.CORMACK, 2/Lt. J. CHADWICK (both at duty) O.R.4 (includes two at duty) 104 M.G.Co. killed O.R.1, wounded 2. 15th Sherwoods Killed O.R.1, wounded 8. 105 M.G.Co. wounded 2/Lt. W.L.FURMSTON, A.V.C. attd. 106 Inf. Bde. H.Q. wounded O.R.1, A.S.C. Div. Train wounded O.R.1, 15th Cheshires wounded O.R.1. **COMMANDS.** Brig. General W.C.STAVELEY, C.B., C.R.A. 35th Divn. evacuated sick on 20/10/17. Brig. General W.R.N.MADOCKS, G.M.G., D.S.O. was appointed C.R.A. on 3.11.17 Captain J.McM.MILLING, M.C., D.A.A.G. to Base sick under G.R.O. 2364 on 26.10.17. T/Captain R.F. BURY, appointed D.A.A.G. of these Division 26.10.17 vice Capt. J.McM.MILLING M.C. Lt.Colonel E.VAUGHAN, D.S.O., O.C. 20th Bn. Lancs. Fus. to Command 2nd Manchesters 31.10.17. Lt.Colonel H.P.F.BICKNELL, D.S.O., Middlesex Regt., assumed Command of 20th Lancashire Fus. on 31.10.17. Major C.M.B.HAMILTON, A.P.M. of the Division evacuated sick 30/10/17, Capt. W.B.LITHERLAND M.C. assumed duties of A.P.M. on 8/11/17 Major G.J.P.GOODWIN, R.E. appointed O.C. 205 Field Co. R.E. 17.10.17. vice Major E. WHITE R.E. to Base as instructor. **MOVES.** 3.10.17. Division moved from Villers Faucon to DUISANS Area. 12.10.17 DUISANS to LEDERZEELE Area. 15.10.17. LEDERZEELE to PROVEN Area. 18.10.17. PROVEN to ELVERDINGHE, 23.10.17. D.H.Q. "A" Echelon ELVERDINGHE to ZOMMERBLOOM CABARET. "B" Echelon ELVERDINGHE to "J" Camp. 25/10/17. "A" Echelon D.H.Q. from ZOMMERBLOOM CABARET to "J" Camp	

NUMBER OF IMMEDIATE HONOURS AWARDED DURING MONTH.

V.C.	M.C.	M.M.
2	3	12

NUMBER OF CASES BROUGHT TO TRIAL BY F.G.C.M. AND CONVICTED.
21.

NUMBER OF CASES BROUGHT TO TRIAL BY G.C.M. AND CONVICTED.
1

H. Farand Lieut-Colonel for Major-General.
Commanding 35th Division.

November 1914

Secret

35th Division.   Administrative Staff.
WAR DIARY
INTELLIGENCE SUMMARY

Army Form C. 2118.

Instructions regarding War Diaries and Intelligence Summaries are contained in F.S. Regs., Part II. and the Staff Manual respectively. Title pages will be prepared in manuscript.

(Erase heading not required.)

Place	Date	Hour	Summary of Events and Information	Remarks and references to Appendices
	1-11-17.		CASUALTIES. 23rd Manchesters wounded O.R.4., Missing 2., 15th Cheshires killed O.R.4., wounded 21., 16th Cheshires wounded O.R.3., 14th Glosters killed O.R.1., wounded 3., 15th Sherwoods wounded 2/Lieut. W.T.C. BLAKE, O.R.4., 18th H.L.I. wounded 2/Lt. J.McGREGOR, 2/Lt. W.L.MOODIE, 19th North'd Fuslrs. wounded Major H.S. DAWSON. M.C., killed O.R.2. wounded 6. missing 1., 203rd Field Coy. R.E. wounded O.R.1., 14th Glosters attached 204th Fd.Coy. R.E. wounded O.R.1., 17th Royal Scots attd. 205th Fd. Coy. R.E. wounded O.R.1., 19th D.L.I. attd. 205th Fd.Coy.R.E. wounded O.R.2., 157th Bde. R.F.A. wounded Capt. (A/Major) J.WEBSTER, 2/Lt. (A/Capt). R.L.WALLER, Lt. (A/Capt). R.C. LYONS, Lt. G.G.D. SCOTT, 2/Lt. S.L. SCOBELL, 2/Lt. C.R.WEATHERELL (First 4 at duty). 159th Bde. R.F.A. wounded O.R.1.,	
	2-11-17.		17th Lancs. Fus. wounded O.R. 1., 18th Lancs. Fus. wounded 2/Lt. G.S. CORMACK, killed O.R.2., wounded 14., 23rd Manchesters wounded O.R.9., 104th M.G.Coy. killed O.R.1., 15th Cheshires wounded O.R.19., 16th Cheshires wounded O.R.4., 14th Glosters killed O.R.2., wounded 5., 15th Sherwoods killed 2/Lt. R.T.WRIGHT, wounded O.R.1., 17th West Yorks wounded Capt. S.L.BELL.M.C. 19th D.L.I. wounded Lt-Col. W.B. GREENWELL (Gassed), wounded O.R. 1., 18th H.L.I. wounded 2/Lt. C.K.R. DEMPSTER O.R.2., 106th M.G.Coy. killed O.R.1., wounded 5., 35th D.A.C. wounded O.R.2., 157th Bde. R.F.A. killed O.R.2., wounded 5., 204th Fd.Coy.R.E. wounded O.R.4., 15th Cheshires attd. 241 M.G.Coy. wounded O.R.1.	
	3-11-17.		15th Cheshires wounded O.R.13., 14th Glosters wounded O.R.3., 17th R.Scots killed O.R.1. wounded 1., 17th West Yorks wounded O.R.1., 19th D.L.I. wounded Capt. J.W RYALL, Major S.HUFFAM, Lt. C.B.PEARSON, 2/Lt. N.WHARTON, 2/Lt. C.J.R. ALLAN, 2/Lt. R.A.EDGAR, 2/Lt. G.M.ALLAN, 2/Lt. C.E. BROWN, 2/Lt. G. PUGH, Capt. H.C.RICE? R.A.M.C., killed O.R.2. wounded 43., 106th M.G.Coy. wounded O.R.2., 19th North'd Fuslrs. wounded O.R.7., Y/35 T.M.B. wounded O.R.3., 157th Bde.R.F.A. wounded O.R.8., 159th Bde.R.F.A. wounded O.R.8., R.A.M.C. 106th Fd. Ambce. wounded O.R.1., 107th Fd. Ambce. wounded O.R.1., 204th Fd. Coy. wounded O.R.7., 205th Fd.Coy.R.E. wounded O.R.1.	
	4-11-17.		15th Cheshires wounded O.R.1., 17th R.Scots wounded O.R.3., 17th West Yorks wounded O.R.4., 19th D.L.I. wounded Capt. W.J. OLIVER, Capt. R.M. MIDDLETON, 2/Lt. G.K.PRIOR, wounded O.R.30., 18th H.L.I. killed O.R. 1, wounded 6., 157th Bde.R.F.A. wounded Lt. G.G.D. SCOTT (At duty) O.R. 3 (At duty), 159th Bde. R.F.A. wounded O.R.5. (At duty), 19th North'd Fus. killed O.R.1. wounded O.R.1., 35th Div. Signals Coy. wounded O.R., R.A.M.C., 105th Fd. Ambce. wounded O.R.5 106th Fd. Ambce. wounded O.R.1., 15th Cheshires attd. 204th Fd. Coy. R.E. wounded O.R.1.	

P.T.O.

Army Form C. 2118.

WAR DIARY
INTELLIGENCE SUMMARY
(Erase heading not required.)

Instructions regarding War Diaries and Intelligence Summaries are contained in F. S. Regs., Part II. and the Staff Manual respectively. Title pages will be prepared in manuscript.

Place	Date	Hour	Summary of Events and Information	Remarks and references to Appendices
	5-11-17.		106th Inf. Bde. H.Q., Bde. Major, Capt. J.N.O.RYCROFT.M.G. (3-11-17) (Gassed)., 17th R.Scots wounded O.R.4., 17th West Yorks wounded 2/Lt. D.C.de LISSA, 157th Bde. R.F.A. killed O.R.5.	
	6-11-17.		17th West Yorks wounded O.R. 4., 19th D.L.I. wounded 2/Lt. E. MILNER, 2/Lt. R.H.WRIGHT, O.R.43., 19th North'd Fus. wounded O.R.2., 157th Bde. R.F.A. killed O.R.1. wounded 2., 159th Bde.R.F.A. wounded O.R.1., 35th Div. Signal Coy. wounded O.R.3., R.A.M.C. wounded Capt. J.YOUNG at.td. 19th D.L.I., 17th Lancs. Fus. wounded 2/Lt. A.ROTHWELL, 15th Sherwoods wounded 2/Lt. G.GALLOW.	
	7-11-17.		16th Cheshires wounded 2/Lt. E.C.OLIVER, 14th Glosters wounded O.R.1., 15th Sherwoods wounded 2/Lt. H.MAXWELL (Shell Shock)., wounded O.R.1. (Accidental)., 17th West Yorks wounded O.R.1., 19th D.L.I. wounded 2/Lt. R.S. BOUTFLOWER,O.R.2.	
	8-11-17.		NIL.	
	9-11-17.		17th Lancs. Fus. wounded O.R.1. (Accidental), 19th North'd Fus. wounded O.R.2.	
	10-11-17.		NIL.	
	11-11-17.		NIL.	
	12-11-17.		NIL.	
	13-11-17.		NIL.	
	14-11-17.		NIL.	
	15-11-17.		19th North'd Fus. wounded O.R.1.	
	16-11-17.		17th R. Scots. wounded O.R.4., 18th H.L.I. wounded 2/Lt. D. IMRIE, 2/Lt.A.W.PAYTON, 106th M.G.C. wounded O.R.1.	
	17-11-17.		14th Glosters wounded O.R.1., 15th Sherwoods wounded O.R.1., 17th R.Scots killed 2/Lt. J.V.WILSON, O.R.7., wounded O.R.9., Missing believed killed O.R.1., 106th M.G.Coy. wounded O.R.1.	
	18-11-17.		17th R.Scots killed O.R.3., 106th M.G.Coy. wounded O.R.2., 4th N.Staffs killed O.R.3., wounded Lt. G.G. HORSLEY, O.R.6., 18th H.L.I. wounded O.R. 1.	
	19-11-17.		15th Cheshires wounded O.R.2., 17th R. Scots wounded O.R.9., R.A.M.C. 105th Fd.Ambce. killed O.R.2., 106th Fd. Ambce. wounded O.R.1., 205th Fd.Coy. R.E. wounded O.R.1.	
	20-11-17.		14th Glosters wounded O.R.1., 17th R.Scots wounded O.R.3., 19th D.L.I. killed O.R.1. wounded 1., 19th North'd Fus. wounded O.R.1., 15th Cheshires wounded O.R.2., (Includes 1 at duty), 205th Fd Coy. R.E. killed O.R.1., wounded 5.	

P.T.O.

Army Form C. 2118.

WAR DIARY

INTELLIGENCE SUMMARY

(Erase heading not required.)

Instructions regarding War Diaries and Intelligence Summaries are contained in F.S. Regs., Part II. and the Staff Manual respectively. Title pages will be prepared in manuscript.

Place	Date	Hour	Summary of Events and Information	Remarks and references to Appendices
	21-11-17.		17th Lancs. Fus. killed O.R.3., 20th Lancs. Fus. wounded O.R.2., 17th R. Scots wounded O.R.2., 19th D.L.I. wounded O.R.3., 18th H.L.I. killed O.R.3. wounded 3 (1 at duty), 203rd Fd. Coy. R.E. wounded O.R.1., 14th Glosters wounded O.R.1.	
	22-11-17.		18th Lancs.Fus. wounded O.R.1. 23rd Manchesters wounded O.R.2., 104th M.G.Coy wounded O.R.2 (includes 1 at duty), 18th H.L.I. Missing O.R.2., 19th Northd. Fus. wounded O.R.1., 241 M.G.Coy. wounded O.R.1.	
	23-11-17.		17th Lancs. Fus. wounded O.R.5., 18th Lancs. Fus. killed O.R.1., 20th Lancs. Fus. wounded O.R.3., 15th Sherwoods wounded Lt. P.W.S. GAMPION (Shell shock), 19th North'd Fus. wounded 2/Lt. S.WALTON, O.R.8. (Includes 1 at duty)., 35th Div. Sigs. killed O.R.1., 18th H.L.I. wounded O.R.1.,	
	24-11-17.		17th Lancs. Fus. wounded O.R.2., 20th Lancs. Fus. wounded O.R.2., 23rd Manchesters wounded O.R3., 19th North'd Fus. wounded O.R.2., 203rd Fd. Coy.R.E. killed Lt. W.S.LAIDLOW, Lt. P.F.M.GAYFORD, wounded 2/Lt. G.D.LANGHAM, F.A.M.C. 107th Fd. Ambce. wounded O.R.1.	
	25-11-17.		18th Lancs. Fus. wounded Lt. W.O.RUSHTON (At duty)., 20th Lancs. Fus. killed 2/Lt. H.M.SMITH, wounded 2/Lt. T.A.CLEGG (At duty), killed O.R.2., wounded 1., 15th Cheshires killed O.R.4., wounded 21., 16th Cheshires killed O.R.2., wounded 2., 205th Fd.Coy. R.E. wounded O.R.1., 241 M.G.Coy. wounded O.R.2.	
	26-11-17.		20th Lancs. Fus. wounded O.P.1. (Self-inflicted), 15th Cheshires killed O.R.1., 16th Cheshires wounded 2/Lt. P.S. JOICE, O.R.3., killed.., wounded O.R. 5 (includes 1 at duty).	
	27-11-17.		20th Lancs. Fus. wounded O.R.6., 16th Cheshires wounded O.R.2., 14th Glosters wounded O.R.1., 15th Sherwoods wounded O.R.9., 105th M.G.Coy. killed O.R.1.	
	28-11-17.		18th Lancs. Fus. wounded O.R.1., 15th Cheshires killed O.R.3., wounded 14., 15th Sherwoods wounded O.R.3., 105th M.G.Coy. wounded O.R.1., 105th Fd. Ambce. wounded O.R.1., 106th Fd. Ambce. wounded O.R.1.	
	29-11-17.		105th M.G.Coy. wounded O.R.1., 19th D.L.I. wounded O.R.1. (at duty)., 157th Bde. R.F.A. wounded O.R.1, 159th Bde. R.F.A. killed O.R.1., wounded 2.	

P.T.O.

Army Form C. 2118.

WAR DIARY
INTELLIGENCE SUMMARY

(Erase heading not required.)

Place	Date	Hour	Summary of Events and Information	Remarks and references to Appendices
	30-11-17.		14th Glosters wounded O.R.1., 15th Cheshires missing O.R.1., 17th R.Scots killed O.R.3., wounded 3., 4th N.Staffs. killed O.R.8. wounded 10., 19th D.L.I. missing O.R.1., 19th North'd Fuslrs. wounded O.R.1., 241 M.G.Coy. wounded O.R.4., R.A.M.C. 106th Fd. Ambce. killed O.R.1., A.S.C. M.T. Attd. 105th Fd. Ambce. wounded O.R.1., 35th Div. Sigs. wounded O.R.1., 203rd Fd. Coy. R.E. wounded O.R."2., 204th Fd. Coy. wounded O.R.1. (At duty), 35th D.A.C. killed O.R.1. wounded 1.	

Major-General,
Commanding 35th Division.

35th Division.
WAR DIARY
INTELLIGENCE SUMMARY.
(Erase heading not required.)

December 1914.
Administrative Staffs. 35170 Army Form C. 2118.

Place	Date	Hour	Summary of Events and Information	Remarks and references to Appendices
Sent	1-12-17.		CASUALTIES. 17th Lancs. Fus. wounded O.R.1., 23rd Manchesters wounded O.R.1., 104th M.G.Coy. wounded O.R.1., 4th N.Staffs killed O.R.1., wounded 8., 19th D.L.I. wounded O.R.1., 18th H.L.I. wounded O.R.1., R.A.M.C. 106th Fd. Ambce. killed O.R.4., wounded 2., 15th Cheshires attd. 204th Fd. Coy. R.E. wounded O.R.2.,	
	2-12-17.		17th R.Scots. wounded O.R. 2., 4th N.Staffs killed O.R.6. wounded 2., 241 M.G.Coy. wounded O.R.1. at duty, 204th Fd.Coy.R.E. wounded O.R.5., 17th Lancs. Fus. attd. 203rd Fd.Coy.R.E. wounded O.R.1., 15th Cheshires attd. 204th Fd.Coy.R.E. wounded O.R.2.	
	3-12-17.		17th Lancs. Fus. wounded O.R.1., 18th Lancs. Fus. wounded O.R. 2., 17th R.Scots missing O.R.1., 4th N.Staffs killed O.R.1., wounded O.R.2., 18th H.L.I. wounded O.R.2., 19th North'd Fus. wounded O.R.3.	
	4-12-17.		17th Lancs. Fus. wounded O.R.1., 18th Lancs. Fus. wounded O.R. 4 (Includes 1 accidental), 23rd Manchesters wounded O.R. 1 (Accidental), 19th North'd Fus. wounded O.R.1., The 10.R. 17th R. Scots reported missing on 3-12-17 now in Hospital - Gassed.	
	5-12-17.		18th Lancs. Fus. wounded O.R.1., 23rd Manchesters killed 2/Lt. G.W.GRAY, wounded O.R.7., 14th Glosters attd. 204th Fd.Coy. R.E. wounded O.R.1.	
	6-12-17.		14th Glosters wounded O.F.2., 19th North'd. Fus. wounded O.F.1., 241 M.G.Coy. killed O.R.1. wounded 2 (includes 1 at duty), R.A.M.C. 107th Fd. Ambce. wounded O.R.2.	
	7-12-17.		20th Lancs. Fus. wounded O.R.1. (at duty), 16th Cheshires wounded O.R.1., 15th Sherwoods wounded O.R.1.	
	8-12-17. 9-12-17.		NIL. 16th Cheshires wounded O.R.6., missing 1., 19th North. Fus. wounded O.R.1. (at duty).	
	10-12-17.		14th Glosters. wounded O.R.4., 19th North'd. Fus. wounded O.R.1.	
	11-12-17. 12-12-17. 13-12-17.		19th North'd Fus. wounded O.R.2. (at duty). NIL. 17th Lancs. Fus. wounded O.R.1. 19th North'd Fus. wounded O. R.1.	

P.T.O.

Army Form C. 2118.

WAR DIARY
~~INTELLIGENCE~~ SUMMARY.

(Erase heading not required.)

Instructions regarding War Diaries and Intelligence Summaries are contained in F. S. Regs., Part II. and the Staff Manual respectively. Title pages will be prepared in manuscript.

Place	Date	Hour	Summary of Events and Information	Remarks and references to Appendices
	14-12-17.		205th Fd.Coy. R.E. killed O.R.1., wounded 1.	
	15-12-17.		NIL.	
	16-12-17.		NIL.	
	17-12-17.		NIL.	
	18-12-17.		205th Fd.Coy.R.E. killed O.R.L.	
	19-12-17.		NIL.	
	20-12-17.		NIL.	
	21-12-17.		NIL.	
	22-12-17.		NIL.	
	23-12-17.		204th Fd.Coy.R.E. wounded O.R.l.	
	24-12-17.		NIL.	
	25-12-17.		NIL.	
	26-12-17.		NIL.	
	27-12-17.		NIL.	
	28-12-17.		NIL.	
	29-12-17.		NIL.	
	30-12-17.		16th Cheshires wounded O.R.L., 4th N.Staffs wounded O.R.L. (accidental), 19th Northd.Fus. wounded O.R.L.	
	31-12-17.		NIL.	

Major-General,
Commanding 35th Division.

SECRET.

Army Form C. 2118.

WAR DIARY
INTELLIGENCE SUMMARY.

35th Divn. Administrative Staff.

(Erase heading not required.)

Instructions regarding War Diaries and Intelligence Summaries are contained in F. S. Regs., Part II and the Staff Manual respectively. Title pages will be prepared in manuscript.

Place	Date	Hour	Summary of Events and Information	Remarks and references to Appendices
			CASUALTIES.	
	1-1-18.		NIL.	
	2-1-18.		NIL.	
	3-1-18.		NIL.	
	4-1-18.		NIL.	
	5-1-18.		NIL.	
	6-1-18.		14th Gloucesters wounded Lieut. E. BILLINGTON (At duty).	
	7-1-18.		19th Northumberland Fus. wounded O.R.1. (Gassed).	
	8-1-18.		NIL.	
	9-1-18.		17th Lancs. Fuslrs. wounded O.R.1., 20th Lancs. Fuslrs. killed O.R.4., wounded 13. 23rd Manchesters wounded O.R.3., 104th M.G.Coy. wounded O.R.1., 104th T.M.B. wounded Capt. R.J.S. TYHURST.M.C. (17th Lancs. Fuslrs).	
	10-1-18.		18th Lancs. Fuslrs. wounded O.R.1. (accidental). 20th Lancs. Fuslrs. killed O.R.2., 4th N.Staffs wounded O.R.2. (accidental). 18th H.L.I. killed O.R.1., wounded 3.	
	11-1-18.		203rd Field Coy. R.E. wounded O.R.1. (at duty)., 20th Lancs. Fuslrs. killed O.R.1. wounded 3. 18th H.L.I. Missing O.R.1.	
	12-1-18.		18th Lancs. Fusrs. wounded O.R.1., 20th Lancs. Fuslrs. wounded O.R. 4(includes 3 at duty).	
	13-1-18.		17th Lancs. Fuslrs. wounded O.R.1., 104th M.G.Coy. killed O.R.1., 19th N.Fus. wounded O.R.1.	
	14-1-18.		205th Field Coy. R.E. wounded O.R.1., 20th Lancs. Fusrs wounded O.R.3., 18th H.L.I. wounded O.R.3., 19th Northd. Fus. wounded O.R.1.	
	15-1-18.		23rd Manchesters wounded O.R.2., 104th M.G.Coy. wounded O.R.1. (at duty). 17th Royal Scots wounded O.R.2. (includes 1 at duty)., 4th N. Staffs. wounded O.R.1.5th Cheshires attd. 19th Northd. Fus. wounded Lieut. T.O.M. FFOULKES (at duty).	
	16-1-18.		203rd Field Coy. R.E. wounded O.R.1. (N.Y.D. Gassed). 205th Field Coy. R.E. wounded O.R.L. (at duty). 20th Lancs. Fus.rs. wounded O.R.1. 104th M.G.Coy. killed O.R.1. (accidentally drowned).	
	17-1-18.		18th Lancs. Fusrs. wounded O.R.4., 20th Lancs. Fus. wounded 2/Lieut. S.C. St. C. ELLIOTT. 4th N.Staffs. wounded O.R.4., 18th H.L.I. wounded O.R.1. 241 M.G.Coy. wounded O.R.1.	
	18-1-18.		17th Lancs. Fus.rs wounded O.R.1. (accidental)., 5th Sherwood For. attd. 15th Sherwood For. killed 2/Lieut. G.S. HOPKINSON., 1/2nd Bn. Sherwood For. attd. 15th Sherwood For. wounded Major W.A. McCLELLAND (Died of wounds).	
	19-1-18.		205th Fild Coy. R.E. wounded O.R.1. (at duty). 159th Bde. R.F.A. wounded O.R.4. (Slightly gassed). 15th Cheshires wounded O.r. 1., 16th Cheshires wounded O.R.1. (at duty)., 14th Glosters wounded O.R.1., 15th Sherwood For. wounded O.F.9., 19th N. Fus. wounded O.R.2.,	

P.T.OL

Army Form C. 2118.

WAR DIARY
INTELLIGENCE SUMMARY

(Erase heading not required.)

Instructions regarding War Diaries and Intelligence Summaries are contained in F. S. Regs., Part II. and the Staff Manual respectively. Title pages will be prepared in manuscript.

Place	Date	Hour	Summary of Events and Information	Remarks and references to Appendices
	20-1-18.		203rd Field Coy. R.E. killed O.R.1., 159th Bde. R.F.A. wounded O.R.1., 17th Lancs. Fus. killed O.R.1., wounded 9. 15th Cheshires killed O.R.1. wounded 2., 15th Sherwood For. wounded O.R.2.	
	21-1-18.		203rd Field Coy. R.E. wounded O.R.3., 17th Lancs. Fus. wounded O.R.1. (at duty). 107th Field Ambulance killed O.R.1. 241 M.G.Coy. wounded O.R.1.	
	22-1-18.		157th Bde. R.F.A. killed 2/Lieut. N. BEWICK. 15th Sherwood For. wounded O.R.4.,	
	23-1-18.		157th Bde. R.F.A. wounded O.R.2., 35th D.A.C. wounded O.R.1. (at duty)., 18th Lancs. Furs. wounded O.R.1. (gassed)., 23rd Manchesters wounded O.R.1. (self-inflicted)., 16th Cheshires killed O.R., 5 wounded 1., 19th D.L.I. wounded O.R.1. (accidental).	
	24-1-18.		23rd Manchesters attd. 203 Field Coy. R.E. wounded O.R.1., 15th Cheshires killed O.R.3, 15th Sherwood For. wounded Lieut. G.H. BOOT O.R.3.	
	25-1-18.		157th Bde. R.F.A. wounded O.R.2., 18th H.L.I. wounded O.R.1., 18th Lancs Fuslrs. attd. R.E. wounded O.R.2., 20th Lancs. Fuslrs. wounded 2/Lieut. L. TAYLOR. O.R.5., 23rd Manchesters attd. R.E. wounded O.R.1., 104th M.G.Coy. wounded O.R.1., wounded 2/Lieut. W.A. TWEDDLE. 15th Sherwood For. killed 2/Lieut. S.R. PRICE, 2/Lieut. A.A. HOGAN,(latter belongs 1/2nd Bn. S.F.)., O.R.2.,	
	26-1-18.		17th Royal Scots attd. 106th T.M.B. wounded O.R.1., 19th D.L.I. wounded O.R.1. (accidental).	
	27-1-18.		203 Field Coy. R.E. wounded O.R.1., 20th Lancs. Fus. wounded O.R.1., 23rd Manchesters missing O.R.3. (Believed prisoners)., 17th Royal Scots killed O.R.1., 23rd Manchesters attd. 203 Fd. Coy. R.E. wounded O.R.1., 18th Lancs. Fuslrs. attd. 203 Fd.Coy. R.E. wounded O.R.2.	
	28-1-18.		23rd Manchesters wounded 2/Lieut. H.J.MASON M.C. (Belongs 1/2nd Bn). O.R.4., (includes one S.I.). 17th Royal Scots wounded O.R.1.	
	29-1-18.		204 Fd. Coy. R.E. wounded O.R.1., 20th Lancs. Fus. wounded O.R.1., 23rd Manchesters wounded O.R.1.	
	30-1-18.		17th Lancs. Fuslrs. wounded O.R.3. (Gassed)., 18th Lancs. Fuslrs. wounded O.R.1. (S.I.) 23rd Manchesters wounded O.R.2. (Gas shell). (one since died of wounds)., 17th R. Scots wounded O.R.2. 4th North Staffs wounded O.R.5., 241 M.G.Coy. wounded O.R.1. (at duty).	
	31-1-18.		157th Bde. R.F.A. wounded O.R.2., 205th Field Coy. R.E. wounded O.R.1., 17th Lancs. Fus. wounded O.R.4., 18th Lancs. Fus. wounded O.R.4., 20th Lancs. Fus. attd. 203 Field Coy. R.E. wounded O.R.3. (includes one at duty). 16th Cheshires wounded O.R.1., 241 M.G.Coy. wounded O.R.1.	
	19-2-18.			

Commanding 35th Division.

SECRET.

Army Form C. 2118.

WAR DIARY 35th Divl. Administrative Staff.
INTELLIGENCE SUMMARY.

(Erase heading not required.)

Instructions regarding War Diaries and Intelligence Summaries are contained in F.S. Regs, Part II. and the Staff Manual respectively. Title pages will be prepared in manuscript.

Place	Date	Hour	Summary of Events and Information	Remarks and references to Appendices
			CASUALTIES.	
	1-2-18.		17th Lancs. Fus. wounded O.R.2., 23rd Manchesters killed O.R.1., 104th M.G.C. wounded O.R.1.	
	2-2-18.		20th Lancs. attd. 203 Fd. Coy. R.E. wounded O.R.3., 15th Cheshires Missing O.R.2., 105th M.G.C. wounded 2/Lieut. E.C. BRADFIELD M.C., 19th Durham L.I. wounded O.R.1.	
	3-2-18.		16th Cheshires killed O.R.1., wounded O.R.1., 15th Sherwoods wounded O.R.1.	
	4-2-18.		203 Fd. Coy. R.E. wounded O.R.1., 15th Cheshires killed O.R.1., wounded 1., 14th Glosters wounded O.R.1., 18th H.L.I. killed O.R.1. wounded 1.	
	5-2-18.		15th Cheshires killed O.R.1. wounded 4., 14th Glosters killed O.R.3., wounded 7., 17th R. Scots killed O.R.1. wounded 1., 18th H.L.I. killed O.R.1. wounded 2.	
	6-2-18.		5th Sherwood Foresters attd. 15th Sherwoods wounded 2/Lieut. F. HURST, 18th Lancs. Fus. wounded O.R.1., 19th Northd. Fus. wounded O.R.1.	
	7-2-18.		18th Lancs. Fus. attd. 104 T.M.B. wounded O.R.1., 17th Royal Scots killed O.R.1. wounded 6., 15th Sherwoods wounded O.R.1., 4th North Staffs killed O.R.1. wounded 2.	
	8-2-18.		X/35 T.M.B. killed O.R.1. wounded 1.	
	9-2-18.		18th Highland L.I. wounded Lieut. G.R. McCOLL (At duty), 106th M.G.Coy. wounded O.R.1.	
	10-2-18.		17th Lancs. Fus. killed O.R.1. wounded 8., 19th Durham L.I. wounded O.R.6., 4th North Staffs wounded O.R.1.;	
	11-2-18.		17th Lancs. Fus. missing O.R.1. 18th Lancs. Fus. killed O.R.1.	
	12-2-18.		18th Highland L.I. wounded O.R.1., 19th Northd. Fus wounded O.R.1.	
	13-2-18.		19th D.L.I. wounded O.R.1.	
	14-2-18.		NIL.	
	15-2-18.		203 Fd. Coy. R.E. wounded O.R.1., 19th Durham L.I. wounded O.R.1., 159th Bde. R.F.A. wounded O.R.1.	
	16-2-18.		18th Lancs. Fus.wounded 2/Lieut. H.C. FRANKS, 2/Lieut. H.J. PLENDERLEITH, 2/Lieut. E.L. BAULD (All at duty), wounded O.R. 12, missing O.R.3., 19th Durham L.I. killed O.R.1., 159th Bde.R.F.A. wounded O.R.6.	
	17-2-18.		35th D.A.C. wounded O.R.1. 203 Fd. Coy. R.E. wounded O.R.1., 204 Fd. Coy. R. E. wounded O.R.4.	
	18-2-18.		17th Royal Scots wounded O.R.1., 18th H.L.I. wounded O.R.1.,	
	19-2-18.		18th Lancs. Fus. wounded O.R.2., 12th Highland L.I. wounded O.R.4.,	
	20-2-18.		18th Lancs. Fus. wounded O.R.1., 17th R. Scots wounded O.R.4.	
	21-2-18.		19th North'd Fus. wounded O.R.1.	
			18th Lancs. Fus. attd R.E. wounded O.R.1., 17th R. Scots wounded O.R.1., 18th H.L.I. wounded O.R.3.	

P.T.O.

Army Form C. 2118.

WAR DIARY
~~INTELLIGENCE SUMMARY~~
(Erase heading not required.)

Place	Date	Hour	Summary of Events and Information	Remarks and references to Appendices
	22-2-18.		V/35 T.M.B. wounded O.R.1., 17th R. Scots attd. R.E. wounded O.R.1. 35th Blv. Signal Coy. wounded O.R.2.	
	23-2-18.		17th R. Scots wounded O.R.1., 106th M.G.C. wounded O.R. 2., 15th Sherwoods killed O.R.2., wounded 1.	
	24-2-18.		159th Bde. R.F.A. wounded 2/Lieut. M.V. DIXON.	
	25-2-18.		157th Bde. R.F.A. killed 2/Lieut. J.M.S. WRIGHT, 15th Cheshires attd. R.E. wounded O.R.1. 15th Cheshires wounded O.R.2., 4th N. Staffs killed O.R.1. wounded 5.	
	26-2-18.		4th N. Staffs killed O.R.1. wounded 5, missing 1.	
	27-2-18.		15th Cheshires wounded O.R.1. 15th Sherwoods wounded O.R.5., 4th N. Staffs killed O.R.1. wounded 8., 19th Northd Fus. wounded O.R.1., R.A.M.C., 105th Fd. Amb. wounded O.R.1.	
	28-2-18.		157th Bde. R.F.A. wounded O.R.1., 15th Cheshires killed O.R.3., 15th Sherwoods wounded O.R.3., 4th N. Staffs killed O.R.1., wounded 13. (10 since died., 35th M.G. Battalion wounded O.R.1.	

HONOURS & REWARDS DURING THE MONTH.

    MILITARY CROSS. 1.
    D. C. M. 3.
    MILITARY MEDAL. 12.

NUMBER OF CASES BROUGHT TO TRIAL BY F.G.C.M. AND CONVICTED DURING THE MONTH.   10.

REORGANISATIONS.

    Reorganisation of Division, Commenced 29-1-18.
                                      Completed 15-2-18.

    Reorganisation of Pioneer Bn. Commenced 13-2-18.
                                           Completed 21-2-18.

	2-3-18.		Formation of M.G. Battalion. Commenced 22-2-18. Completed 2-3-18.	

H. Farmar Lieut Colonel
for
Major-General.
Commanding 35th Division.

35th Division Administrative.

A. & Q.

35th DIVISION.

MARCH 1918

D.A.G.
3rd Echelon.

35th Div. No. A.A. 21.

        Herewith War Diary for the Administrative Branch of this Division for the month of March 1918.

23rd April, 1918.
EAH.

                      Major-General,
              Commanding 35th Division.

SECRET.

Army Form C. 2118.

WAR DIARY
or
INTELLIGENCE SUMMARY

Administrative Branch
35th Division.

(Erase heading not required.)

Instructions regarding War Diaries and Intelligence Summaries are contained in F.S. Regs., Part II. and the Staff Manual respectively. Title pages will be prepared in manuscript.

Place	Date 1918.	Hour	Summary of Events and Information	Remarks and references to Appendices
At CANAL BANK.	March 1st to March 11th		Div. Headquarters moved from CANAL BANK near YPRES, to St. SIXTE near LOVIE	
	March 22nd		Orders received from II Corps for 35th Division to be prepared to entrain after mid-night 22/23rd March.	
	March 23rd.	3 a.m.	Entrainment commenced at PROVEN, ROUSBRUGGE and PESELHOEK (34 Trains - Infantry first Artillery last - Journey 12 hours) for Fifth Army Area. Detraining Stations CORBIE - HEILLY and MERICOURT L'ABBE.	
	March 24th		Orders were received for Infantry to be taken forward in buses to BRAY-SUR-SOMME from thence marched into action. In some cases no lorries were made available and the troops marched the whole distance. Advanced Div. H.Q. MARICOURT. Rear Div. H.Q. MERICOURT-SUR-SOMME. The Division came under the VII Corps.	
	March 25th	7 a.m.	Div. H.Q. (complete) opened at BRAY-SUR-SOMME. All three Infantry Brigades and Pioneer Battalion holding the line East of MARICOURT.	
	March 26th	10 p.m.	Divisional Headquarters opened at SAILLY LAURETTE.	
	March 26th		Losses and requirements in Ordnance Stores having been anticipated, shortly after arrival on the line of the ANCRE, the Division was completed with its requirements in Vickers Guns (16) Lewis Guns (29), spare parts, lubricants and flanellette. Div. H.Q. HENENCOURT CHATEAU.	
	March 27th		Major General FRANKS left the Division, Brig-General MARINDIN was placed in temporary Command by the G.O.C. VII Corps.	
	March 28th) 29th) 30th)		Line of the River ANCRE held.	

WAR DIARY SECRET.
or
~~INTELLIGENCE SUMMARY~~

(Erase heading not required.)

Army Form C. 2118.

Administrative Branch
35th Division.

Place	Date	Hour	Summary of Events and Information	Remarks and references to Appendices
	March 31st		35th Division (less Artillery) withdrawn from the line being relieved by the 3rd and 4th Australian Divisions, and was located in the following area :-	
			PONT NOYELLES - Div. H.Q. LA HOUSSOYE - 104th & 105th Infantry Brigades. HEILLY - 106th Infantry Brigade.	
			No. of Decorations awarded - 15. No. of Cases brought to trial by Court Martial and Convicted. 14.	
			Casualties (approximately).	
			Officers. O.Rs. 113 3089	
			Owing to the ~~precipitous advent of active operations~~ *Italian nature of the situation*, with the consequent scarcity of Transport, the whole of the office stores had of necessity to be dumped and thereafter burned to prevent them falling into the hands of the enemy. These stores included the information for the compilation of the War Diary. The information regarding Casualties, Honours and Awards and Courts-Martial, is very approximate, the correctness of which cannot be vouched for.	
			[signature] Major-General, Commanding 35th Division.	
			23rd April, 1918.	

SECRET.

WAR DIARY
or
INTELLIGENCE SUMMARY.
(Erase heading not required.)

Army Form C. 2118.

Administrative Branch.
35th Division.

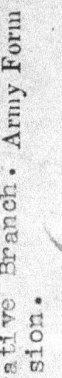

Instructions regarding War Diaries and Intelligence Summaries are contained in F.S. Regs., Part II. and the Staff Manual respectively. Title pages will be prepared in manuscript.

Place	Date 1918.	Hour	Summary of Events and Information	Remarks and references to Appendices
	April 5th.		157th Bde. R.F.A., wounded 2 O.R., 159th Bde. R.F.A. killed O.R. 2, wounded 4. 35th Div. Sig. Co. R.E. attd. H.Q. 35th Div. Arty. wounded O.R.1. 205th Field Co. R.E. killed O.R. 2, wounded 8.(includes 1 at duty) 4th N.Staffs. wounded O.R. 5, missing 6. 17th R. Scots killed Lieut. F.A. Raynes, M.C. (28.3.18.) 12th H.L.I. killed Capt. R.L.HANNAH, M.C. (25.3.18.) wounded 2/Lieut. W.L. DUNLOP (25.3.18.).	
	April 6th		17th Lan. Fus. 1 O.R. wounded, 18th Lan. Fus. 2 O.R. wounded, 19th D.L.I. 8 O.R. wounded (includes 6 gassed). 18th H.L.I. 1 O.R. wounded.	
	April 8th		17th Lan. Fus. 2/Lieut. W.W. COTTON wounded (at duty) 2/Lieut. H.E.TUPLING wounded., Wounded O.R. 3. 19th D.L.I. wounded 2/Lt. C. MOSLEY (gassed) other ranks 1. 12th H.L.I. wounded 2/Lt. J. BAUCHOP, O.R. 5. 18th H.L.I. wounded O.R. 3.	
	April 9th		48th Army Bde. R.F.A. wounded (gassed) Major C.G.DUFFIN, M.C., Lieut. J.R.GIFFORD, M.C., O.R. 34. 17th Lan. Fus. wounded Lieut. T.G.GRIBBLE O.R. 2 (1 at duty), 18th Lan. Fus. wounded O.R. 2. 4th North Staffs. killed O.R. 1. 17th R. Scots O.R. killed 4, wounded 5, 12th H.L.I. O.R. wounded 7, 18th H.L.I. wounded O.R. 2. 35th Bn. M.G.C. wounded 2/Lt. J.M. BLAIR, 1 O.R.	
	April 10th		48th Army Bde. R.F.A. wounded (all gassed) Lt. B.GIRLING, 2/Lt. F.B.LITTLE, O.R.10. 77th Army Bde. R.F.A. wounded (gassed) Lieut. A.E.COATMAN. 204th Field Co. R.E. killed O.R. 1, wounded 4. 205th Field Co. wounded (allgassed) Lieut. A.H. DOWNES-SHAW, O.R. 14. 15th Ches. R. wounded O.R. 2. 4th N.Staffs. wounded O.R. 10. 17th R. Scots wounded O.R. 4 (includes 1 N.V.D.N.) 12th H.L.I. wounded O.R. 3. 13th H.L.I. wounded O.R. 2 (1 accidental) 35th Bn. M.G.C. wounded 2/Lt. S.E. PEAKE, 2/Lt. A.E.MILNE 9.4.18. (both gassed) O.R. 34 (includes 32 gassed and 1 accidental) 19th Northd. F. wounded O.R. 61 (includes 55 gassed) R.A.M.C. attd. StxxNxStaffxx killed Captain L.A.H.BULKELEY 10.4.18. R.A.M.C. attd. 4 N. Staffs. killed Captain A.L.GARDNER 10.4.18. 15th Cheshires	
			35th Div. Sig. Co. R.E. wounded O.R. 6 (includes 5 gassed)	

WH.G.

Secret.

WAR DIARY
or
INTELLIGENCE SUMMARY
(Erase heading not required.)

Army Form C. 2118.

Administrative Branch
35th Division.

Instructions regarding War Diaries and Intelligence Summaries are contained in F.S. Regs., Part II. and the Staff Manual respectively. Title pages will be prepared in manuscript.

Place	Date 1918.	Hour	Summary of Events and Information	Remarks and references to Appendices
	April 11th		15th Cheshires wounded 2/Lt. R.DONE, O.R. 28 (includes 25 slightly gassed). 15th Sherwoods killed O.R. 4, wounded 6 (includes 4 gassed). 4th N. Staffs. killed 3, wounded 11 (4 gassed) 17th R. Scots wounded 20.R. 12th H.L.I. killed 3 O.R., wounded 7. 18th H.L.I. wounded 8 O.R. 48th A.F.A.Bde. wounded Lt. A.SUTCLIFFE, 18 O.R. (gassed) 77th A.F.A.Bde. wounded (gassed) 3 O.R.	
	April 12th		48th A.F.A.Bde. wounded 2/Lt. M.E.GUERMONT (11.4.18 gassed) Lt. (A/Major) B.J.MOORE, M.C. (10.4.18 gassed) 16 O.R. (gassed) 77th A.F.A.Bde. wounded O.R.l. 204th Field Co. killed O.R.2 wounded Captain A.J.FAWCETT (10.4.18 gassed, at duty) 32 O.R. (all gassed; 8 at duty) 205th Field Co. R.E. 28 O.R. wounded (includes 25 gassed and 1 at duty). 18th Lancs. Fusrs. wounded O.R. 2. 4th N. Staffs. wounded O.R. 2. 18th H.L.I. wounded O.R. 1. 19th Northd. Fus. killed O.R. 4, wounded 13 (1 at duty). R.A.M.C. attached 105th Field Ambulance wounded O.R.4 (gassed)	
	April 13th		204th Field Co. R.E. wounded (gassed) O.R. 3 (2 at duty). R.A.M.C. attached 107th Field Ambulance killed O.R.1. ASC/Mt attd. 107th Field Amb. killed O.R. 1. 17th Lancs. Fus. wounded O.R. 1. Missing 2/Lt. E.C.WEBSTER (12.4.18.) 1 O.R. 18th Lan. Fus. O.R. killed 2, wounded 11. 15th Sherwoods killed O.R.1 wounded 3, 2/Lt. W.B.POLLARD wounded 12.4.18. 77th A.F.A.Bde. wounded Capt. J.W.MASON, M.C. 11.4.18. (gassed) 4th N.Staffs. killed O.R.1. 35th Bn. M.G.C. wounded O.R.1. 19th Northd. Fus. wounded O.R.1.	
	April 14th		157th Bde. R.F.A. wounded O.R.2. 159th Bde. R.F.A. wounded O.R.1. 48th A.F.A.Bde. wounded O.R.3 (gassed) 77th A.F.A.Bde. wounded O.R.1. 15th Sherwoods killed O.R.1, wounded kxxxxxx 7 O.R.(5 gassed) Lieut. E.E.ADSHEAD 12.4.18. (gassed) 19th Northd. Fus. killed O.R.2, wounded 2 (at duty)	
	April 15th		V/35 TMB. wounded O.R.1. 204th Field Co. R.E. wounded O.R.1. (gassed) 17th Lan. F. killed O.R.1. wounded (at duty) 1. 18th Lan. Fus. wounded 2/Lt. E.L.STOREY 13.4.18., O.R.2. 19th D.L.I. wounded O.R.2 (includes 1 gassed) 15th Sherwoods attached 105th TMB. wounded O.R.1. (gassed) 4th N. Staffs. killed O.R.3. wounded 17. 18th H.L.I. wounded O.R.2.	

WHG.

SECRET.

Administrative Branch.Army Form C. 2118.
35th Division.

WAR DIARY
or
INTELLIGENCE SUMMARY

(Erase heading not required.)

Instructions regarding War Diaries and Intelligence Summaries are contained in F. S. Regs. Part II. and the Staff Manual respectively. Title pages will be prepared in manuscript.

Place	Date 1918.	Hour	Summary of Events and Information	Remarks and references to Appendices
	April 16th		17th Lan. Fus. killed O.R.1, wounded 1 (attd. 104 T.M.B.) 18th Lan. Fus. killed O.R.1, wounded 2. (includes 1 S.I.W.) 19th D.L.I. wounded O.R.1, 15th Ches. R. killed O.R.1, wounded 1 (at duty) 15th Sherwoods wounded O.R.2, 4th N.Staffs. killed O.R. 3, wounded 8. Captain E.BACHE (15.4.18) Lieut. S.B.DODMAN (NYDN) (15.4.18) 17th R. Scots, wounded O.R. 4 (2 at duty) 12th H.L.I. wounded 2, 18th H.L.I. wounded (at duty) 2/Lt. A.M.WOODSIDE (14.4.18) 35th Bn. M.G.C. killed O.R.1, wounded 4 (1 at duty) 19th Northd. Fus. wounded O.R. 48 (all gassed) 232 Div. Emp. Co. attached 105th Inf. Bde. H.Q. wounded O.R. 2 (gassed).	
	April 17th		77th A.F.A. Bde. wounded O.R.1, 18th Lan. Fus. killed O.R. 5, wounded 7. 19th D.L.I. killed 2, wounded 2, 15th Cheshires wounded 11 (1 at duty) 12th H.L.I. killed 2, wounded 13, 18th H.L.I. wounded 2 (1 accidental) 35th Bn. M.G.C. killed 2.	
	April 18th		17th Lan. Fus. wounded 1, O.R. 19th D.L.I. killed 1, wounded 2, 15th Ches. wounded 2, 15th Sherwoods wounded 3, 17th R. Scots wounded 1, 18th H.L.I. wounded 2/Lt. A.M. WOODSIDE (17.4.18.) 1 O.R., 12th H.L.I. wounded O.R.1, 35th Bn. M.G.C. wounded 2 O.R., 19th Northd. Fus. wounded 1 O.R.	
	April 19th		15th Ches. wounded 2/Lt. R. BISHOP (18.4.18) O.R. 5 (1 at duty) 15th Sherwoods killed 2/Lt. C.A. NEWMAN (18.4.18), O.R.2, wounded 5, 17th R. Scots wounded 1, 12th H.L.I. wounded 2 (1 accident) 35th Bn. M.G.C. wounded 1 (at duty).	
	April 20th		77th A.F.A. Bde. wounded O.R. 2, wounded 2 (1 at duty) 17th Lan. Fus. wounded 9, 18th Lan. Fus. wounded 2, 19th D.L.I. killed O.R. 4, wounded 5, 2/Lt. B.FISH (19.4.18) 105th Inf. Bde. (G.O.C.) wounded Bt.Lt.Col. (T/Brig-Gen) A.CARTON de WIART, V.C., D.S.O. (20.4.18) 15th Cheshires killed O.R. 4, wounded 2/Lt. W.N.D.TYSON (20.4.18) 13 O.R., Missing believed killed 2 O.R., 15th Sherwoods wounded O.R. 3, 4th N. Staffs, wounded 1, 17th R. Scots wounded 3 (1 at duty) 12th H.L.I. killed 3 wounded 5, 18th H.L.I. wounded (at duty) 2/Lt. J.C.SMEWART (19.4.18) O.R. 2. 35th R.F.G.C. wounded O.R. 3 (1 at duty) A.S.C. 35th Div. Train wounded O.R. 1.	
	April 21st.		35th Div. Sig. Co. R.E. wounded (gassed) 1 O.R., 17th Lan. Fus. wounded O.R. 1, 15th Ches. R. killed O.R. 1, 19th D.L.I. wounded 6 (1 accidental), Missing,believed killed 1 O.R. 15th Sherwoods wounded 1 O.R., 4th N. Staffs O.R. killed 1, wounded 5, 17th R. Scots wounded O.R.2, 12th H.L.I. wounded O.R.1, 19th Northd. Fus. wounded (gassed) O.R.1, 35th Bn. M.G.C. wounded O.R. 2, 105th Field Ambulance O.R. died of wounds 1.	

SECRET.

WAR DIARY
or
INTELLIGENCE SUMMARY

(Erase heading not required.)

Army Form C. 2118.

Administrative Branch
35th Division.

Instructions regarding War Diaries and Intelligence Summaries are contained in F.S. Regs., Part II. and the Staff Manual respectively. Title pages will be prepared in manuscript.

Place	Date 1918.	Hour	Summary of Events and Information	Remarks and references to Appendices
	April 22nd		157 Bde. R.F.A. wounded O.R.1, 77th A.F.A. Bde. wounded O.R.1, X/35 TMB. wounded O.R.1, 18th Lan. Fus. wounded (S.I.) O.R.1, 19th D.L.I. killed O.R.1, wounded 2/Lt. W.C.HAYMAN (22.4.18) O.R.2, 15th Ches. R. wounded O.R. 8 (2 accidental) 15th Sherwoods killed O.R.2, wounded 3, Missing 1, 4th N. Staffs, wounded O.R.1, 12th H.L.I. killed O.R.2, wounded 1, 18th H.L.I. O.R. wounded 2.	
	April 23rd		157th Bde. R.F.A. killed O.R.2, wounded 8, 77th A.F.A. Bde. wounded O.R.2 (1 at duty) 205th Field Co. R.E. wounded O.R.1, 18th Lan. Fus. killed O.R.2, wounded 7, 5th N.Staffs. wounded 5 O.R. 17th R. Scots wounded O.R.4, 19th Northd. Fus. wounded O.R.1.	
	April 24th		159th Bde. R.F.A. wounded 2/Lt. F.A.MITCHELL (23.4.18) 77th A.F.A.Bde. wounded O.R. 3 (1 at duty) 17th Lan. Fus. killed O.R. 4, wounded 6, 18th Lan. Fus. killed O.R.1, wounded Captain B.T.O'GRADY, 2/Lt. M.REEVES, 2/Lt. W.CHADWICK, 8 O.R. (1 S.I.) 19th D.L.I. killed O.R. 4, wounded 6 (1 accidental) 15th Ches. R. killed O.R.1, 4th N. Staffs. wounded O.R.1 17th R. Scots killed O.R. 2, wounded 2. 12th H.L.I. wounded O.R.4, 35th Bn. M.G.C. wounded 3 O.R.	
	April 25th		17th L.F. wounded O.R.2, 18th Lan. Fus. killed 1, wounded 3, 19th D.L.I. killed Capt. C.W.HOWES, 2/Lt. A.C.PATERSON, 2/Lt. J.BELL (22.4.18) 38 O.R., wounded 2/Lt. C.GRUMMITT, 2/Lt. J.RICHARDSON, 2/Lt. R.HALL (22.4.18) O.R. 79, Missing 9 (1 wounded and missing) 15th Ches. R. killed Captain G.G.MILN, M.C., Lt. A.W.HANFORD (22.4.18) O.R.7, wounded Capt. A.E.WENNER, 2/Lt. T.HEAP, M.C. (22.4.18) 38 O.R. (1 at duty) 15th Sherwoods killed 2/Lt. J.H.DICKERSON (22.4.18) 18 O.R., wounded 2/Lt. A.M.SARGENT, 2/Lt. J.SHAW, 2/Lt. F.WHYSALL, 2/Lt. H.GERMAN (22.4.18) 87 O.R., Missing 13 O.R. 17th R. Scots killed 10 O.R. (accidental) 12th H.L.I. wounded 7, 18th H.L.I. wounded 1, 35th Bn. M.G.C. killed O.R. 2, wounded 1.	
	April 26th		35th Div. Sig. Co. R.E. wounded O.R. 1 (gassed) 17th Lan. Fus. wounded O.R.1, 18th L.F. killed 1, wounded 2 (1 accidental) 17th R. Scots killed 1, 12th H.L.I. wounded 3 O.R. 18th H.L.I. wounded Major (T/Lt.Col.) R.R.LAWRENSON, D.S.O. & Bar (26.4.18) Commanding Officer Died of wounds) O.R.2, 35th Bn. M.G.C. killed 2, wounded 1 O.R., XXXXXXXXXXXXXXXXXXXXXXXXXX XXXX	
	April 27th		17th Lan. Fus. wounded (at duty) 2 O.R., 18th Lan. Fus. killed 1, 15th Cheshires wounded 3, 4th N. Staffs. killed 1, wounded 6, 17th R.Scots killed 1, wounded 3 (1 believed S.I.) 12th H.L.I. killed 1, wounded 10 O.R., 18th H.L.I. wounded 1 O.R.	

SECRET.

WAR DIARY
or
INTELLIGENCE SUMMARY.

(Erase heading not required.)

Army Form C. 2118.

Administrative Branch.
35th Division.

Instructions regarding War Diaries and Intelligence Summaries are contained in F.S. Regs., Part II. and the Staff Manual respectively. Title pages will be prepared in manuscript.

Place	Date 1918.	Hour	Summary of Events and Information	Remarks and references to Appendices
	April 28th		159th Bde. R.F.A. wounded O.R.1, 205th Field Co. R.E. wounded 2/Lt. J.S.CHARNLEY (27.4.18) 1 O.R. 15th Ches.R. wounded 2 O.R., 15th Sherwoods wounded 1 O.R. (at duty) 17th R. Scots killed 2/Lt. J.WATSON (27.4.18) 2 O.R., wounded 10 O.R., 12th H.L.I. killed 1 O.R., wounded Lt. G.L.SCOTT (28.4.18) 7 O.R. (1 at duty), 18th H.L.I. wounded O.R.1, 35th Bn. M.G.C. killed 1, wounded 1 O.R.	
	April 29th		15th Cheshires killed O.R.1, wounded 3, Missing 1, 15th Sherwoods wounded O.R. 3 (2 gassed) 17th R. Scots wounded O.R.1, 12th H.L.I. killed O.R.2, wounded 6, 18th H.L.I. wounded 1 O.R. 19th Northd. Fus. wounded 1 O.R. (gassed).	
	April 30th		17th Lan. Fus. wounded O.R.3, 19th D.L.I. wounded 1 (accidental) 15th Sherwoods wounded 2, 4th N. Staffs. Killed 1, wounded 6, 17th R. Scots wounded 2, 18th H.L.I. killed 2 wounded 1. 35th Bn. M.G.C. wounded 2, 107th Field Amb. R.A.M.C. wounded 1.	
			No. of cases brought to trial, during the month, by Court Martial and Convicted.	
			21.	
			No. of decorations awarded during the month.	
			V.C. D.S.O. M.C. D.C.M. M.M.	
			1 9 x 44 " 17 ⌗ 124 @	
			x. Includes 4 Bars.	
			" Includes 6 Bars.	
			⌗ Includes 1 Bar.	
			@ Includes 3 Bars.	

Ralph Ruxy Major GS
35th Division

Army Form C. 2118.

WAR DIARY

ADMINISTRATIVE STAFF, 35th DIVISION.

~~INTELLIGENCE SUMMARY~~

(Erase heading not required.)

Instructions regarding War Diaries and Intelligence Summaries are contained in F.S. Regs., Part II. and the Staff Manual respectively. Title pages will be prepared in manuscript.

Place	Date	Hour	Summary of Events and Information	Remarks and references to Appendices
			CASUALTIES.	
	1-5-18.		159th Bde. R.F.A. wounded O.R.2., 17th Lancs. Fuslrs. wounded O.R.1., 18th Lanc. Fus. wounded O.R.3., 15th Cheshires wounded O.R.3., 4th N. Staffs killed O.R.2 wounded 1, 18th North'd. Fus. wounded O.R.1.	
	2-5-18		159th Bde. R.F.A. wounded Lieut. G.A.HART,DSO (at duty), Lieut. (A/Major) V.W.GOSS (at duty). 18th Lancs. Fus. wounded O.R.4., 19th D.L.I. wounded O.R.1., 12th H.L.I. wounded O.R.1., 18th H.L.I. wounded 2/Lt. A.L. DARE (at duty), 35th Bn. M.G.C. wounded O.R.1.	
	3-5-18.		17th Lancs. Fus. wounded O.R.4., 18th Lancs. Fus. wounded O.R.1.	
	4-5-18.		19th North'd. Fus. wounded O.R.1.	
	5-5-18.		17th R. Scots killed O.R.1.	
	6-5-18.		12th H.L.I. killed O.R.1.	
	7-5-18.		19th D.L.I. wounded O.R.1. (S.I)., 19th North'd. Fus. wounded 2/Lt. G.A. PRIESTMAN.	
	8-5-18.		NIL.	
	9-5-18.		NIL.	
	10-5-18.		NIL.	
	11-5-18.		19th North'd. Fus. wounded O.R.2., 35th Bn. M.G.C. wounded O.R.1.	
	12-5-18.		NIL.	
	13-5-18.		203 Fd. Coy. RE killed O.R.1. wounded 1, 15th Sherwoods wounded O.R.3., 19th N. Fus. wounded O.R.1. (at duty).	
	14-5-18.		204 Fd. Coy. R.E. wounded O.R.1., 12th H.L.I. killed O.R.1., wounded 1, 18th H.L.I. wounded 1.	
	15-5-18.		35th Bn. M.G.C. wounded O.R.1. (accidental).	
	16-5-18.		NIL.	
	17-5-18.		NIL.	
	18-5-18.		NIL.	
	19-5-18.		NIL.	
	20-5-18.		17th R. Scots killed O.R.2., wounded 9., 18th H.L.I. killed Capt. R.J.W. RITCHIE O.R.2., wounded 7., 106th TMB. wounded N.Y.D.N. O.R.2.	
	21-5-18.		157th Bde. RFA wounded O.R.2., 159th Bde. RFA wounded O.R.2., 35th Div. Sig. Co. RE. wounded O.R.1., 15th Cheshires wounded O.R.20., 15th Sherwoods wounded O.R.1., 4th N. Staffs wounded Lieut. J. CHARLES, 2/Lt. J. SPILSBURY, O.R.44., 17th R. Scots killed O.R.1., wounded 5, 12th HLI. wounded Capt. P.H. CAMPBELL, M.C., Lieut. H.E. BETHUNE, Lieut. A. ANDERSON, O.R.23., 18th H.L.I. killed O.R.7., wounded 2.	
	22-5-18.		159th Bde. R.F.A. wounded O.R.2., 35th Div. Sig.Co.RE wounded O.R.2, (1 at duty), 17th Lancs. Fus. killed O.R.1., 18th Lancs. killed O.R.1. wounded 7., 19th D.L.I. wwounded O.R.2., P.T.O.	

WAR DIARY
INTELLIGENCE SUMMARY

(Erase heading not required.)

Place	Date	Hour	Summary of Events and Information	Remarks and references to Appendices
	22-5-18.		Continued. 15th Cheshires wounded O.R., 14., 15th Sherwoods wounded O.R.1., 4th N.Staffs wounded O.R.29., 17th R.Scots killed O.R.1., wounded 1., 12th HLI. wounded Capt. D.G.WATSON.M.C., Lieut. W.F. BURTON, O.R.64., 106th TMB. wounded O.R.2., 19th Northd. Fus. wounded O.R.6., 35th Bn. M.G.Corps wounded O.R.1., RAMC. attd. 15th Cheshires wounded Capt. D.A.A. DAVIS (AMC).	
	23-5-18.		157th Bde. RFA. wounded O.R.1., 17th Lancs. Fus. wounded O.R.2., missing 2., 18th Lancs. Fus. wounded O.R.3., 19th D.L.I. wounded O.R.7., 15th Cheshires wounded O.R.3., 4th N.Staffs killed O.R.1. wounded 2., 12th HLI. wounded 1 O.R., 19th Northd. Fus. wounded O.R.3., 35th Bn. MGC. wounded O.R.7.	
	24-5-18.		17th Lancs. Fus. wounded 2/Lieut. G.H. DRANSFIELD O.R.5., 18th Lancs. Fus. killed O.R.2. wounded 2., 19th DLI. wounded O.R.1., 15th Cheshires wounded O.R.2., 15th Sherwoods killed O.R.2., wounded 5., 4th N.Staffs wounded Capt. S. JEPSON O.R.4., 12th HLI wounded O.R.3., 35th Bn. MGC wounded 9.	
	25-5-18.		17th Lancs. Fus. wounded 2/Lt. E.E. BENSON, O.R.13, 18th Lancs. Fus. killed O.R.1. wounded 2/Lt. T. COOPER O.R.18., 19th DLI wounded O.R.3., 15th Cheshires killed O.R.2. wounded 11., 15th Sherwoods wounded O.R.3., 4th N.Staffs wounded O.R.1., 17th R. Scots wounded Lieut. S. SINCLAIR O.R.1., 12th HLI wounded 2/Lieut. J.E. LAING O.R.3., 18th HLI wounded O.R.2., 19th Northd. Fus. killed O.R.1. wounded 5., RAMC attd. 17th R. Scots wounded Capt. G.G. CHARTERS.	
	26-5-18.		17th Lancs. Fus. wounded O.R.1., 18th Lancs. Fus. wounded O.R.3., 15th Cheshires killed O.R.1. wounded 2., 15th Sherwoods wounded O.R.3., 4th N. Staffs wounded O.R.1., 17th R. Scots killed accidentally O.R.1., 12th HLI killed O.R.1., wounded Lieut. S.J. HARRIS, O.R.3., 18th HLI wounded O.R.1. (at duty)., 19th Northd. Fus. wounded at duty O.R.1., 35th Bn. MGC wounded O.R.1.	
	27-5-18.		157th Bde. RFA. wounded at duty Lieut. H.R. COOPER, X/35 TMB wounded O.R.3 (1 at duty)., 17th Lancs. Fus. killed O.R.5. wounded Capt. F.L. WAINWRIGHT. M.C., Lieut. H.G. LEAVER. M.C., O.R.4., 15th 19th DLI killed O.R.4. wounded 2/Lieut. T.Y. HAWKIN, Hon. Capt. & Qr. G. JACKSON, O.R.23., 18th HLI Cheshires killed O.R.5. wounded O.R.2., wounded 9., 12th HLI wounded 2/Lieut. H. COWAN O.R.23., 18th HLI 17th R.Scots killed O.R.1. wounded 12 (includes 4 NYDN)., 19th Northd. Fus. wounded at duty O.R.1. killed O.R.1. wounded O.R.	
	28-5-18.		17th Lancs. Fus. wounded 2/Lieut. H.R. PATRICK, 2/Lieut. W. BROOKES, 2/Lieut. J. EDWARDS, 2/Lieut. T.B. LUCEY, (Brookes and Edwards at duty)., O.R.1., 18th Lancs. Fus. killed O.R.1. 15th Cheshires wounded O.R.4., 4th N.Staffs wounded O.R.1., 12th HLI wounded O.R.4., 18th HLI wounded O.R.2., 35th Bn. MGC wounded O.R.1.	
	29-5-18.		18th Lancs. Fus. wounded O.R.1. 19th DLI wounded O.R.1. 15th Cheshires wounded 2/Lieut. F.G. ALLISON O.R.1., 15th Sherwoods wounded O.R.1., 4th N.Staffs wounded O.R.2., 17th R.Scots wounded O.R.2.,	

P.T.O.

Army Form C. 2118.

WAR DIARY
INTELLIGENCE SUMMARY.
(Erase heading not required.)

Instructions regarding War Diaries and Intelligence Summaries are contained in F. S. Regs., Part II. and the Staff Manual respectively. Title pages will be prepared in manuscript.

Place	Date	Hour	Summary of Events and Information	Remarks and references to Appendices
	29-5-18.		Continued. 12th HLI wounded Lieut. A. McDOUGALL. M.C., O.R.2., 18th HLI wounded Capt. L.G.AITKEN 19th North'd. Fus. wounded O.R.1.	
	30-5-18.		H.Q. RE., wounded O.R.2., 17th Lancs. Fus. wounded O.R.2., 15th Cheshires wounded O.R.1., 15th Sherwoods killed O.R.2., 18th HLI wounded O.R.4.	
	31-5-18.		157th Bde. RFA. wounded O.R.3., 203 Fd. Coy. RE. wounded O.R.1., 204th Fd. Coy. RE wounded O.R.4., 205th Fd. Coy. RE wounded at duty O.R.1., 17th Lancs. Fus. wounded 2/Lieut. H.W. PRYCE O.R.4., 18th Lancs. Fus. wounded O.R.1., 105th Inf.Bde. HQ. wounded at duty (Staff Captain) Capt. W.H. ROBSON, 15th Cheshires wounded O.R.5, 15th Sherwoods killed O.R.1. wounded 5., 4th N. Staffs killed O.R.1. wounded 2/Lt. C.F. THOMPSON, O.R.6., 17th R. Scots wounded O.R.1., 12th HLI wounded O.R.1., 19th Northd. Fus. wounded O.R.4., (includes 2 at duty)., 35th Bn. M.G.C. wounded O.R.1.	

COURTS - MARTIAL.

No. of cases brought to trial during the month, and convicted. - 40.

HONOURS & AWARDS.

No. of decorations awarded during the month.

MILITARY CROSS.	D.C.M.	MILITARY MEDAL.
2 x	2	20 ø

x includes 1 Bar.
ø includes 1 Bar.

[signature]
Major-General.
Commanding 35th Division.

8th June, 1918.

Army Form C. 2118.

WAR DIARY

Administrative Staff, 35th Division.

INTELLIGENCE SUMMARY

(Erase heading not required.)

PAGE 1.

Instructions regarding War Diaries and Intelligence Summaries are contained in F.S. Regs., Part II. and the Staff Manual respectively. Title pages will be prepared in manuscript.

Place	Date	Hour	Summary of Events and Information	Remarks and references to Appendices
			CASUALTIES.	
	1-6-18.		159th Bde. R.F.A. wounded O.R.1, 203rd Field Coy. R.E. killed O.R.1., wounded 5 (includes 1 at duty)., 17th Lancs. Fuslrs. wounded Capt. R.S. HEAPE. M.C., Lieut. J.A. SHEARSTON, 2/Lieut. P.Mc. GIVENEY, 2/Lieut. J.H. CARTWRIGHT., wounded O.R.1., 19th Durham L.I. wounded O.R.1., 15th Cheshires wounded O.R., 6., 15th Sherwoods wounded O.R.1., 17th Royal Scots wounded O.R.1., 12th H.L.I. wounded O.R.1., 18th H.L.I. killed 2/Lt. C.S. WEIR., 35th Bn. M.G.Corps killed O.R.1., wounded 1.	
	2-6-18.		157th Bde. R.F.A. wounded O.R.1. (at duty). 203 Fd. Coy. R.E. wounded O.R.4., missing O.R.1.4., (includes 1 wounded & missing)., R.A.M.C. wounded O.R.3., RAMC (M.O.R.C.) U.S.A. attached 18th Lancs. Fuslrs. wounded Capt. C.H. ARNOLD. 17th Lancs. Fuslrs. killed O.R.5., wounded 2/Lieut. C. COOP., 2/Lt. R.L. KEANE wounded O.R.62, missing O.R.15 (includes 2 wounded & missing)., 19th Durham L.I. wounded O.R.1., 15th Cheshires killed Capt. (A/Major) H.J. DRESSER wounded Major A.E.Y. TRESTRAIL (at duty) O.R.5. (includes 3 gassed)., 15th Sherwood Foresters killed O.R.1., wounded O.R.9., missing 5 (believed wounded and admitted to hospital)., 4th North Staffs wounded O.R.3., 17th Royal Scots wounded wounded O.R.2., 12th HLI killed O.R.2., wounded O.R.4., 106th Inf. Bde. wounded Capt. G.C. LYLE (Gas)., 19th Northumberland Fusiliers killed O.R.1., wounded 28 (includes 4 at duty)., 35th Bn M.G.C. wounded 2/Lt. E. STAINTON O.R.12. missing O.R.1.	
	3-6-18.		18th Lancs. Fuslrs. killed Capt. W.S. MORRIS 2/Lt. C. THOMPSON O.R.17., wounded Lieut. H.F. WARD, M.C. 2/Lt. A. CROWDER 2/Lt. E.L. PARRY 2/Lt. R.H. TURNBULL 2/Lt. G.E.K. PRITCHETT 2/Lt. W.H. GRESTY (at duty), O.R. 131., Wounded and missing 2/Lt. H.B. ALMOND, wounded 2/Lt. T.C. CRAWSHAW. Missing 73 includes 12 wounded and missing, 203 Field Coy. R.E. killed O.R.1., 17th Lancs. Fus. wounded Lieut. (A/CApt). W.A. CALDWELL (at duty) O.R.1. (at duty)., 18th Lancs. Fus. O.R.3., 20th Lancs. rus. 2/Lt. M. ANDREW, wounded., 15th Cheshires wounded O.R.4., 15th Sherwood Foresters killed O.R.1., wounded 4., 17th R. Scots wounded 2/Lt. C. WILLIAMSON, O.R.2., 12th H.L.I. wounded O.R.1., 18th H.L.I. killed O.R.1., wounded 10., 19th Northumberland Fusiliers killed O.R.2., 35th Bn. M.G.C. killed O.R.1. wounded 8.,	
	4-6-18.		157th Bde. R.F.A. wounded O.R.1., 34th A.F.A. Bde. wounded O.R.3., (includes 2 gassed)., 19th Durham L.I. killed O.R.8., wounded 2/Lt. H.R. CUNLIFFE wounded O.R. 44, missing 4 (includes 3 wounded and missing., 15th Sherwood Foresters wounder O.R.1. (includes 1 gassed and 1 NYD)., 4th North Staffs killed O.R.1. wounded 2., 17th Royal Scots wounded 3 (includes 1 at duty)., 12th H.L.I. wounded O.R.3., 18th H.L.I. killed O.R.1. wounded O.R.6., 19th N.F. wounded O.R.6. No missing 24 (Includes 1 missing believed killed and 4 believed wounded).	

Army Form C. 2118.

WAR DIARY
INTELLIGENCE SUMMARY

(Erase heading not required.)

Instructions regarding War Diaries and Intelligence Summaries are contained in F.S. Regs., Part II. and the Staff Manual respectively. Title pages will be prepared in manuscript.

Place	Date	Hour	Summary of Events and Information	Remarks and references to Appendices
	5-6-18.		204 Fd. Coy. R.E. wounded O.R.1., 15th Cheshires wounded O.R.2., 15th Sherwoods killed O.R.1. wounded 4., 4th North Staffs wounded O.R.1., 12th High.L.I. wounded O.R.2., 18th High.L.I. wounded O.R.7., 35th Bn. M.G. Corps wounded O.R.1., 105th Fd. Ambce. RAMC. wounded O.R.1.	
	6-6-18.		17th Lancs. Fus. wounded O.R.1., 19th D.L.I. wounded O.R.5. (includes 1 accidental)., 15th Cheshires wounded Capt. R. FROST 2/Lt. R.C. CANNON O.R.1., 4th N. Staffs wounded O.R.2 (1 S.I.). 17th R. Scots wounded O.R.5., 12th H.L.I. killed Lt. (A/Capt) D.R. SILLARS wounded Lt.Col. J.N.O. RYCROFT, (at duty), Lt. W.T. McKELLAR, Lt. H.G. NICHOLSON O.R.1., 18th High.L.I. wounded 2/Lt. A.P CURRIE,M.C. O.R.2., 19th Northd. Fus. O.R.1., 35th Bn. M.G.C. O.R.2. wounded. (1 at duty).	
	7-6-18.		157th Bde. R.F.A. wounded Capt. (A/Major) C.H. MORTIMER, (Gas)., 203 Fd. Coy. R.E. killed O.R.5. wounded O.R.1., 19th Durham L.I. wounded O.R.3., 17th Royal Scots wounded O.R.1., 12th High.L.I. killed O.R.1. wounded 4., 35th Bn. M.G.C. wounded O.R.1.	
	8-6-18.		157th Bde. R.F.A. wounded O.R.2., 17th Lancs. Fus Killed O.R.1., wounded 2/Lt. M. LANCASTER, 2/Lt. E.H. GUY, O.R.2., 18th Lancs. Fus. killed O.R.1., 19th D.L.I. wounded O.R.2., 15th Cheshires wounded O.R.4. (includes 3 at duty)., 17th Royal Scots wounded O.R.7., 12th H.L.I. killed O.R.2., wounded 2/Lt. E.T.R. HANNAH, 2/Lt. S. DUNCAN., O.R.23., 18th High.L.I. wounded 2/Lt. J.G.M. BAIRD O.R., 2., 19th Northumberland Fus. wounded O.R.3. (includes 1 at duty)., 35th Bn, MG.Corps wounded Lieut. N.W. AKHURST, 2/Lt. W.E.W. HAWKINS. O.R.2.,	
	9-6-18.		X/35 T.M.B. wounded O.R.1., 17th Lancs. Fuslrs. Wounded Lieut. A. POWELL O.R.2., 18th Lancs. Fus. killed O.R.1., 15th Cheshires wounded O.R.3., 17th Royal Scots killed O.R.2. wounded 2/Lt. J. MOYES, 12th High.L.I. killed O.R.3., wounded 15., 18th High.L.I. killed O.R.1. wounded 11.	
	10-6-18.		203 Fd. Coy. R.E. wounded O.R.2., 17th Lancs. Fus. wounded O.R.1., 18th Lancs. Fus. killed O.R.2., wounded 3., 15th Cheshires wounded O.R.4. (includes 2 at duty), 15th Sherwood Foresters wounded Lieut. W.J. MORGAN, 4th North Staffs wounded O.R.1., 17th R. Scots wounded O.R.2., 12th High.L.I. killed O.R.1., wounded 2/Lt. F.S. SUTHERLAND O.R.1., 19th Northd. Fus. wounded O.R.1., 18th High. L.I. wounded O.R.1., 35th Bn. M.G.Corps wounded O.R.2.	
	11-6-18.		157 Bde. R.F.A. wounded O.R.3., 159 Bde. R.F.A. wounded O.R.1., 17th Lancs. Fus. wounded O.R.2., 18th Lancs. Fus. killed O.R.2., wounded 11., 15th Cheshires wounded O.R.2., 15th Sherwoods wounded O.R.10.	P.T.O.

Army Form C. 2118.

WAR DIARY
INTELLIGENCE SUMMARY.
(Erase heading not required.)

Instructions regarding War Diaries and Intelligence Summaries are contained in F.S. Regs., Part II. and the Staff Manual respectively. Title pages will be prepared in manuscript.

Place	Date	Hour	Summary of Events and Information	Remarks and references to Appendices
	11-6-18.		Continued. 4th North Staffs wounded O.R.2., 17th Royal Scots wounded O.R.3, 12th High.L.I. wounded O.R.3., 18th High.L.I. wounded O.R.1., 35th Bn. M.G.Corps wounded O.R.1.	
	12-6-18.		X/35 T.M.B. wounded O.R.1. 18th Lancs. Fus. wounded O.R.1. 15th Sherwood Foresters wounded 2/Lt. W.B. WALKER O.R.8., 4th North Staffs wounded 2/Lt. A.G. KING O.R.2., 17th R. Scots killed O.R.1. wounded 2., 12th Highland L.I. wounded O.R.8. missing 2., 106th T.M.B. wounded O.R.1.	
	13-6-18.		18th Lancs. Fus. wounded O.R.4., 15th Cheshires wounded O.R.1., 15th Sherwood Foresters wounded O.R.1. (at duty)., 17th R. Scots wounded O.R.1., 12th H.L.I. wounded O.R.4. (includes 1 accidental)., 18th H.L.I. wounded O.R.1.	
	14-6-18.		157 Bde. RFA wounded O.R.1., 17th Lancs. Fus. wounded O.R.2., 18th Lancs. Fus. killed O.R.5., wounded 4., 19th D.L.I. killed O.R.1. wounded 3., 15th Cheshires wounded O.R.1., 17th R.Scots wounded O.R.3., 12th H.L.I. wounded O.R.1., 18th H.L.I. wounded O.R.3.,	
	15-6-18.		17th Lancs.Killed O.R.1., 18th Lancs. Fus. wounded 8., 18th Lancs. Fus. wounded O.R.1., 19th D.L.I. wounded O.R.14. 17th R. Scots wounded O.R.7 (2 accidental)., Missing O.R.1., 12th Highland L.I. wounded O.R.4., 18th H.L.I. wounded O.R.3., 106th T.M.B. wounded O.R.1.	
	16-6-18.		X/35 T.M.B. wounded O.R.1., 17th Lancs. Fus. wounded O.R.1., 17th R.Scots wounded O.R.2., 12th H.L.I. wounded O.R.1., 18th H.L.I. wounded O.R.2., 19th Northd. Fus. Killed O.R.1. wounded 1.	
	17-6-18.		17th Lancs. Fus. killed O.R.2. wounded 3 (1 S.I.)., 19th D.L.I. Killed O.R.1. wounded O.R.3. (2 at duty).	
	18-6-18.		203 Fd. Coy. R.E. wounded O.R.2.	
	19-6-18.		NIL.	
	20-6-18.		NIL.	
	21-6-18.		15th Cheshires killed O.R.1. wounded 1., 15th Sherwood Foresters killed O.R.1., 4th North Staffs wounded O.R.1., 35th Bn. M.G. Corps wounded O.R.9.	
	22-6-18.		106th T.M.B. wounded O.R.1., 35th Bn. M.G.Corps wounded at duty O.R.1.	
	23-6-18.		15th Cheshires wounded O.R.2. (accidental)., 4th North Staffs wounded 2/Lt. R.C. BUTTERS.	
	24-6-18.		NIL.	
	25-6-18.		NIL.	

Army Form C. 2118

WAR DIARY
INTELLIGENCE SUMMARY
(Erase heading not required.)

-3-

Instructions regarding War Diaries and Intelligence Summaries are contained in F.S. Regs., Part II. and the Staff Manual respectively. Title Pages will be prepared in manuscript.

Place	Date	Hour	Summary of Events and Information	Remarks and references to Appendices
	26-6-18		18th Lancs. Fus. O.R. wounded 4 (accidentally)., 35th D.A.C. wounded O.R.1.	
	27-6-18		NIL.	
	28-6-18		NIL.	
	29-6-18		232 Div. Emp. Co. Wounded O.R.1., 17th Lancs. Fus. wounded O.R.3. (1 at duty)., 19th D.L.I. wounded O.R.2, 19th Northd. F. killed 2/Lt. R.E. WILLIAMS.	
	30-6-18		NIL.	
			HONOURS AND REWARDS.	
			D.S.O. M.C. D.C.M. M.M.	
			1 12 2 46	
			1 Bar. 4 Bars.	
			COURTS-MARTIAL.	
			Number of Courts-Martial during month :- 35.	

H. Forward
Lieut.Colonel
for Major-General.
Commanding 35th Division.

Army Form C. 2118.

WAR DIARY
~~INTELLIGENCE~~ SUMMARY.

ADMINISTRATIVE STAFF, 35th DIVISION.

(Erase heading not required.)

Instructions regarding War Diaries and Intelligence Summaries are contained in F. S. Regs, Part II and the Staff Manual respectively. Title pages will be prepared in manuscript.

Place	Date	Hour	Summary of Events and Information	Remarks and references to Appendices
	1-7-18.		NIL.	
	2-7-18.		NIL.	
	3-7-18.		NIL.	
	4-7-18.		NIL.	
	5-7-18.		NIL.	
	6-7-18.		NIL.	
	7-7-18.		35th Div. Sig. Co. R.E. killed Lieut. E.M. SUTTON (24-3-18)., 18th Lancs. Fus. wounded S.L. O.R.1 15th Cheshires.killed O.R.1., wounded Lieut. A. WALKER (at duty). 159 Bde. R.F.A wounded O.R.2., 17th Lancs. Fus. killed O.R.1. wounded O.R.3., 18th Lancs. Fus. killed O.R.1. Wounded O.R.3., 19th D.L.I. wounded 2/Lt. H.V. TYLER (Shell Shock)., 4th North Staffs killed O.R.1. wounded 1., 18th H.L.I. killed O.R.1. wounded 1.	
	8-7-18.		17th Lancs. Fus. killed O.R.1. wounded 2., 18th Lancs. wounded Lieut. E.B. KEATING O.R.3., 18th H.L.I. wounded O.R.1., 35th Bn. M.G.C. wounded 2/Lt. O.A. WILCOX (at duty) O.R.2., 35th Div. H.Q. wounded O.R.1.,	
	9-7-18.		18th Lancs. Fus. wounded O.R.1.(1 S.I.).15th Cheshires wounded O.R.2. (1 S.I.) 17th R.Scots wounded O.R.3., 35th EN. M.G.Corps killed O.R.1.	
	10-7-18.		35th Div. H.Q. wounded O.R.1. (at duty)., 35th Div. Sig. Co.RE. wounded O.R.4. 157 Bde. R.F.A. wounded O.R.1., 159 Bde. R.F.A. wounded O.R.2., 15th Cheshires wounded O.R.5., 15th Sherwood Foresters wounded O.R.2., (S.I.)., 17th R.Scots wounded O.R.1., 18th H.L.I. wounded O.R.2.	
	11-7-18.		18th Lancs. Fus. wounded O.R.2., 15th Sherwood For. killed O.R.1. wounded O.R.2., 4th North Staffs. wounded O.R.1.	
	12-7-18.		157 Bde. R.F.A. wounded O.R.2., 159 Bde. R.F.A. wounded O.R.5., 203 Fd. Coy. R.E. killed O.R.1., 18th Lancs. Fus. wounded 2/Lt. L. CLARK O.P.2., 19th D.L.I. wounded O.R.2., 4th North Staffs killed O.R.1. wounded O.R.3., 17th R. Scots wounded O.R.2.	
	13-7-18.		159 Bde. R.F.A. wounded O.R.1., 17th Lancs. Fus. wounded O.R.1., 19th D.L.I. wounded O.R.2.,(1 at duty)., 4th North Staffs killed O.R.1., 17th R. Scots wounded O.R.1. 12th H.L.I. wounded O.R.1., 35th Bn. M.G.Corps wounded O.R.1.	
	14-7-18.		159 Bde. R.F.A. wounded O.R.1., 17th Lancs. Fus. wounded O.R.1., 19th D.L.I. wounded O.R.7., 15th Sherwood Foresters killed O.R.4., wounded 5., missing 3., 17th R.Scots wounded O.R.2., 12th H.L.I. wounded O.R.1.	
	15-7-18.		203 Fd.Coy. RE. killed O.R.1., 18th Lancs.Fus. wounded 2/Lt. T.C.A. HILL O.R.8. missing 1., 19th D.L.I. killed O.R.2., wounded 2/Lt. R. HADFIELD, 2/Lt. W.R. BRUCE, O.R.6., 15th Sherwood Foresters killed O.R.1. wounded 6., 17th R. Scots killed O.R.2. wounded 2., 12th H.L.I wounded O.R.3.	

P.T.O.

Army Form C. 2118.

WAR DIARY
or
INTELLIGENCE SUMMARY
(Erase heading not required.)

Instructions regarding War Diaries and Intelligence Summaries are contained in F. S. Regs., Part II. and the Staff Manual respectively. Title pages will be prepared in manuscript.

Place	Date	Hour	Summary of Events and Information	Remarks and references to Appendices
	16th.7.18.		17th Lan. Fus. wounded O.R. 1 (SI), 19th D.L.I. wounded 3, 15th Sherwoods killed 1, wounded 3, missing 4, 17th R.Scots wounded 2 (1 accidental), 12th H.L.I. wounded 1.	
	17.7.18.		203 field Co. R.E. wounded O.R. 2 (1 at duty) 17th Lan. Fus. wounded 3, 18th Lan. Fus. killed 6, wounded 11, 19th D.L.I. wounded 1, 15th Cheshires killed 16.7.18. 2/Lt. H.A.WAINWRIGHT, wounded 2/Lt. H.D.GALLAGHER, M.C. killed O.R.4 wounded 14. 15th Sherwoods killed 6, wounded 4, missing 1, 35th Bn. M.G.C. killed 2 wounded 4, 107th Field Ambce. wounded 1.	
	18.7.18.		203 Field Co. killed 1, wounded 2 (1 NYD), 17th Lan. Fus. killed 6, wounded 6, 18th Lan. Fus. wounded 6, 15th Cheshires wounded 4 (1 S.I.), 17th R. Scots killed 2/Lt. A.WILSON 16.7.18., O.R. 4, wounded 9, 12th H.L.I. killed 1., 35th Bn. M.G.C. wounded 2 (1 at duty)	
	19.7.18.		15th Ches. killed O.r. 2, wounded 3 (1 NYD), 15th Sherwoods wounded at duty 1, 19th N.F. killed 1, wounded at duty 1, 18th Lan. Fus. wounded 2 (1 NYD, 1 SIW), 12th H.L.I. wounded 8, missing 1, 18th H.L.I. wounded 5, 35th Bn. M.G.C. wounded 1.	
	20.7.18.		157 Bde. R.F.A. wounded 1, 159 Bde. RFA. wounded 1, 17th Lan. Fus. killed 2/Lt. T.W.M.GREENWELL 19.7.18., wounded O.R. 4, 15th Ches. wounded 4, 12th H.L.I. wounded 1 accidentally 18th H.L.I. killed 1, wounded 5 (1 accidental), 35th Bn. M.G.C. wounded 1.	
	21.7.18.		17th Lan. Fus. wounded 2/Lt. W.H.BREARLEY (19.7.18.) killed O.R. 2, wounded 3, 4th N.Staffs. wounded 2 (1 S.I.), 12th H.L.I. wounded Lt. H.M.SCOTT (18.7.18.), 35th Bn. M.G.C. wounded 1.	
	22.7.18.		17th Lan. Fus. missing 2, 18th Lan. Fus. wounded 6, 19th D.L.I. killed 1, wounded 3, 15th Sherwoods wounded 5, 4th N.Staffs. wounded 1, 17th R. Scots wounded 1, 12th H.L.I. wounded 2, 18th H.L.I. wounded 1, 19th N.Fus. wounded 4 (1 at duty)	
	23.7.18.		159 Bde. RFA. wounded 1 (accidental), 18th Lan. Fus. killed 1, wounded 2, 12th H.L.I. wounded 2,	
	24.7.18.		18th Lan. Fus. wounded 6, 19th D.L.I. wounded 5, 4th N.Staffs. killed 3, wounded 8, 17th R.Scots wounded accidentally 3, 18th H.L.I. wounded 4, 35th Bn. M.G.C. killed 1, wounded 2	

Army Form C. 2118.

WAR DIARY
or
INTELLIGENCE SUMMARY.
(Erase heading not required.)

Instructions regarding War Diaries and Intelligence Summaries are contained in F. S. Regs., Part II. and the Staff Manual respectively. Title pages will be prepared in manuscript.

Place	Date	Hour	Summary of Events and Information	Remarks and references to Appendices
	25.7.18.		157 Bde. R.F.A. wounded O.R.1, 15th Sherwoods killed 1, wounded 3 (2 at duty), missing 2/Lt. C.E.MANSHI (24.7.18.) O.R.2, 4th N.Staffs, killed 1, wounded 8 (1 S.I.), 17th R. Scots wounded 2, 18th H.L.I. killed 1, wounded 5, 19th N.F. killed 2, wounded 6 (3 at duty)	
	26.7.18.		203 Field Co. R.E. wounded O.R. 2 (1 at duty), 15th Sherwoods wounded 1, 18th H.L.I. wounded 4, 35th Bn. M.G.C. wounded 1 (Gas)	
	27.7.18.		203 Field Co. wounded accidentally 2/Lt. L.HOLDEN (18.7.18.), 19th D.L.I. killed 1, wounded 1(SI) 15th Ches. wounded 1, 15th Sherwoods wounded 5, 35th Bn. M.G.C. wounded 2/Lt. C.A.WILCOX (26.7.18.) wounded O.R.1, 232 Div. Emp. Co. wounded 3.	
	28.7.18.		159 Bde. R.F.A. wounded O.R.4, 35th Div. Sig. Co. wounded 2, 17th Lan. Fus. killed 5, wounded 2 19th D.L.I. wounded Captain J.W.RIAL, Captain K.SMITH, 2/Lt. G.DYER, M.C., 2/Lt. H.W.JORDAN (27.7.18.) (3 at duty) wounded O.R. 24, 15th Ches. wounded 1, 15th Sherwood Fores. killed 2/Lt. C.E.WOODROFFE (27.7.18.) killed O.R.1, wounded 2.	
	29.7.18.		203 Field Co. missing O.R.1, 17th Lan. Fus. killed O.R.1, wounded 2/Lt. E.E.BENSON (29.7.18.) 15th Ches. killed O.R. 2, 15th Sherwoods killed 1, wounded 1 (SI), 19th N.F. wounded 3 (2 at duty) 35th Bn. M.G.C. killed 1, wounded 1.	
	30.7.18.		159 Bde. R.F.A. wounded O.R.1, 17th Lan. Fus. wounded 1, 18th Lan. Fus. wounded 1, 4th N.Staffs. wounded (at duty) T/Lt. J.J.HUGHES, wounded (at duty) O.R. 2,	
	31.7.18.		157 Bde. R.F.A. wounded O.R. 4 (1 at duty), 18th Lan. Fus. killed O.R. 2, wounded 2/Lt.J.WHITE (30.7.18.), wounded O.R. 3, 15th Ches. wounded O.R.1, missing 3, 4th N.Staffs. wounded O.R.4, 19th N.F. wounded O.R. 11 (1 at duty), 35th Bn. M.G.C. wounded 3.	

HONOURS & REWARDS.

M.C. M.M.
 1   3

COURTS-MARTIAL.

27 during month.

H. Farnal Lieut-Colonel
for Major-General.
Commanding 35th Division.

D.A.G., 3rd Echelon.

Herewith War Diary for the Administrative Branch, 35th Division, for the month of August, 1918.

8th September, 1918.
PH.

[Signature]
Major-General.
Commanding 35th Division.

Army Form C. 2118.

WAR DIARY or INTELLIGENCE SUMMARY

35th Division Administrative Branch.

(Erase heading not required.)

Instructions regarding War Diaries and Intelligence Summaries are contained in F.S. Regs., Part II. and the Staff Manual respectively. Title pages will be prepared in manuscript.

Place	Date	Hour	Summary of Events and Information	Remarks and references to Appendices
			CASUALTIES.	
	1-8-18.		17th Lancs. Fus. wounded O.R.9., (includes 6 at duty)., 15th Cheshires wounded O.R.6. (1 S.I.). 203 Fd. Co. R.E. wounded O.R.2.	
	2-8-18.		203 Fd.Co. R.E. wounded O.R.1. (at duty)., 17th Lancs. Fus. wounded O.R.3. (2 at duty)., 106th Light T.M.B. (19th D.L.I.) T/Lieut. W.V. FALKINER, M.G. wounded., 19th North'd. Fus. wounded O.R.4. (1 at duty & 1 accidental).	
	3-8-18.		157 Bde. RfrA. wounded O.R.1., 35th D.A.C. wounded O.R.1., 15th Cheshires wounded O.R.1., 15th Sherwood Foresters wounded O.R.1.	
	4-8-18.		17th Lancs. Fus. killed O.R.2. wounded 2., 15th Sherwoods wounded O.R.1. at duty, 4th North Staffs wounded O.R.1., 12th High. L.I. wounded O.R.2., 18th High. L.I. wounded O.R.1.,killed O.R.1. (both accidental)., 35th Bn. M.G.Corps wounded O.R.2.	
	5-8-18.		X/35 T.M.B. wounded O.R.1. (accidental)., 17th Lancs. Fus. killed O.R.1. wounded 2., 18th Lancs Fuslrs. killed O.R.1., wounded 9., Missing 2., 2/Lt. W.J. HENDERSON, wounded., 15th Sherwoods wounded O.R.1., 4th North Staffs wounded O.R.2. (1 S.I.)., 17th Royal S ets wounded O.R.1., 19th North'd. Fuslrs. wounded O.R.3. (2 at duty)., 35th Bn. M.G.Corps killed O.R.1. wounded 8.	
	6-8-18.		203 Fd. Co. R.E. wounded O.R.1. (at duty)., Missing O.R.1., 18th Lancs. Fus. wounded O.R.10 (includes 2 at duty)., 19th D.L.I. wounded O.R.3., 17th R. Scots wounded O.R.5. (1 accidental)., 19th North'd. Fus. wounded O.R.1., 35th Bn. M.G. Corps wounded O.R.1.	
	7-8-18.		17th Lancs. Fus. killed O.R.1. wounded 4., 19th D.L.I. wounded O.R.1., 15th Cheshires wounded O.R.1., 17th R. Scots wounded O.R.1.	
	8-8-18.		35th D.A.C. killed O.R.4. wounded 2., X/35 T.M.B. killed O.R.1., Y/35 T.M.B. wounded O.R.4. (1 at duty)., 204 Fd. Co. R.E. wounded O.R.1., 15th Cheshires wounded Lieut. H. ARNFIELD, Capt. C.E. CUNNINGHAM (at duty)., O.R.2., 15th Sherwoods wounded O.R.1., 4th North Staffs wounded O.R.2., 17th R. Scots wounded O.R.2., 12th H.L.I. wounded O.R.4., 19th North'd. Fus. wounded O.R.3.	
	9-8-18.		19th D.L.I. killed O.R.3., wounded 11., 17th R. Scots wounded O.R.5., 12th High. L.I. killed O.R.1. wounded 4., 35th Bn. M.G. Corps wounded O.R.1.	
	10-8-18.		NIL.	
	11-8-18.		17th R. Scots wounded O.R.1. (at duty).	
	12-8-18.		NIL.	
	13-8-18.		203 Fd. Co. R.E. wounded O.R.1. (at duty)., 35th Divl. Train. killed O.R.2., wounded 1.	
	14-8-18.		35th D.A.C. wounded O.R.1. (S.I)., 18th Lancs. Fus. wounded Capt. M.Y. NUNNERLEY M.C. (accidentally at duty)., 19th North'd. Fuslrs. wounded O.R.1.	
	15-8-18.		NIL.	
	16-8-18.		NIL.	

F.T.O.

Army Form C. 2118.

WAR DIARY

INTELLIGENCE SUMMARY

(Erase heading not required.)

Instructions regarding War Diaries and Intelligence Summaries are contained in F. S. Regs., Part II. and the Staff Manual respectively. Title pages will be prepared in manuscript.

Place	Date	Hour	Summary of Events and Information	Remarks and references to Appendices
	17-8-18.		159 Bde. R.F.A. wounded O.R.5.,	
	18-8-18.		NIL.	
	19-8-18.		NIL.	
	20-8-18.		NIL.	
	21-8-18.		15th Sherwoods wounded O.R.1. 19th Northd. Fus. killed O.R.1. wounded 5.	
	22-8-18.		35th Bn. M.G. Corps wounded O.R.2 (includes 1st duty).	
	23-8-18.		19th Northd. Fus. killed O.R. 5 wounded 8 (4 at duty)., 35th BN. M.G. Corps wounded O.R.8.	
	24-8-18.		19th Northfd. Fus. killed O.R.2. wounded 1.	
	25-8-18.		157 Bde. R.F.A. killed O.R.2., wounded Lieut. G.P. DOUGLASS. M.C. O.R.3. 19th Northd. Fus. wounded O.R.2. (1 at duty).	
	26-8-18.		NIL.	
	27-8-18.		NIL.	
	28-8-18.		NIL.	
	29-8-18.		NIL.	
	30-8-18.		NIL.	
	31-8-18.		NIL.	

HONOURS AND REWARDS.

MILITARY CROSS.   D.C.M.   MILITARY MEDAL.
      4   2 and 1 Bar.   12

COURTS-MARTIAL.

48 cases tried.

8-9-18.
PH.

Major-General.
Commanding 35th Division.

Army Form C. 2118.

WAR DIARY
or
INTELLIGENCE SUMMARY.

35th Divl. Administrative Staff.

(Erase heading not required.)

Instructions regarding War Diaries and Intelligence Summaries are contained in F.S. Regs., Part II. and the Staff Manual respectively. Title pages will be prepared in manuscript.

Place	Date	Hour	Summary of Events and Information	Remarks and references to Appendices
			CASUALTIES.	
	1-9-18.		17th R. Scots wounded accidentally O.R.1., 18th High. L.I. wounded O.R.1.	
	2-9-18.		NIL.	
	3-9-18.		35th Bn. M.G. Corps wounded O.R.3.	
	4-9-18.		203 Field Co. Accidentally Injured 2/Lt. G. LEGG, R.E., 12th Highland L.I. wounded O.R.4., 18th Highland L.I. wounded Capt. J.N. FERGUSON, O.R.7.	
	5-9-18.		15th Cheshires wounded O.R.1., LXXX 4th North Staffs Wounded (Gas) O.R.17., 12th High L.I. wounded O.R.22 (19 gassed)., 18th Highland L.I. killed O.R.1. wounded 6.	
	6-9-18.		15th Cheshires wounded O.R.1., 4th North Staffs wounded O.R.8. (6 gassed)., 12th High. L.I. killed O.R.2. wounded at duty Lieut. H.E. BETHUNE O.R. 14 (1 gassed and 1 accidental). 17th R. Scots wounded O.R.2. (1 gassed)., 106th T.M.B. wounded O.R.2., 105th Fd. Ambce RAMC. wounded O.R.2.	
	7-9-18.		15th Cheshires wounded O.R.4., 15th Sherwoods killed O.R.1. wounded 2., 17th R.Scots wounded O.R.2., 12th Highland L.I. Killed Lieut. H.M. Scott, O.R.2., wounded O.R.4. (1 accidental) Missing O.R.1., 18th Highland L.I. wounded O.R.1. (1 gassed).	
	8-9-18.		157 Bde. RFA. wounded O.R.2. (1 at duty)., 35th Div. Sig.Co.RE. wounded Gas O.R.3., 15th Sherwoods wounded O.R.3. (Gas)., 4th North Staffs wounded O.R.2. (1 gassed)., 17th R. Scots wounded O.R.6. (1 accidental)., 12th High. L.I. wounded O.R.2. (Gas)., 18th High. L.I. killed O.R.2. wounded 6 (1 at duty & 3 gassed)., 19th North. Fus. injured accidentally O.R.1.	
	9-9-18.		159 Bde. RFA. wounded O.R.1., 35th Div. Sig. Co.RE. wounded Gas O.R.1., 17th Lancs. Fus. Missing O.R.3., 18th Lancs. Fus. killed O.R.1. wounded 1., 19th Durham L.I. wounded O.R.1., 15th Sherwoods wounded Gas O.R.1., 4th N. Staffs wounded O.R.2., 17th R.Scots wounded O.R.5., 35th Bn. MG. wounded O.R.2. (1 at duty).	
	10-9-18.		17th Lancs. Fus. killed O.R.7. wounded 2/Lieut. J. Edwards, O.R.1. (at duty)., 15th Sherwoods wounded Gas O.R.3., 17th R.Scots wounded Gas 2/Lt. J.D. Crawford, O.R.4 (1 accidental and 1 Gassed).	
	11-9-18.		18th Lancs. Fus. killed O.R.2., 17th R. Scots wounded accidentally O.R.1., 12th High. L.I. wounded O.R.2., 19th N.F. wounded O.R.1. accidentally injured O.R.1.	
	12-9-18.		204 Fd. Co.RE. KX Injured accidentally O.R.1., 17th Lancs. Fus. wounded O.R.1. 18th Lancs. Fus. wounded O.R.2., 17th R. Scots wounded O.R.3., 12th highland L.I. wounded O.R.1., 19th Northd. Fus. wounded O.R.2., (1 at duty).	

P.T.O.

Army Form C. 2118.

WAR DIARY
INTELLIGENCE SUMMARY

(Erase heading not required.)

Instructions regarding War Diaries and Intelligence Summaries are contained in F.S. Regs., Part II and the Staff Manual respectively. Title pages will be prepared in manuscript.

Place	Date	Hour	Summary of Events and Information	Remarks and references to Appendices
	13-9-18.		204 Fd. Co. RE. wounded O.R.1, 205 Fd.Co.RE. wounded O.R.3., 17th Lancs. Fus. wounded O.R.1., 18th Lancs.Fus. wounded O.R.3., 19th Durham L.I. Killed O.R.2., wounded 1., 15th Sherwoods wounded O.R.1., 4th N.Staffs Killed O.R.1., wounded 5. (1 S.I)., 17th R. Scots killed O.R.l., 19th Northd. Fus. Killed O.R.1. wounded 4., 35th Bn. M.G.Corps wounded O.R.1.	
	14-9-18.		18th Lancs. Fus. Killed O.R.1. 19th Durham L.I. wounded O.R.1., 15th Sherwoods wounded at duty O.R.1., 19th Northd. Fus. accidentally injured O.R.1., 35th bn. M.G.Corps wounded O.R.2.	
	15-9-18.		157 Bde. RFA. accidentally injured O.R.1., 19th Durham L.I. wounded at duty O.R.1., 15th Sherwoods wounded O.R.4. (1 gassed), 4th N.Staffs wounded O.R.1., 17th R.Scots wounded O.R.1., 19th Northd. Killed O.R.1. wounded at duty O.R.1., 35th Bn. M.G.Corps wounded O.R.1.	
	16-9-18.		203 Fd.Co.RE. killed O.R.1., 18th Lancs. Fus. wounded O.R.3. (1 at duty), 19th Durham L.I. Killed 2/Lt. J. REID O.R.4., wounded O.R.7., 104 T.M.B. wounded Lieut. G.B. Pearson O.R.1. at duty.	
	17-9-18.		157 Bde. RFA. wounded O.R.1., 15th Sherwoods wounded O.R.4., 17th R.Scots wounded O.R.3., 18th High.L.I. wounded 2/Lt. H.J. Cross,M.M., O.R.1., 35th Bn. M.G. wounded O.R.4.	
	18-9-18.		203 Fd.Co.RE. Killed O.R.1., 205 Fd.Co.RE. wounded 2/Lt. W.G.Hill, O.R.3., 19th Northd. Fus. wounded O.R.2., 15th Sherwoods Killed O.R.2., 35th Bn. M.G. Corps. wounded at duty O.R.1.	
	19-9-18.		17th Lancs. Fus. wounded O.R.1., 15th Cheshires Killed Lieut. W.G.Stott, O.R.1., wounded O.R.6 (2 at duty)., 15th Sherwoods wounded O.R.3., 17th R.Scots killed Major (A/Lt-Col) A.G. SOUGAL,M.C., O.R., wounded 2/Lieut. G. Mann, O.R.12, (1 at duty and 3 gassed)., 12th High. L.I. wounded O.R.1. 18th Highland L.I. wounded O.R.6., ASG.M.T., Attd. 105th Fd.Ambce.RAMC. wounded O.R.1.	
	20-9-18.		35th D.A.C. accidentally injured O.R.1., 205 Fd.Co.RE. killed O.R.1., 15th Sherwoods wounded O.R.2., 17th R.Scots wounded O.R.2., 18th High. L.I. wounded O.R.3., 35th Bn. M.G.C. wounded O.R.2 (1 at duty).	
	21-9-18.		203 Fd.Co.RE. wounded at duty O.R.1., 205 Fd.Co.RE. wounded at duty O.R.1., 18th Lancs.Fus. wounded Lieut. A.T. Sheahan, 17th R.Scots wounded O.R.10 (2 at duty)., 12th High.L.I. wounded O.R.19. (2 at duty)., 18th High. L.I. wounded O.R.1.	
	22-9-18.		157 Bde. RFA. wounded at duty O.R.2., 35th DAC. wounded O.R.1., 205 Fd.Co.Re. wounded at duty O.R.1., 17th Lancs. Fus. wounded accidentally O.R.1., 17th R.Scots killed O.R.1. wounded 2., 12th High.L.I. wounded O.R.1., 18th High. L.I. wounded O.R.3., 12th H.L.I. Attd. 106th TMB. wounded O.R.1. (at duty)., 35th Bn. M.G.C. wounded O.R.1.	
	23-9-18.		157 Bde. RFA. wounded 2/Lt. (A/Capt) P.M.Leckie, O.R.2. (1 gassed), 159 Bde. RFA. wounded O.R.1., 17th Lancs. Fus. killed O.R.1. wounded 2., 15th 203 Fd.Co.RE. wounded O.R.2., 18th R.Scots wounded O.R.1. Sherwoods wounded O.R.2.,	

PTO

WAR DIARY
INTELLIGENCE SUMMARY.
(Erase heading not required.)

Army Form C. 2118.

Place	Date	Hour	Summary of Events and Information	Remarks and references to Appendices
	24-9-18.		12th E.L.I. Killed O.R. wounded O.R.1., 18th H.L.I. killed O.R.1. wounded 2/Lt. J. BAIRD, O.R.10., 157 Bde. RFA. wounded O.R.2. (1 at duty).	
	25-9-18.		17th Lancs. Fus. killed O.R.3. wounded at duty O.R.1., 18th Lancs. wounded O.R.2., 19th Durham L.I. wounded O.R.14 (2 at duty)., Missing O.R.1., 15th Cheshires killed O.R.1. wounded 2/Lt. J.H. Slater, O.R.2., 15th Sherwoods wounded O.R.1., 17th R.Scots killed O.R.1. wounded 2/Lt. A.S. ASQUITH, O.R.8.; 12th H.L.I. wounded O.R.5., 19th Northd. Fus. wounded O.R.1., 35th Bn. M.G.Corps wounded O.R.2.	
	26-9-18.		17th R.Scots wounded at duty O.R.1., 12th H.L.I. killed O.R.1., 19th North. Fus. wounded Gas O.R.90.	
	27-9-18.		157 Bde. RFA. killed O.R.1., 17th R.Scots wounded O.R.4. (3 gas, 1 accidental)., 19th Northd. Fus. wounded O.R.1.	
	28-9-18.		X/35 T.M.B. accidentally injured Lieut. R.F. Spalding, 203 Fd.Co. R.E. killed O.R.2., 4th N.Staffs wounded Capt. W.L. 9., 15th Cheshires killed O.R.2., wounded 10 (1 at duty)., 19th Northd. Fus. killed O.R.2., wounded Capt. Harrild, 2/Lt. H.D. Brand, Capt. M.D.Gib (at duty)., 19th Northd. Fus. killed O.R.17., wounded 10 (3 at duty)., 232 Div.Emp.Co. wounded O.R.1., 17th Lancs. Fus. Killed O.R.21., wounded 2/Lt. W. Brookes, O.R.130 (6 atduty)., Missing 8., 18th Lancs. Fus. killed O.R.17., wounded 2/Lt. H.J. Plenderleith M.C., 2/Lt. A.W.E. Stabler, Capt. M.T.Nunnerley,M.C., 2/Lt. (A/Capt.) A.J. Ferris, 2/Lt. W.H. Gresty, O.R.127., Missing 20., 19th Durham L.I. Killed O.R.17., wounded 2/Lt. W.H. Edwards, 2/Lt. G.S. Leach, O.R.106, Missing 18., 35th Bn. M.G.Corps Killed O.R.9., Missing 4, wounded 53 (3 at duty)., 15th Cheshires Killed O.R.13., wounded 106 (1 at duty), Missing 8., 15th Sherwood Foresters Killed O.R.26., Wounded Capt. B.J. Ross MC., 2/Lt. R.H. Barton, 2/Lt. A.B.Griffiths, O.R.88 (3 at duty)., Missing 16., 4th North Staffs Killed 2/Lt. B.C.Whistler, O.R.30., Wounded Capt. S.J.Worsley, MC., Lt. B.C.Q.A.Norman, 2/Lt. T.H. Presten, 2/Lt. S.Williams, 2/Lt. A.L. Johnson, 2/Lt. J.E.Hudson, (2/Lt. S.Williams at duty)., O.R.182 (1 at duty)., Missing 10., 17th R.Scots Killed Capt. S.McKnight, Lieut. W.A.Cairns, O.R.27., wounded Lieut. (A/Capt) J.R. Craig, 2/Lt. L.W. Hamlet, 2/Lt. J.Kennedy, 2/Lt. Errekxxxx., A.T.Tait,MC., 2/Lt. A.C.Syme,MM., 2/Lt. P.Bourhill, 2/Lt. A.Rushton, O.R.245, Missing 2/Lt. A.I. Grant, 2/Lt. A. Benniem O.R.66., 12th High.L.I. Killed Capt. P.B.Milligan, Lieut. E.E. Bethune, O.R.20, wounded Capt. R.F. Mather, 2/Lt. T.F.Murray, O.R.100, Missing 58., 18th H.L.I. Killed Lieut. H. Fleming, O.R. 22, Wounded 2/Lt. A.Hose, A.F.McGubbin, Lieut. R.J. Hutchison, J.McGhurll, MC., 2/Lt. G.E.Missen, Lieut. G.McDonald, 2/Lt. J.C.Stewart, R.D.Orr, Lt.Col. V.E.Goederson,DSO, (at duty)., O.R.120, Missing 32.	

PTO.

Army Form C. 2118.

WAR DIARY
INTELLIGENCE SUMMARY.

(Erase heading not required.)

Instructions regarding War Diaries and Intelligence Summaries are contained in F. S. Regs., Part II. and the Staff Manual respectively. Title pages will be prepared in manuscript.

Place	Date	Hour	Summary of Events and Information	Remarks and references to Appendices
	29-9-18.		157 Bde. RFA. killed O.R.3., wounded O.R.16., 159 Bde. RFA. killed O.R.2. wounded 2/Lt. W.G. Noakes, O.R.14., Missing O.R.1., 19th N.Fus. wounded O.R.9., 35th Bn. M.G.C. killed O.R.5., wounded O.R.14., 23 2 Div. Emp.Co. wounded O.R.1.	
	30-9-18.		NIL.	

HONOURS AND AWARDS.

MILITARY CROSS.

3

MILITARY MEDAL.

14

COURTS-MARTIAL.

21

Major-General.
Commanding 35th Division.

-1-

Army Form C. 2118.

WAR DIARY

INTELLIGENCE SUMMARY. 35th Divn. Administrative Staff.

(Erase heading not required.)

Instructions regarding War Diaries and Intelligence Summaries are contained in F.S. Regs., Part II. and the Staff Manual respectively. Title pages will be prepared in manuscript.

Place	Date	Hour	Summary of Events and Information	Remarks and references to Appendices
			CASUALTIES.	
	1-10-18.		159 Bde. RFA. wounded 2/Lt. J.W. Thompson, 35th Div.Sig.Co.RE. killed O.R.1. wounded 1., 17th Lancs. Fus. wounded O.R.1., killed accidentally Capt. R.S.Heape,MG., Lieut. J.A. Shearsten, Lieut, A. BELL, 18th Lancs. Fus. wounded Capt. S.H.A. Parry, Lieut. F.W. HOBSON, 2/Lieut. J.E. Coutts, 35th Bn. M.G.Corps killed 2/Lt. J. Tayler, AM. O.R.5., wounded Lieut. P.G.B. Stringer, O.R.8.,	
	2-10-18.		157 Bde. RFA. wounded O.R.15 (1 at duty, 35th D.A.C. (Indians), O.R.4 accidentall, 12th High. L.I. killed Major J.A. Cox, DSO, 19th Nrthd. Fus. wounded O.R.1., 35th Bn. M.G.C Killed O.R.4., wounded 2/Lt. N.H.Parry, 2/Lt. H. Barr, O.R.16. Missing 2.,	
	3-10-18.		157 Bde. RFA. Killed O.R.1. wounded 2., 15th Cheshires killed Lieut. W.N.D. Tysen, wounded 2/Lt. A.G. West, 2/Lt. C.S. Joslyn, 232 Div.Emp.Co. wounded O.R.1.	
	4-10-18.		NIL.	
	5-10-18.		NIL.	
	6-10-18.		NIL.	
	7-10-18.		35th Div.Sig.Co.RE. wounded O.R.1., 17th Lancs. Fus. wounded 2/Lt. J. Galbreatj, 18th Lancs. Fus. Killed O.R.2. wounded 18, Missing 1., 105 Bde. H.Q. wounded at duty T/Capt. G.W. Hedgkirnsen, 15th Sherwood Foresters wounded O.R.1., 18th High. L.I. wounded 2/Lt. G.B.Mason, 3 5th Bn. M.G.Corps killed O.R.4. wounded 12.	
	8-10-18.		157 Bde. RFA. wounded O.R.1., 203 Fd. Co.RE. wounded O.R.1., 17th Lancs. Fus. wounded O.R.1., 15th Sherwood Foresters killed O.R.1. wounded Capt. (T/Lt-Col) W.A.W. GRELLIN, DSO, (since died), 2/Lt. B. Hornby, O.R.9. (3 at duty), Missing 1., 12th Highland L.I. wounded O.R.1., 18th High. L.I. killed Capt. J.James (RAMC. attd)., wounded Capt. A.C. Balfour, O.R.3., 35th Bn. M.G.Corps wounded O.R.17.	
	9-10-18.		35th D.A.C. wounded O.R.2., 12th Highland L.I. wounded O.R.2. (1 accidental), 18th High. L.I. killed O.R.1. wounded 7., 19th Nrthd. Fus. wounded accidentally O.R.1., 35th Bn. M.G.Corps wounded O.R.1.	
	10-10-18.		12th High.L.I. wounded O.R.1., 35th Bn. M.G.Corps wounded O.R.1.	
	11-10-18.		18th High. L.I. killed O.R.5. wounded 1., 254 Div. Emp.Co. wounded O.R.1.	
	12-10-18.		19th D.L.I. accidentally injured 2/Lt. C.Q. Farmer, O.R.3 wounded, (2 accidental), 19th Northd. Fus. wounded O.R.3. (1 at duty)., 35th Bn. M.G.Corps wounded O.R.1.	
	13-10-18.		17th Lancs. Fus. wounded O.R.2., killed O.R.1.	
	14-10-18.		157 Bds. RFA. wounded 2/Lt. H.R. Cooper.	

PTO.

WAR DIARY
INTELLIGENCE SUMMARY.
(Erase heading not required.)

Army Form C. 2118.

Instructions regarding War Diaries and Intelligence Summaries are contained in F.S. Regs., Part II. and the Staff Manual respectively. Title pages will be prepared in manuscript.

Place	Date	Hour	Summary of Events and Information	Remarks and references to Appendices
	15-10-18.		157 Bde. RFA. Killed O.R.1. wounded 4., 159 Bde. RFA. wounded at duty 2/Lt. F.V.Dutch, O.R. wounded 12 (2 gassed), Missing 1., 35th DAC. wounded O.R.2.,203 Fd.Co. RE. wounded O.R.2., 17th Lanc s. Fus. Killed Lt-Col. J. Hones, MC., 2/Lt. F. Aspden, 2/Lt. F.T. Leigh, wounded 2/Lt. J.P.Pender, 2/Lt. S.R.Williams, 2/Lt. J. Cooke, 15th Cheshires Killed O.R.1, wounded 36, Missing 3., 4th North Staffs wounded O.R.5 (4 gassed), 17th R.Scots wounded O.R.5., 12th High.L.I. Killed O.R.3. wounded 15., 18th High. L.I. Killed O.R.5., 19th Northd. Fus. Killed O.R.2., wounded Lieut. R.E. Hicks, O.R.10., 35th Bn. M.G.Corps Killed O.R.6., Wounded Lieut. R.N. Neritz, O.R.12., Missing O.R.3.	
	16-10-18.		159 Bde. RFA. Wounded 2/Lt. R.A. Bernhard, O.R. 2, 35th DAC. Killed O.R.1., 4th North Staffs Killed Capt. A.L.Johnson, wounded 2/Lt. J. Dutton, Capt. N.G.P.de C. Tronson, Capt D.C.B.Cotes, 2/Lt. S.G.Burgess, 2/Lt. H.H. Pickford, 2/Lt. W.G.Barnes.	
	17-10-18.		18th High. L.I. Killed O.R.1. wounded 10.	
	18-10-18.		157 Bde. RFA. wounded O.R.8 (2 at duty), Missing 2.	
	19-10-18.		204 Fd. Co. RE. wounded 2/Lt. S. Welsh, 19th Durham L.I. wounded Capt. K.Smith,MC. 2/Lt. H.W. Jordan, Lieut. H.L.Dale, 15th Cheshires Killed Lieut. J.Miller, O.R.19, wounded Lieut. O.N. Sidebottom, Lieut. A.Walker, 2/Lt. A. Wyon, O.R.79., Missing 16., 15th Sherwood Foresters Killed Capt. G.S. Sewter, 2/Lt. F.H. Burton,O.R.22., wounded Capt. M.M.Harvey,DSO,MC., 2/Lt. L.Lewis, 2/Lt. J.H.Dickinson, 2/ Lt. W.B.Walker, O.R.120, Missing 23., 4th North Staffs Killed O.R.9., wounded 92, Missing 12., 12th Highland L.I. wounded Lieut. H.S.D. Smith, 18th Highland L.I. Killed O.R.1. wounded 10, 35th Bn. M.G.Corps wounded O.R.3.	
	20-10-18.		205 Fd. Co. RE. wounded Gas O.R.1., 204 Fd.Co.RE. wounded O.R.3.,(2 at duty), 19th Northd. Fus. killed O.R.9., wounded 15 (1 at duty).	
	21-10-18.		159 Bde. RFA. wounded O.R.1. wounded 3 (1 at duty), X/35 T.M.B. wounded 2/Lt. H. Playle, 35th D.A.C. accidentally injured O.R.1., 17th Lancs. Fus. Killed O.R.18 wounded 103, Missing 7. 18th Lancs. Fus. Killed O.R.16, wounded Capt. R. Farnham, 2/Lt. A.E.F. Stafford, Capt. E.V. Finch, MC., O.R.62., Missing 24., 19th Durham L.I. Killed O.R.10., wounded 60, Missing 21.	
	22-10-18.		203 Fd.Coy.Re. wounded O.R.2., 205 Fu.C. Killed O.R.10., wounded 2/Lt. S.L.Luker, 15th Cheshires Killed 2/Lt. J.S. Brown, O.R.7., wounded Lieut. S.Whitney,DCM, (Gas), 2/Lt. T.LLOYD, O.R.39., 15th Sherwood Foresters Killed O.R.13., wounded Capt. W.M.Robinson, Capt. J.A.Player, 3/Lt. G.Witten, 2/Lt. J.F.Powell, 2/Lt. C.C.Tinley, 2/Lt. E.D.Brittain, 2/Lt.W.Watson, 2/Lt. W.C.O.Wade, Lieut. T.Williamson Missing,O.R.wounded 34, Missing 17., 35th Bn.M.G.C. wounded 7.	
	23-10-18.		17th Lancs. Fus. Killed O.R.1. wounded 8 (1 accidentally), 18th Lancs. Fus. Killed 4, wounded 7. wounded 2/Lt. G.S. Cormack, 2/Lt. P.Merrick,O.R.21., 19th D.L.I. Killed 4, wounded 11, missing 2. PTO.	

Army Form C. 2118.

WAR DIARY
INTELLIGENCE SUMMARY.

(Erase heading not required.)

Instructions regarding War Diaries and Intelligence Summaries are contained in F. S. Regs., Part II. and the Staff Manual respectively. Title pages will be prepared in manuscript.

Place	Date	Hour	Summary of Events and Information	Remarks and references to Appendices
	23-10-18.		Cont'd. 4th N. Staffs Killed O.R.14, wounded Capt. G.Richards, Lieut. W.Procter, 2/Lt. W.Stoneley, O.R.73, missing 7.	
	24-10-18.		15th Sherwoods Killed O.R.1, wounded O.R.1., 17th R.Scots Killed O.R.1. wounded Lieut. H.R. Harvey, O.R.7., 12th High. L.I. Killed O.R.1. wounded 2/Lt. J. Callan, MC., O.R.26, Missing 7., 18th High. L.I. wounded O.R.3.;	
	25-10-18.		18th Lanc s. Fus. Wounded Gas 2/Lt. A.H.Holford., 15th Sherwoods Killed O.R.1, wounded 2 (1 at duty)., 12th High. L.I. wounded accidentally O.R.1.	
	26-10-18.		NIL.	
	27-10-18.		18th Lanc s. Fus. killed O.R.1., wounded 2/Lt. J.A. Sheddick O.R.10., 17th R.Scots wounded O.R.1., 18th Highland L.I. killed O.R.1., wounded 2.	
	28-10-18.		17th Lancs. Fus. wounded O.R.4., 17th R.Scots wounded O.B.1.	
	29-10-18.		35th Div.Sig.Co.RE. wounded O.R.1., 17th Lanc s. Fus. killed O.R.5. wounded 29, Missing 11. 15th Lancs. Fus. killed O.R.2. wounded 8., 19th Durham L.I. wounded O.R.10., 17th R.Scots. killed O.R.1., wounded 12, 18th Highland L.I. wounded O.R.2 (1 at duty)., 35th Ba. M.G.Corps wounded O.R.1.	
	30-10-18.		205 Fd.Co.RE. Wounded at duty Lieut. D.A.Davidson, 19th Durham L.I. Killed O.R.1. wounded 4., 15th Cheshires wounded GasO.R.l., accidentally injured O.R.1., 15th Sherwoods wounded O.R.1., 15th Chesh. at td. 105 T.M.B. wounded at duty 2/Lt. T.H. Oliver, 17th R.Scots wounded O.R.3., 35th Bn. l.G.Corps wounded O.R.15 (13 gassed).	
	31-10-18.		15th Sherwoods wounded 2/Lt. E.V.Calverley, 17th R.Scots killed O.R.1. wounded 7, 18th High.L.I. killed O.R.4. wounded 5., 35th Bn. M.G.Corps Killed 2/Lt. T.H. Hammend, wounded at duty Lieut. T.J. Forbe s, Lieut. H.J.M. Jackson, wounded 2/Lieut. H.G.Bilicliffe, Killed O.R.2. wounded 16., 35th Div. Train wounded O.R.1.	

HONOURS AND AWARDS.

D.S.O.	M.C.	D.C.M.	M.M.
2	36	11	151

COURTS-MARTIAL.

8

8-11-18.

Major-General
Commanding 35th Division.

H.Q.
35th DIVISION.
("A")
No. A26/170.
3-4-19

Vol 33 to 36
37.

WAR DIARY.

OF

Headquarters 35 Division
Administrative Staff

From Novr 1918
To March 1919.

Army Form C. 2118.

WAR DIARY

Headquarters 35th (British) Division,
Administrative Staff.

(Erase heading not required.)

Place	Date	Hour	Summary of Events and Information	Remarks and references to Appendices
	1918.			
	1st to 14th Nov.		"A & Q" office at QUAREMONT.	
	14/11/18.		"A & Q" office moved from QUAREMONT to HARLEBEKE.	
	20/11/18		do. do. do HARLEBEKE to VOGELTJE and arrived same day.	
	30/11/18.		do. do. do VOGELTJE to APERLECQUES and arrived in new billets same day.	
	Decr.		"A & Q" office remained at EPERLECQUES during the month. Nothing of importance to record during the month.	
	1919. Jan.		"A & Q" office remained at EPERLECQUES. Demobilization of Coalminers, Demobilizers and Pivotal men commenced.	
	Feby. 6.2.19.		"A & Q" office at EPERLECQUES during the whole month. Demobilization carried on. Major J.M.McTAVISH, MC. D.A.A.G. died in No.3 Canadian Stationary hospital. Major W.H.TALLOR, R.A.V.C. D.A.D.V.S. died in No.3 Canadian Stationary hospital.	
	25.2.19		Lt-Col. L.M.JONES, DSO. A.A. & Q.M.G. left to assume appointment as A.A.G. Fourth Army.	
	March. 18.3.19.		"A & Q" office at EPERLECQUES during the whole month. Maj-Gen.A.H.MARINDIN DSO. relinquished command of the Division and proceeded to assume command of 187th Inf.Bde and Brig-Gen.J.W.SANDILANDS, CMG.DSO. assumed command of 35th Division.	
	18.3.19.		Lt-Col.N.H.C.SHERBROOKE, DSO. GSO.1 admitted to hospital and evacuated to England 19.3.19.	

Brig-General.
Commanding 35th Division.

Army Form C. 2118.

WAR DIARY
or
INTELLIGENCE SUMMARY.

(Erase heading not required.)

Headquarters 35th (British) Division,
Administrative Staff.

Instructions regarding War Diaries and Intelligence Summaries are contained in F. S. Regs., Part II. and the Staff Manual respectively. Title pages will be prepared in manuscript.

Place	Date	Hour	Summary of Events and Information	Remarks and references to Appendices
	1918.			
	1st to 14th Nov.		"A & Q" Office at QUAREMONT.	
	14/11/18.		"A & Q" Office moved from QUAREMONT to HARLEBEKE.	
	20/11/18		do. do. do HARLEBEKE to VOGELTJE and arrived same day.	
	30/11/18.		do. do. do VOGELTJE to APERLECQUES and arrived in new billets same day.	
	Decr.		"A & Q" Office remained at EPERLECQUES during the month. Nothing of importance to record during the month.	
	1919. Jan.		"A & Q" Office remained at EPERLECQUES. Demobilization of Coalminers, Demobilizers and Pivotal men commenced.	
	Feby.		"A & Q" Office at EPERLECQUES during the whole month. Demobilization carried on.	
	6.2.19.		Major J.W.McTAVISH, MC. D.A.A.G. died in No.5 Canadian Stationary Hospital. Major W.H.TAYLOR, R.A.V.C. D.A.D.V.S died in No. 3 Canadian Stationary Hospital.	
	25.2.19.		Lt-Col.L.M.JONES, DSO. A.A. & Q.M.G. left to assume appointment as A.A.G. Fourth Army.	
	March.		"A & Q" Office at EPERLECQUES during the whole month.	
	18.3.19.		Maj-Gen.A.H.MARINDIN DSO. relinquished command of the Division and proceeded to assume command of 187th Inf.Bde and Brig-Gen.J.W.SANDILANDS, CMG.DSO. assumed command of 35th Division.	
	19.3.19.		Lt-Col.N.H.C.SHERBROOKE, DSO. GSO.1 admitted to hospital and evacuated to England 19.3.19.	

Brig-General.
Commanding 35th Division.

www.ingramcontent.com/pod-product-compliance
Lightning Source LLC
Chambersburg PA
CBHW081542160426
43191CB00011B/1814